LIBERTY EQUALITY FASHION

Robe à Carreaux. Fichu tenant au Tablier.

LIBERTY
EQUALITY
FASHION

The Women Who Styled
the French Revolution

ANNE HIGONNET

W. W. NORTON & COMPANY
Independent Publishers Since 1923

For information about permission to reproduce selections from this book, write to
Permissions, W. W. Norton & Company, Inc., 500 Fifth Avenue, New York, NY 10110

For information about special discounts for bulk purchases, please contact
W. W. Norton Special Sales at specialsales@wwnorton.com or 800-233-4830

Manufacturing by Versa Press
Book design by Marysarah Quinn
Production manager: Lauren Abbate

ISBN 978-0-393-86795-4

W. W. Norton & Company, Inc., 500 Fifth Avenue, New York, N.Y. 10110
www.wwnorton.com

W. W. Norton & Company Ltd., 15 Carlisle Street, London W1D 3BS

1 2 3 4 5 6 7 8 9 0

Contents

PART III:

AFTER THE REVOLUTION

Cast of Characters

BARRAS, PAUL-FRANÇOIS-JEAN-NICOLAS, VICOMTE DE (1755–1829)
Leader of the Directory government and lover of Térézia Tallien.

BEAUHARNAIS, ALEXANDRE-FRANÇOIS-MARIE, VICOMTE DE (1760–94)
First husband of Joséphine Bonaparte.

BONAPARTE, JOSÉPHINE (1763–1814)
Born Marie Josèphe Rose Tascher de La Pagerie. Married to Alexandre de Beauharnais in 1779. Mother of Eugène de Beauharnais, born 1781, and Hortense de Beauharnais, born 1783. Widowed in 1794. Married to Napoléon Bonaparte in 1796, known afterward as Joséphine. Repudiated by Napoléon Bonaparte in 1810.

BONAPARTE, NAPOLÉON (1769–1821)
Second husband of Joséphine Bonaparte, married in 1796. Seizes control of French government in 1799, becomes emperor of France in 1804. Abdicates 1814, returns to power 1815, exiled 1815.

CHATEAUBRIAND, FRANÇOIS-RENÉ-AUGUSTE, VICOMTE DE (1768–1848)
Prominent Romantic writer, memoirist, and politician. Closely associated with Juliette Récamier.

CONSTANT DE REBECQUE, HENRI-BENJAMIN (1767–1830)
Prominent Romantic writer and politician. Closely associated with Germaine de Staël.

DAVID, JACQUES-LOUIS (1748–1825)
Painter.

GÉRARD, FRANÇOIS-PASCAL-SIMON (1770–1837)
Painter.

ISABEY, JEAN-BAPTISTE (1767–1855)
Style leader and painter of miniatures.

MARIE ANTOINETTE (1755–93)
Queen of France.

OUVRARD, GABRIEL-JULIEN (1770–1846)
Financier and lover of Térézia Tallien.

RÉCAMIER, JULIETTE (1777–1849)
Born Jeanne Françoise Julie Adélaïde Bernard. Married to Jacques-Rose Récamier in 1793.

ROBESPIERRE, MAXIMILIEN-FRANÇOIS-MARIE-ISIDORE (1758–94)
Leader of the Terror government, 1793–94.

STAËL, GERMAINE DE (1766–1817)
Born Anne Louise Germaine Necker in 1766. Married to Baron Erik Magnus Staël von Holstein in 1786. Prominent Romantic writer and political theorist.

TALLEYRAND-PÉRIGORD, CHARLES-MAURICE DE (1754–1836)
Diplomat and politician during all phases of the Revolution.

TALLIEN, JEAN-LAMBERT (1769–1825)
Lover during the Terror and second husband during the Directory and Consulate of Térézia Tallien.

TALLIEN, TÉRÉZIA (1773–1835)
Born Juana María Ignacia Teresa Cabarrus y Galabert. Married to Jean Jacques Devin, marquis de Fontenay, in 1788, divorced in 1791. Married to Jean-Lambert Tallien in 1794, divorced in 1802. Lover of Paul Barras and Gabriel Ouvrard during the Directory and Consulate. Married to François-Joseph-Philippe de Riquet, comte de Caraman, later prince de Chimay, in 1805. Mother of eleven children, born between 1789 and 1815, of whom nine survived.

VIGÉE LEBRUN, ELISABETH LOUISE (1755–1842)
Painter.

An Approximate
Guide to Money

MONEY

20 sous = 1 livre

20 livres = 1 écu

As of the Revolution, 1 livre = 1 franc

ANNUAL INCOMES, IN LIVRES

100–300	laboring poor women at the low end of the range
300–1,000	salaried manual or skilled work women at the very low end of the range
1,000–3,000	professional worker or office holder
5,000–20,000	salaried professionals and those with investment income
40,000–100,000	nobles
Over 100,000	princely nobles

Source: J. Sgard, "L'Échelle des revenus," Dix-Huitième Siècle *14 (1982): 425–33.*

French Revolution

TIMELINE

1789   **1790**   **1791**   **1792**   **1793**   **1794**

May:
Assembly of the Estates General, with representatives elected from the clerical and noble First Estate, the noble Second Estate, and the common Third Estate

June:
Representatives vow to form an elected government

July:
Formation of the National Constituent Assembly government (a constitutional monarchy)
July 14:
Fall of the Bastille, symbol of royal authority, to a popular mob

August:
Declaration of the Rights of Man and of the Citizen (in effect a constitution)

July:
Fête de la Fédération, celebrating constitutional government

September:
Adoption of the first constitution (for a constitutional monarchy)

October:
Formation of the National Assembly government (a constitutional monarchy)

September:
Massacres in Paris prisons

–

War begins against European monarchies

–

Formation of the National Convention government (an entirely elected government)

January:
Execution of King Louis XVI

April:
Beginning of the arbitrary rule of the Committee of Public Safety led by Robespierre

October:
Execution of Queen Marie Antoinette

July:
End of the rule of the Committee of Public Safety

–

Return to power of the elected National Convention government

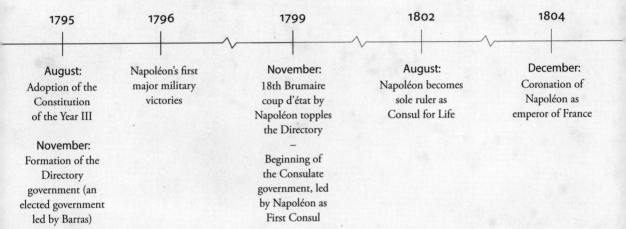

1795

August:
Adoption of the
Constitution
of the Year III

November:
Formation of the
Directory
government (an
elected government
led by Barras)

1796

Napoléon's first
major military
victories

1799

November:
18th Brumaire
coup d'état by
Napoléon topples
the Directory
—
Beginning of
the Consulate
government, led
by Napoléon as
First Consul

1802

August:
Napoléon becomes
sole ruler as
Consul for Life

1804

December:
Coronation of
Napoléon as
emperor of France

Garnitures de Velours appliqué.

Introduction

GUARDED within the gated storage facility of a great Paris museum, locked into a metal drawer, reverently wrapped in tissue paper, nestle the shoes of three women. The shoes were collected and given to the museum in honor of a legend. Side by side now in their resting place, their silver embroidery tarnished and their fine leather stiff, but their line still elegant, they once walked through revolution, and stepped into international celebrity.

This is the story of the style mavericks who wore those shoes. The French Revolution of 1789 redirected the whole world by overthrowing the principles of monarchy and declaring universal human rights. It included a fashion revolution, led by Joséphine Bonaparte, future empress of France, Térézia Tallien, the most beautiful woman in Europe, and Juliette Récamier, iconic muse of intellectuals.

Everywhere a fashion magazine could reach, women imitated what was then called "the new style." They rebelled against confinement in massive, rigid garments; women moved and everyone could see them move. A century before couturier Paul Poiret banned the Victorian corset, well over a hundred years before couturière Coco Chanel championed supple knit dresses, more than two hundred years before social media influencers, these three revolutionary Frenchwomen, Joséphine, Térézia, and Juliette, abandoned underwear cages and slipped into light, graceful one-piece dresses. They affirmed the physical presence of the female body in public, accessorized with tailored jackets and shawls, hair cropped short, and the first handbags over their wrists. The motto of the French Revolution was "Liberty, Equality, Fraternity." I set out to show it could also have been "Liberty, Equality, Fashion."

Along my way to the shoes, I studied many scattered documents and artifacts. The first were a lost treasure trove of extremely rare fashion plates. A quirky catalogue entry brought me to the serene reading room of the Morgan Library in New York. I looked at one plate after another, hundreds of them, published every ten days. Suddenly, I leapt to my feet and shouted. A myth had dissolved before my eyes. The totality of the plates proved beyond any doubt that a supposedly indecent episode of outrageous exposure had instead been a decade of women's creative independence.

The true story began during the worst violence of the French Revolution, in a Paris prison cell.

It was irresistible for the jailors to strip Térézia Cabarrus naked. Along with all of France, they had heard the rumors of her beauty. They gloated over the curves universally described as those of a "goddess." Then the jailors hacked off her jet-black hair, tossed her a rough chemise undergarment, and locked her in a stinking cell. Straw rotted in a mixture of urine and feces on the floor; moisture seeped through cracks in the stone walls. She remained there in the dark for twenty-five days.

When Térézia arrived at the prison, she had been wearing an edifice of conical boned stays, layered petticoats, and three-piece silken gown, whose skirt fabric alone cost years of a working woman's wages. Her apparel was a spectacle of power. Its materials and scale announced social superiority. It demanded deference. Now she was reduced to almost nothing: a plain straight sheath, which she cinched with a plaid cotton kerchief.

Térézia had wholeheartedly supported the start of the Revolution whose twisted course had landed her in a dungeon. At first, the French Revolution of 1789 intended to topple monarchy and correct the worst abuses of a decadent aristocracy. A newly elected government proclaimed the *Declaration of the Rights of Man and of the Citizen*: to this day the fundamental principle of political equality. By 1793, however, the Revolution had devolved into the Reign of Terror, ruled by an implacable Committee of Public Safety, presided over by Maximilien Robespierre. Like thousands of others, Térézia was arbitrarily arrested and condemned. Her principal offense was against the prudish sexual morals of Robespierre himself. He believed she had undermined his authority in the city of Bordeaux by using her wiles to seduce his appointed envoy, Jean-Lambert Tallien. No man could resist her, Robespierre was told.

On the thirty-first of May, 1794, the Committee of Public Safety was busy passing judgments, but not so busy that its members didn't enjoy obliging Térézia to sit in front of them all day, with nothing to eat or drink, while they laughed and were served their lunch. In the end, her trial didn't take long. Besides being guilty of sexual seduction, she was guilty of being noble. Never mind that she was born a commoner, the daughter of a middle-class Spanish banker; never mind that her family traded her in marriage at the age of fourteen for a breach into the aristocracy; or that the Vicomtes de Fontenay were a fake old aristocratic family; or that her marginally noble husband abused her, so much so that she took advantage of a radical revolutionary law to divorce him. The Committee of Public Safety deemed her a counterrevolutionary. Robespierre personally demanded her solitary confinement. Soldiers shoved her into a carriage, which lurched over the cobblestones of Paris all evening long, searching for an available cell. They passed the Place de la Révolution on their way (previously the Place Royale, today the Place de la Concorde). The soldiers thrust her head through the carriage window toward the looming hulk of the guillotine. "You will be next," they roared.

Actually, Robespierre was next. On July 27, 1794, he and the Committee of Public Safety were overthrown in a coup d'état called Thermidor, led by Térézia's Bordeaux lover, Jean-Lambert Tallien. Robespierre was guillotined the next day. In the continued belief that Térézia could cause a man to do anything, even while she was locked away in prison, she was credited with having instigated Thermidor and freed France from the Terror. She emerged from prison the darling of Europe.

Térézia also emerged from prison with no husband, no title, no formal education, no skills, and no money. Her entire fortune had been confiscated. But she had an idea about clothing, one of the few zones of expertise women were allowed. Society had been turned upside down. What if she did the same to fashion? What if she pronounced the

Vigée Lebrun painted Queen Marie Antoinette in 1783 wearing the sumptuous finery reserved for her rank.

pathetic chemise she had been reduced to in prison the ultimate Paris chic? She was France's most glamorous victim of the Terror, so why not dress that role with brilliant *éclat*? She would declare nothing the new everything. In one stroke she would vanquish the stays, the petticoats, the three-piece gowns, the silk brocades, the massive skirts, the lace, the baubles, and the towering coiffures. She would decapitate aristocratic style.

Before the Revolution, the queen of fashion was a true queen, Marie Antoinette. Térézia intended to rule fashion on new terms fought for by the Revolution. Rather than rely on inherited rank or royal court position, her celebrity would be self-made. We know where inspiration first came to her, because once she had succeeded, she commissioned a formal oil portrait of her style invention as if she were still in jail, holding her shorn hair in her lap.

She put the portrait on public display. Paris was stunned. The world was stunned. She had turned trauma into triumph. No one had ever imagined a woman could wear so little and look so gorgeous.

Térézia staged this portrait by Laneuville in 1796 to show the original prison inspiration for her radical style.

apeau de paille Blanche. ample Voile. Spencer de drap.

PART I

THREE PARIS SHOPPING TRIPS

Vue de Frascati.

CHAPTER 1

SUMPTUARY DICTATES

(Joséphine)

THREE GIRLS WENT SHOPPING in Paris during the last decade of a monarchy. The right clothes, their families hoped, would help them marry well, so they were led to the intimidating center of European style by their mothers or aunts. Little did the girls know that when a revolution changed everything in 1789, they would become the leaders of the fashion world to which they were being introduced.

Paris boutiques beckoned. Inside a carriage rattling over cobblestone streets sat a sixteen-year-old girl who would one day marry Napoléon Bonaparte and become Empress Joséphine of France. In 1779, she was called Rose, and was being taken by her aunt, Madame Désirée de Renaudin, for a complete Paris makeover. The style in which she had been raised was utterly incorrect.

Rose had come to mainland France from the island colony of Martinique. She was accompanied by a mixed-race servant named Euphémie, who probably still wore clothing brought from the Antilles, as the French called their Caribbean territories. French aristocracy, however, demanded a completely different way of dressing. Rose was never going to forget Martinique style. Even if she was stunned by Paris fashion, with its confidence in its superiority, its centuries of accumulated craft skill, its haughty codes, and its opulent materials, in the back of her mind memories of another kind of elegance lingered.

She had been born on June 23, 1763, named Marie Josèphe Rose Tascher de La Pagerie, and nicknamed Yéyette by her mixed-race nurse, Marion. She lived surrounded by house-servants on one of the many sugar plantations brutally managed by White colonists on the Caribbean islands that French military power had conquered. An intercontinental trade supplied plantation masters with enslaved African labor. On the five-hundred-hectare Martinique estate owned by the Tascher de La Pagerie family, some 330 enslaved Africans labored in cane fields and in the sugar-boiling building, while a few worked in the family house as personal servants. The plantation's area was called "la petite Guinée," Little Guinea, after the part of Africa from which the enslaved had been taken. It was also called "Les Trois Islets" because it was located near three small islands.

The young Rose could not ignore the enslaved people her father owned. When she was very young she was tended day to day by Marion, whom she freed after she became empress. The entire Tascher de La Pagerie family lived literally directly above slave labor. Rose probably could not remember the separate, wooden, house in which her family had lived for the first three years of her life. In 1766, a hurricane blew the wooden house down, inflicting so much financial loss on the plantation that her parents could not afford to rebuild the house and moved into the second floor of their brick sugar-factory building. The first floor housed the plantation's sugar-boiling vats. On a typical Antilles sugar plantation, especially during the harvest season, some enslaved laborers worked night shifts at the boiling vats after day shifts in the cane fields. During these intense night shifts, called *veillées*, exhaustion frequently led to accidents, in which men lost limbs to the mill cylinders or fell into the vats.

Moulin. 2. Fourneaux 3. Formes 4. Vinaigrerie. 5. Cannes SVCRERIE 6. Cros 7. Latanir. 8. Pajomirioba 9. Choux 10. Cafes 11 Figuir. 12t.
et Chaudieres.   de Juire   Carambos. de Negres.

The Black or mixed-race women and men on the Tascher de La Pagerie plantation were among the approximately 85,000 enslaved and about 5,000 nominally free people on Martinique ruled by 11,000 White people, according to a 1685 French royal edict later named the Code Noir. Although the Code Noir ostensibly put limits on torture, the separation of mothers from children, and arbitrary execution, the spirit of the law exempted Whites from punishment for infractions. In 1806, for instance, Rose's mother accused an enslaved house-servant named Emilie of attempting to poison her. Madame Tascher de La Pagerie turned Emilie over to the island tribunal. The interrogation took place one day, the condemnation two days later. For the crime of poisoning a White master, the punishment was death by burning. Execution of the sentence took place the next day.

The Code Noir also governed the clothing of the enslaved. For centuries, sumptuary laws in mainland France had regulated who was allowed to wear what materials, according to a strict hierarchy with the king at the top, aristocrats sternly ranked at the next level, professionals

Eighteenth-century sugar plantation on Saint Domingue (now Haiti). The brick building on the back right resembles the building the Tascher de la Pagerie family lived in during Joséphine's childhood. The enslaved wear minimal clothing, while the plantation overseer wears a hat, shirt, and breeches—and carries a gun.

in the middle, and peasants at the bottom. In 1685 an even lower rank was added for France's colonies by the Code Noir. Plantation masters were obliged to provide each enslaved person with two outfits of the coarsest linen or cotton fabric, *toile* (canvas), or else to provide four *aunes* (ells, equal to roughly 1.15 yards) of such cloth a year. Four and a half yards of fabric would barely have been enough for two straight, sleeveless shifts that would not reach much past the knees.

In 1685, this one Code Noir sumptuary edict applied to all the enslaved imported from Africa. As the decades passed, however, the racial character of the islands became more complicated, as Joséphine knew from Marion and Euphémie, among other house-servants on her family's plantation. The rape of enslaved women had done its heinous work and inadvertently produced a group in between Black and White. To deal with this demographic development, the French government decreed a dedicated sumptuary edict on June 4, 1720, six years before Joséphine's grandfather settled in Martinique. Like the Code Noir, the 1720 edict allocated the coarsest types of cotton to the enslaved. In addition to a modification of the old category, "negroes, mulattos, and indigenous [Carib] Indians," the 1720 edict inserted a new category: "mulattos and freed or born free [Carib] indians or negroes." Those in this category were allowed cast-off clothes from their masters and household liveries with silver trim, but forbidden any gold, gems, silk, ribbons, or lace.

Only thirty-four years later, another sumptuary edict was pronounced. It expressed mounting White anxieties about how clothing identified race. By 1754 some mixed-race people in the Antilles were very light-skinned, as well as free and skilled. The more racial boundaries blurred, the more urgently White colonists tried to sharpen boundaries with clothing. The 1754 edict divided people of color into three clothing categories: field- or garden-slaves, house-slaves, and mixed-race free people. To each category was assigned a different quality of cotton. Though the edict decreed that free mixed-race people were still not supposed to wear gold, gems, silk, ribbons, or lace, it conceded that they could if the materials were "of little value."

Sumptuary laws were not merely guidelines; penalties for breaking the laws were extreme. A free person could lose their freedom for wearing a forbidden item of clothing; field-slaves were threatened with prison. Joséphine grew up surrounded by the causes and the effects of the 1754 edict. She knew from experience how fearsome sumptuary regulations could be, and also how they could be creatively circumvented.

The 1754 sumptuary edict reflected how women of color had pushed against the limits of the 1720 sumptuary edict. As a child, Joséphine saw, all day every day, the contrast between what the field-slaves on her family's plantation wore and what the house-servants she lived with wore. Women like Marion, who attended her personally on Martinique, and Euphémie, who accompanied her to the mainland, strove against sumptuary restrictions. Differences between cotton textures and colors

Le Masurier's *Marché à Saint Pierre de la Martinique* shows the full range of clothing worn on Joséphine's native Martinique between 1750 and 1780, from the barely clad enslaved to the opulently garbed White plantation owners.

that to us might be imperceptible, to them were crucial: harsh knee-length sleeveless shifts or sleeved long shifts versus smooth long gathered skirts, blouses, and jackets; cheap "gros guingas" or "grosse indienne" cotton fabric versus the better "Morlaix"; coarse solid off-white fabric versus finer blue-and-white stripes; plain versus two-color-plaid versus three-color-plaid square madras scarves; one-scarf head-wraps versus multiple-scarf head-wraps. Sundays and holidays occasioned the finest that could be obtained. An eminent historian of the French Antilles, Frédéric Régent, has called it "vestimentary bidding."

When Joséphine left home and went to town, strolling through marketplaces or along the docks, she witnessed the most audacious styling of all. There, she encountered women in the third category established by the 1754 edict: the very light-skinned free women of color, who dared to invent an entirely new kind of women's clothing. Technically, the invention abided by the 1754 edict because it was made of cotton. It evaded sumptuary laws by being neither the privileged three-part gown nor the humble skirt-and-jacket combination. It was instead a one-piece dress called a *gole*, sometimes spelled *gaulle*. This dress dramatically replaced the fitted tops and bell-shaped skirts of conventional women's clothing with a straight silhouette from shoulder to ankle, while retaining the long, fitted sleeves of gown bodices. Made of fine, diaphanous cotton, a gole was always worn over a slip. Slips were sometimes white, sometimes pink, light blue, or peach. When worn over a pastel slip, the body of the white gole appeared delicately tinted. To keep them modest, these new gole dresses were also worn with big, sheer white cotton square scarves, folded diagonally, draped around the throat, and tucked in or tied.

Every detail of complete gole attire just barely slid by sumptuary restrictions, with substitutes for lace, precious embroideries, and *passementerie*. A cotton ruffle, for example, was embroidered white on white with cotton thread, to render it almost, but not quite, like lace. Exuberant cotton knots or bows replaced ribbons. Though gold and gems were banned, discretely small jewelry, "of little value," escaped censors.

Forced by law to innovate within the parameters of cotton, women of color in the Antilles fundamentally altered the history of fashion. Centuries of European sumptuary regulations had allocated rank to clothing according to the value of materials, but the women Joséphine grew up in the midst of had invented a fashion ecology independent of materials. Moreover, Antilles style allowed Joséphine to assume that anyone could design and construct their own clothes, because on the Antilles there were no guilds. Entrepreneurial tailors, of whom many were mixed race, could experiment without fear of guild reprisal. Elegance, Joséphine saw, could be achieved entirely through imaginative design.

Proud, light-skinned, mixed-race women in gole dresses dominated the style ecology of the islands. Trailed by male admirers or chatting with one another, accompanied by their own servants hold-

Sometime between 1770 and 1790, Brunias catalogued the cotton styles worn by women of color in the French Antilles, from coarse wraps to long, striped skirts with blouses and plaid kerchiefs, to straight *gole* dresses with slips, white kerchiefs, and towering head-wraps.

ing aloft brightly colored sunshades, they steered confidently through crowds of women in thick sturdy cotton skirts and blouses, whose more practical head-wraps and neck-scarves tended toward blue and red plaids, probably stained with the sweat of labor. The most elegant women in the Antilles, with their towering white head-wraps adorned with huge asymmetric bows and graceful *fichu* scarves swathing their throats, offered a mobile alternative to rigid mainland silhouettes.

How do we know what Joséphine saw? Luckily for us, one artist who made many small paintings on a nearby Caribbean island was fascinated by women's clothing. Agostino Brunias arrived on Dominica, located snugly between the French islands of Guadeloupe and Martinique, sometime between 1764 and 1770. When he arrived, Dominica had been British only since 1763, the year of Joséphine's birth. The sumptuary system Brunias encountered had been formed by French law. Brunias represented every nuance of cotton quality and accessories, while keying them to subtle differences in skin color, as if he were illustrating French sumptuary law. His paintings show us exactly what fashion Joséphine experienced until the age of sixteen.

However comfortable and strangely appealing straight white cotton gole dresses might have seemed to Joséphine, it was out of the question for her, as a White child on Martinique, to wear one outside the home, or on any formal occasion. White women in the Antilles knew it would be inconceivable for White women on the mainland of France to ever be seen in public in a gole. Glimpses might be caught of a few White women dressed in goles at home in the French port cities of Nantes, Lorient, or Bordeaux, where families in transatlantic trade clustered. Yet a gole was a serious fashion faux pas. It signaled Creole, and therefore social inferiority. To the mainland French, Creole meant anyone raised in the colonies.

The Tascher de La Pagerie family longed to escape their Creole status. They were very minor nobility, rendered yet more marginal within the French aristocracy by their residence in Martinique. The most ambitious and enterprising member of the family, Rose's father's sister Désirée de Renaudin, escaped the Antilles to live flagrantly for many years with a noble lover: François de Beauharnais, Marquis de la Ferté-Beauharnais. Though her lover was dearly attached to her, and would in fact marry her much later, when he was eighty-two and both their spouses had died, her situation before 1779 was irregular. To consolidate her place in the family, she announced that one of her Martinique brother's three daughters must marry her lover's heir. It didn't matter which niece. "We must have one of your children."

The middle Tascher de La Pagerie sister was first designated because at thirteen, she was considered the right age, but then she died of disease. Next selected was the youngest sister, but after thinking it over, Monsieur and Madame Tascher de La Pagerie felt eleven was too young. That left Rose, the eldest, who was then fifteen. If only, Rose's family must have thought as they plotted, the girl could have been born with a pink-and-white porcelain complexion, classical face, and soft smooth curves. She was not very pretty by the standards of the eighteenth century, with small sharp features, matte complexion, bad teeth, and fine dark hair. Regardless, she was adequate to the family's purpose.

The marriage terms were settled. Rose was shipped off to France with Euphémie to take care of her. She was married to the vicomte Alexandre de Beauharnais in December of 1779, and thus became Rose, Vicomtesse de Beauharnais. Rose's new in-laws agreed she was amenably docile, luckily, because she needed polish. She had not received much formal education, and what little she had learned from nuns on Martinique was provincial by Paris standards. Her husband hoped she could be improved. He wrote his father, "She may seem less pretty than you expected."

The Beauharnais family felt its own social insecurities. It did not rank much higher on the social scale than the Tascher de La Pagerie family. All too recently, members of the Beauharnais family had been in trade, or in law. Yet according to the minutely calibrated competition among French nobles, a mainland marquis was superior to a colonial seigneur. In 1786, Alexandre de Beauharnais petitioned to be presented at the royal court of Versailles, only to be devastatingly snubbed by an etiquette-enforcer, who passed on the verdict of a court genealogist: "M. de Beauharnais is not suitable for the Court Honors he solicits." One of the branches of his family had been convicted of being "usurpers" of their title—in 1667.

Madame de Renaudin, therefore, had an urgent shopping task in Paris. Rose must begin to appear noble—as noble as sumptuary law would allow. Madame de Renaudin was not going to take any chances. If she shopped carefully in the right Paris clothing boutiques, her niece could meet expectations. Madame de Renaudin had about 20,000 livres to spend on the bride's trousseau: the clothing and linens that equipped girls to become wives. Status signs played such a major role in any arranged marriage that this money was most of what the Tascher de La Pagerie family paid up front for their daughter's dowry; payment of the rest of the dowry was vaguely promised for the future. Compared with the 400,000 livres that the empress of Austria had paid for her daughter Marie Antoinette's royal trousseau, 20,000 livres was paltry. Compared with the 270 livres a skilled working woman could earn in a year, however, the sum was definitely aristocratic.

Foundations first. Aunt and niece gazed through their carriage windows, scanning the many wrought-iron signboards for the name of the little boutique on their list, and the image that indicated the stays tailor they were looking for. When their carriage stopped and they descended, they paused to look at a few specimens of the *tailleur de corps* craft though small leaded glass windows on either side of its narrow, carved wood door. They entered a dim space with nothing for sale to be seen, because nothing was ready-made; everything was ordered according to the specifications of the master craftsman who reigned over the boutique. He had risen to his position after years of training at every level of his craft, from apprentice to *compagnon* (journeyman) and finally to *maître* (master). Now, he, in turn, was in command, and greeted his customers into his realm with a bow, while calculating in his head what materials he would offer ladies of their particular rank. The shop was lined on three sides with wood counters, behind which stood a few assistants, who bowed, too, deferentially but not obsequiously. Even the least experienced, like their master, could instantly recognize what rank their customers belonged to by their clothing, and these two ladies did not warrant obsequious.

Anyone who was a lady, however, must have some version of the stiff conical undergarments the shop provided, no matter what materials they were made of. A woman with the slightest pretension to respectability would never dream of meeting guests at home, let alone venturing away from home, without being laced into a *corps*. The French word *corps*, which translates into "body," signaled a substitution for the natural body. (The undergarment was called *stays* in English and in the next century *corset*.) The corps indeed functioned as a second skin, the surface society imposed on women's torsos.

Despite the tailleur de corps boutique being dedicated to intimate feminine undergarments, its master and underlings were men. Men controlled all the ancient craft guilds, including the powerful clothing guilds. Since 1268, when guild regulations had been codified by the *Établissements des métiers de Paris*, usually called the *Livre des métiers*, the guilds had structured the entire skilled labor force of the kingdom, in France as in every European monarchy. The master tailleur de corps felt part of the collective authority of more than a hundred French crafts. In eighteenth-century Paris, he was one of

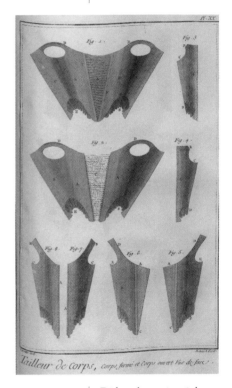

Diderot's magisterial collection of knowledge, the 1751–72 *Encyclopédie*, included this diagram of a women's whale baleen–stiffened *corps* foundation garment.

between 30,000 and 40,000 masters, who with their apprentices and journeymen numbered over 100,000, out of a total Parisian population of about 600,000–650,000. Masters enforced strict quality standards, none more stringently than the clothing-guild masters of Paris. So when the master tailleur de corps approached Madame de Renaudin and her niece, of course he showed the respect due from a craftsman to a noble. But he did not feel the slightest doubt about what his expert knowledge and the skill of his workers would produce. He knew exactly how a Paris corps should be made.

First, the new customer must be meticulously measured. A good corps had to fit the torso exactly to discipline it correctly. Rose's body was not ideal, with its long skinny straight shape, but then again, all natural bodies posed challenges to the tailor of a corps. His task was to transform nature into elegant artifice. After the measurements, and some negotiation over the quality of linen fabric, Madame de Renaudin and the fledgling vicomtesse de Beauharnais left the boutique. In a workshop right behind the salesroom, construction of the corps began. A craftsman inserted strips of whale baleen between straight channels of stitches to stiffen it. Tiny holes down the edges of the back were rimmed with sturdy stitches to withstand the pull of laces by a maid, which would perfect the hieratic cone shape. At every step, work was checked to ensure it met the tailleur de corps guild standards, as well as the master's finishing instructions. When the order was complete, it would be delivered by a lowly boy to the Beauharnais residence. Because the Beauharnais women were not such highly ranked customers that their patronage was a favor to the boutique, they would be expected to pay their bill.

Meanwhile, many shopping stops lay ahead. The young bride had never imagined such variety or quality. Nothing in Martinique had prepared her for this. Each guild had perfected its particular product. Together, the clothing guilds constituted a Paris fashion system, reinforced by intermarriages and shared neighborhoods. Just to start at the alphabetical top of the list of crafts: Bootmakers (*bottiers*) turned leather into sturdy footwear that reached above the ankle. Bootmakers were not to be confused with shoemakers (*cordonniers*), who plied a significantly different set of skills, turning both leather and fabric into more delicate shoes that covered only the foot. The list went on: braid makers, button makers, cleaners, dressmakers, drapers, dyers, embroiderers, fashion merchants, feather dressers, furriers, gauze makers, girdlers, glovers, hairdressers, hatters, hosiers, haberdashers, leather crafters (not for footwear), linen drapers, mercers, pin and needle makers, perfumers, purse makers, ribbon weavers, secondhand dealers, skinners and furriers, skullcap makers, soap makers, tailors, wig makers. To each of these Madame de Renaudin and the bride in her charge would eventually pay a call. The stakes were highest at the dressmaker's because the choice of silk fabrics was so crucial.

Rose had no doubt dreamt of French silk before her marriage. The most prestigious gowns in the colony of Martinique were made of French silk brocade. Wearing a silk gown, fitted over your corps, turned you into a lady. All your senses told you so. The silk glowed, its lustrous gleam especially impressive by candlelight. It was so smooth to the touch, yet strong, and your fingers could feel where the flowers were because of the delicate long threads that passed over the background weave. It was hot in the summer months, but then again you had servants to fetch and carry. Perhaps it smelled a bit, because you had worn it for years and it couldn't be washed, only dabbed with cleaning fluids, but those servants laundered your linen chemise so

Rose de Beauharnais aspired to this sort of French silk *robe à la française*, exported in the 1760s. Even without embroidery or *passementerie* trim, the quality of the brocade fabric made it an expensive investment.

often that the clean chemise smell prevailed. And when food tempted you with its taste, your silk reminded you to eat daintily.

Silk merited investment. Madame de Renaudin sought silks crafted so well that Rose could wear them for the rest of her life, then hand them down to her heiresses. Though styles might change in a decade or two, a gown made with heirloom-quality fabric could be gently altered. Not all silks, however, were created equal. Silks, like French aristocrats, came in a wide range of value. Gold-thread brocades lorded over sprigged floral silks. When the future Joséphine, empress of France, entered the dressmaker's shop in 1779, a guild master would again have rapidly assessed her status, and signaled his subordinates behind another set of wooden counters to unfurl only the silks suitable for a newly minted vicomtesse.

In every boutique she entered, she discovered clothing materials forbidden to her, even after her marriage into the mainland nobility. In Paris, the young Joséphine was confronted with the upper registers of the sumptuary laws whose lowest rungs she had grown up with. No doubt to her dismay, she, who had been at the top of a local hierarchy in Martinique, suddenly realized she was nowhere near the top of the whole French sumptuary system.

Not for a mere vicomtesse the truly splendid silks woven in France's second-biggest city, Lyon. With their shimmering precious-metal-wrapped threads, grand arabesque patterns, and intricate color combinations, those were reserved for the upper echelons of the aristocracy, dominated by pedigreed counts and countesses, dukes and duchesses, princes and princesses. Elite silks included as many as twelve colors and six types of precious-metal thread, along with technically difficult contrasts between smooth and ribbed textures. The skilled women who helped their families weave such imposing silks were unlikely to earn as much in their whole lives as it cost to buy a formal skirt's worth of this most precious fabric.

Nor would a master dressmaker bother to mention to a Madame

de Renaudin or a vicomtesse de Beauharnais the most magnificent embroidery his fellow master in the embroidery guild could supply. Such embroidery also used gold or silver thread, sometimes combined with gems and pearls. Ladies at the vicomtesse level could be satisfied with quite marvelously lifelike and textured embroideries in pure silk that would spread their foliage, pistils, stamens, petals, and palmettes across the gowns he was dedicated to assembling.

The master dressmaker would also have astutely modulated his suggestions for how to adorn the gown with *passementerie*: an untranslatable French word for woven, braided, knotted, twisted, coiled, wired, tasseled, or intertwined trims. It was a waste of his time and perhaps just a bit condescending to mention that one formal court gown alone could require three and a half *aunes* of trim embroidered with gold and silver thread at 100 livres an aune (an aune was very roughly a yard), three aunes of silver fringe, rhinestones, ribbons, five and a half aunes of ribbon embroidered with spangles, gold tassels, nine and a half aunes of lace, silver fringe and tassels, and three aunes of trim fabric with gold dots. The cost of such finery—just the *passementerie*, not counting the gown's silk fabric—totaled 1,400 livres, plus 110 livres for the relatively cheap labor: the price of ten gowns appropriate for someone like Rose de Beauharnais.

The master dressmaker might have added a proposal for a moderate quantity of new lace to animate the throat and sleeves of the gown, supposing the two customers did not have their own lace already, perhaps handed down from previous generations. Though lace looked essential to gowns, it was not actually integral to them, being only loosely basted to the silk, so it could be easily removed for gentle laundering. To the consternation of all guild masters, lace was not controlled the way their venerable crafts were. Outstanding lace, microscopically knotted bas-relief linen-thread sculpture, had been produced in France for only a little over a century. King Louis XIV's great finance minister Colbert himself had grown impatient with the hemorrhage of French money to

The British Countess of Hertford and the Germanic Count von Dehn commemorated the splendor of their French court costume with portraits.

Italy for the best lace. In 1665, he had organized a domestic lace industry under the direct aegis of the Crown. This did not bode well for the authority of the medieval guilds, yet fashion mavens agreed French lace had developed a charmingly ethereal and fluttering flat style of its own.

Madame de Renaudin and the dubious vicomtesse de Beauharnais could only dream of the most magnificent clothing Parisian tailors, dressmakers, embroiderers, and jewelers created: the legendary court *habit à la française* for men and court *robe à la française* for women. If they were lucky or clever enough to be admitted into the residences of the sort of nobles who had the birthright to be presented at court, they were likely to see portraits hung on walls to commemorate these outfits of a lifetime. Nobles from every corner of Europe had their Versailles court regalia made by the supreme Paris guilds to ensure maximum *éclat*. The guilds designed and executed skirts thirty yards around, hung on wicker or metal cages called *panniers*. It was rumored that some skirts could not fit through the doors of the Versailles palace, obliging the highnesses of Europe to sidle into rooms at angles. Jewels paved the triangular stomacher pieces of their three-part gowns. Waterfalls of lace cascaded from their throats and sleeves, and sometimes swagged across their bodices and skirts.

The Beauharnais and Tascher de La Pagerie families were painfully aware they were not allowed to wear these magnificent costumes. It seemed as if sumptuary laws had governed Europe since time immemorial, because some of them dated back to the fourteenth century. In 1337, the English Crown proclaimed that only the royal family, the highest church officials, earls, barons, knights, and ladies could wear fur. In 1463, English decrees ordered that "no person under the state of a lord" could "wear any manner of cloth or silk being of the color of purple." In 1533 an "Act for the Reformation of Excess in Apparel" reserved crimson, scarlet, and blue silk velvets for dukes, marquises, and earls. A particularly rapid-fire series of edicts were decreed in seventeenth-century France to restrict the use of gold and silver thread: in 1601, 1606, 1613, 1620, 1634, 1665, 1677, and 1680.

Needless to say, families like the Beauharnais and Tascher de La Pagerie clans wanted to cheat as much as they could without getting caught. But by and large, people obeyed sumptuary laws simply because they could not afford to break them. While the members of the aristocracy policed its internal hierarchy with fanatic jealousy, and the range of annual income within that hierarchy was vast, from as low as 10,000 livres to over 100,000 livres, as a class the aristocracy occupied a different order of existence than the rest of the kingdom's subjects. The laboring poor, by far the majority of the population, earned as little as 100 livres a year. Estimates vary, but historians have calculated that between 1 percent and 0.5 percent of France's approximately twenty-three million people in 1789 had noble titles, and only 5 percent of those titles dated back to the feudal era before about 1500. The clerical and secular nobility of France—called the First and Second Estates—paid no taxes, thanks to what were bluntly named "privileges" (though everyone in the Third Estate scrambled for the royal favor of privileged exemption from taxes, sometimes successfully), and controlled the French government, military, and church with absolute authority, an authority encoded in elaborate costumes.

The bodies of nobles were transformed by their apparel into cosmic apparitions, the bodies of monarchs most splendidly of all. Marie Antoinette, the reigning queen, had a stupendous budget at her disposal. In 1783, she enjoyed an annual clothing allocation of 120,000 livres. In 1785, she spent 258,002 livres, more than twice her budget. Monarchic splendor justified the renewal of Marie Antoinette's wardrobe with thirty-six new outfits every trimester: twelve *grands habits*, twelve *robes à la française*, and twelve less formal gowns.

A fairy tale expressed how clothing seemed to perform magic on royal bodies. "Peau d'âne" ("Donkey Skin"), published in 1694 by the great French folklore gatherer Charles Perrault, tells how a king wants his own daughter to marry him. The princess, hoping to avoid his demands, asks that he first give her gowns so impossibly celestial they are like the "blue sky," the "moon," and the "sun." To her dismay, her royal father's craftspeople manage to create the celestial gowns. (But in the end the princess does escape incest.)

When Rose vicomtesse de Beauharnais eventually became Joséphine Bonaparte, empress of France, she did acquire a fairy-tale wardrobe. In 1779, while she was still a sixteen-year-old bride, her Paris shopping trip made her feel that at least she was on her way in that direction. As she looked in the mirror, she could see a fundamental difference between the *before* of Martinique and the *after* of Paris. The difference was caused by her new clothes, and by how those clothes changed her body. She discovered that style is not only a formal question of aesthetics, or about how craft transforms materials, or even about how one person can compose the elements of a style most harmoniously or strikingly. Style, she learned by switching from one dress code to another, is also about social power. If ever she took her own status on Martinique for granted, in Paris she learned how clothing gives authority to some people over others.

Every morning, the daily ritual of the toilette taught her body the posture of aristocracy. Over a thin linen chemise, servants tied her petticoats around her waist, for formal occasions topped by a *pannier* armature. When she was laced into her first Paris corps, she may have felt she could hardly breathe, let alone twist or bend, but she knew she must acquire the calm, dignified bearing befitting her new rank—and her new gowns. After her skirt was lowered onto its base, she had to stand very still while the rigid triangular stomacher was pinned to her corps, lest the sharp pins prick her. More straight pins fastened the bodice, with or without tails and back drapery, to the sides of the stomacher. The bodice was fit on the corps so meticulously that the bodice looked as if it too were a geometric solid. Every tiny piece had been precisely cut and seamed. The three parts of the gown—stomacher, skirt, and bodice—seemed to be one garment, so carefully had they been coordinated.

At last, she appeared as her family hoped. Her attire had turned her into a French aristocrat in the eyes of the world. She had learned just how much a person's sense of self could be changed by their clothing.

Toquet à Pointes. Robe de Madras.

CHAPTER 2

STYLE ENTERPRISE

(Térézia)

H OWEVER UNAVOWABLE colonial trade might be, it was irrevocably transforming the French economy and French clothing. Joséphine's Tascher de La Pagerie family happened to be bad at business, but it was part of a global commercial system generating enormous profits. Those profits paid for fashion. When Térézia went to Paris to shop, she discovered an alternative to the ancient guilds. She could see in the trendiest boutiques how cotton was supplanting silk, and how new style trends rivaled the authority of court etiquette. Parisiennes cared as much about whether the shapes of their *indienne* fabric gowns were *à la mode* that season as how long the fabric would last, and as much about which *marchande de modes* had designed the gowns as about which duchess had endorsed them.

Sugar from plantations like the one that belonged to Joséphine's father was shipped to Europe, where Europeans invested sugar profits both in the Atlantic slave trade and in cotton from India. The high returns on that commerce paid for newly invented machines and expanding textile factories, primarily in Great Britain, which

In 1678, the style magazine *Le Mercure galant* ran the first visual advertisement for a boutique that escaped guild specialization.

further increased European profits on raw cotton from India. Intercontinental trade voyages required major capital investments and complex financial packages. So did the textile factories that launched industrialization. Bankers handled the money behind all these transactions, and took their cuts.

Like many noble families, the Tascher de La Pagerie and Beauharnais families clung to archaic social status while unwittingly fueling capitalism. They held bankers in contempt at the same time that they contributed to banking fortunes. Aristocratic rank and its privileges remained superior, the nobility reassured itself. Why else would those brash arriviste families use their filthy lucre to marry into the nobility?

Térézia Cabarrus's family provides the archetypal example. Her father was an extremely successful self-made eighteenth-century financier, who cofounded the national bank of Spain. No Spanish Catholic noble would contemplate such a demeaning occupation, relegated to despised people like Basques and Jews. François Cabarrus came from the Basque stronghold of Bayonne, and had joined the Freemasons (like many of the founding fathers of the United States). Yet despite his secret club engagement with Enlightenment philosophy, and his public career in capitalist finance, Monsieur Cabarrus aspired to nobility for himself and his children.

Luck handed Monsieur Cabarrus an extraordinary asset to bargain with. His first child, born July 31, 1773, and officially named Juana María Ignacia Teresa Cabarrus y Galabert, turned into a remarkably beautiful girl. Everyone who met her exclaimed over her classical features, a dramatic contrast between raven-black hair and flawless pale-white skin, and the harmonious proportions of her strikingly tall body; she seemed more divine than human. Moreover, the child exuded a wild energy that defied conventional feminine modesty. Térézia (as she signed herself when she reached adulthood) later claimed to have been raised by a goat. In fact, a brief stint in Paris with family friends polished her just a little bit. The older she grew, the more attractive she became. Her sexuality exerted a magnetic force field. With men of all ages buzzing around her, François Cabarrus decided to marry her advantageously sooner rather than later. Térézia was twelve years old.

Térézia's parents were keenly aware that Spanish style would get their daughter nowhere on the French noble marriage market. Only by being outfitted in Paris could a common girl compensate for the lack of a title, even one as rich and naturally lovely as Térézia. Like Joséphine, Térézia needed a total makeover. In summer 1785, Térézia's mother was charged with taking her daughter back to Paris. A shopping spree in the capital of fashion was probably not a hardship mission for Madame Cabarrus, herself not yet thirty years old. Monsieur Cabarrus stayed behind in Madrid to gather the kind of impressive dowry required to attract a noble suitor, so the trip would be a mother-daughter shopping expedition, with clothes to be bought and a bride to sell.

Though the Cabarrus family was just as eager as the Tascher de La Pagerie family to marry into mainland French aristocracy, they approached Paris style in a different spirit. Minor colonial Antilles nobility was still French nobility, whereas the Cabarrus family were common foreigners, therefore twice as unlikely to have internalized the attitudes of Gallic aristocracy. The atmosphere of banking inclined them instead to risk and novelty. Tracking current global commercial developments and seizing new opportunities was, after all, how financiers made money in the eighteenth century. Madame and Mademoiselle

Cabarrus were going to devote more attention to what was changing in the domain of clothing than what was sanctioned by custom.

The world of Paris clothing had been changing at an accelerating pace since the 1670s. The same fundamentally modern forces that drove the Tascher de La Pagerie colonial sugar plantation and the banking career of François Cabarrus were threatening the medieval guild system of Paris style.

When people like Térézia and her mother shopped in Paris, they headed straight to the rue Saint Honoré (still today called on the internet "the heart of Paris luxury"), bypassing traditional guild boutiques in favor of the rogue boutiques run by *marchands merciers*. Denis Diderot, whose leading Enlightenment ideas the Cabarrus family probably knew, said this new sort of merchant "made nothing and sold everything." The Cabarrus women might have been alerted back home in Spain to *marchands merciers* by the first illustrated lifestyle magazines and fashion plates, especially the *Mercure Galant*, which had been promoting new buying habits since the 1670s. Now they could browse the latest Paris fashion in person. They joined glamorous cosmopolitan customers who considered a tempting array of lace, fabric, and accessories such as shoes or fans, with no obligation to buy. These customers did not commission craft. They consumed commodities.

Women from a banking family, convinced that natural laws of supply and demand should govern markets, rather than medieval guild regulations, likely approved of the *marchand mercier* challenge to archaic shopping. Along with others in their social position, they might well have felt that the guilds had ossified, and no longer promoted solidarity or reciprocity, but rather used their monopolies to gouge both labor and customers. From a capitalist point of view, exemptions and corruption jammed mobility within guilds. No wonder stagnant journeymen had grown disaffected, and the training logic of apprenticeship had devolved into indentured servitude. All over Paris, shoppers found clandestine or brazenly illegal stores, which accepted the risk of fines, confiscation, or imprisonment. Financiers like Monsieur Cabarrus sided with a school of economists called the physiocrats, who explained that guilds obstructed the freedom of workers. They were disappointed when the entrenched power of the guilds fought back successfully against a first wave of reform the physiocrats won in 1776.

Despite determined resistance from the guilds, Térézia and her mother would discover as they continued to shop, some major changes in the Paris fashion world had proved inexorable. Some bold shops were run by women. In 1652, the tailors' guild of the French provincial city Aix-en-Provence had accepted female members. In 1675, seamstresses in Paris and Rouen, another important provincial urban center, were allowed to found independent guilds. This new seamstress guild was allowed to sew dresses and linen underwear (but no stays). The mother-daughter duo probably felt all the more at ease in a boutique run by *couturières* because they knew that only women and children were allowed to shop there.

Fashion was changing so fast (by pre-revolutionary standards) that a phenomenon as novel as the *couturières* had already, by 1785, been outrun by another commercial innovation. In the same spirit of defiance against the specialization of the guilds, a type of business called *marchandes de modes*, also run by women, put the parts of a total outfit together for women clients. Surely a family whose father was a Freemason knew Diderot's 1751–72 *Encyclopédie*, a notorious compendium of Enlightenment information. In it, Diderot dedicated an entry to the *marchandes de modes*, announcing that they had stopped offering a variety of goods and dedicated themselves to fashion: "These merchants have been established and called by this name a very short time; it's only since they entirely gave up the business of *la mercerie* to adopt the business of *la mode*." *La mode* was all about the excitement of discarding last season's favorite for a brand-new style. *La mode* appealed to a dynamic, impatient twelve-year-old adolescent.

Diderot's 1751–72 *Ency-clopédie* revealed the latest trend in women's shopping: the *marchande de modes*.

In a *marchande de modes* boutique, customers like Térézia were introduced to the latest styles and urged to experiment with them. Certainly the *marchande* suggested she try a gown made of cotton. No material was more *à la mode*. The fabric with which women of color in the Antilles had disrupted the history of clothing connected continents. Most cotton came from India. It grew indigenously in the French Antilles island colonies when slavery began there, but sugar produced with slave labor yielded higher profits, so cotton was imported to the Antilles from India, and some from West Asia, then called the Levant. Not only did the enslaved in the Antilles wear imported Indian cotton, some of them had been traded in Africa for Indian cotton. One late eighteenth-century French trader in Indian cotton went so far as to claim: "It was the establishment of colonies and the slave trade which gave birth to this branch of commerce with [India]. . . . If the colonies of the Antilles cease to buy slaves, one can say without doubt, this article [cotton] will decline more and more." An especially coarse cotton was even named *Guinée* after the African region from which many of the enslaved came—the same name as the location of Joséphine's family plantation on Martinique.

In the fashionable boutiques of 1785 Paris, cotton seemed new, but it had been a staple of the Indian economy since around 1300, when climate and regional specialization in the fiber made Indian cotton the best in the world. All financiers, like Térézia's father, knew the lucrative profits that had been made since the seventeenth century by investing in long-distance maritime trade voyages to obtain superior quality. They also knew that to control Indian markets, investment companies had the military might of the most powerful European nation-states behind them. The British East India Company and the French East Indies Company essentially conquered India and divided it between them. Most of their business was in textiles, and the overwhelming majority of those were cottons. By the first decades of the eighteenth century, the French East Indies Company imported between one hundred thousand and three hundred thousand pieces a year of white, blue-dyed, or printed cottons from India. Not all that long before Térézia and her mother came to town, in the middle of the eighteenth century, France lost most of its Indian colonies to Britain, but it retained some key trading posts, notably Pondicherry, and rogue French merchants continued to expand the cotton trade. Textiles remained the French East Indies Company's biggest business.

A bewildering plethora of Indian weights, fibers, and weaves were unfurled on the counters Térézia and her mother sat at in Paris boutiques. One hundred sixteen types of cotton came from Chandernagor (now Chandannagar in West Bengal) alone, sixty-six from Dhaka (now the capital of Bangladesh). Customers had to feel quality with their fingers to avoid being fooled by their eyes. Some simpler woven and dyed goods came from Gugarat in western India; finer pieces from Punjab and Pradesh in the north, and the Coromandel coast in the southeast; cottons so fine they were almost transparent, called muslins, came from Bengal. It was impossible to forget these many cottons all came from

India, because their French names designated their origins: *calico*, for instance, from the city Calicut; and *madras*, from the city Madras. The "*indiennes*" were self-explanatory.

So in 1785 the Paris *couturiers* and *marchandes de modes* were amply stocked with printed or painted cotton, which they proposed to turn into gowns in the very same styles as the silk ones required for ladies of noble rank. The same seamstress would charge 144 to 155 livres for a fine silk taffeta gown, 72 to 130 livres for a gown of lesser silk, 90 to 100 livres for a fine calico gown, and 60 to 84 livres for a gown of lesser cotton. Labor was cheap: about 6 to 8 livres per gown. Cottons were a bargain.

Cottons were also fascinatingly exotic, yet somehow familiar too. Late eighteenth-century customers and *marchandes* could hardly remember that ever since seventeenth-century French merchants had begun to trade in bulk with Indian cotton producers, they had suggested design modifications to encourage further sales. What consumers believed to be foreign Indian patterns were actually what merchants thought consumers would find exotic, altered by local Indian interpretation, which spiraled through successive feedback loops of design translation until styles fused. The red and blue patterns seemed fashionably fresh, yet not outlandish.

As the *marchandes de modes* pointed out to potential customers like Térézia and her mother, the most astonishing thing about these appealing "indienne" prints was that they could be washed over and over without their designs fading. French printers, led by the *toile de Jouy* manufactory, scrambled to emulate superior Indian indigo and madder dyes, fixative mordants, and wax or resin resist-dye techniques. "Indiennes" sold, whether imported or imitated. Someone like Térézia who chafed against all physical constraints would have been thrilled to think that she could wear a gown and not worry too much about staying perfectly neat and tidy. She could eat and move without the worries silk provoked. And she could stay cool throughout the hot months in a cotton gown. Even as she tried it on for the first time, her skin could feel the fabric breathe.

For anyone progressive, furthermore, wearing cottons was a pleasant form of economic sedition. Louis XIV, the Sun King of the previous century, had noticed noblewomen wearing cottons at the palace of Versailles and he had not approved; cottons undermined the sumptuary supremacy of his court, and they siphoned business away from the guilds under his aegis. Cotton menaced the French wool industry and the French linen industry. The silk weavers' and drapers' guilds were also still very powerful at the end of the seventeenth century. Imported cotton had therefore been banned by Louis XIV in 1686. Britain also partially outlawed imported cotton, but the French Crown forbade importation of the raw material, importation of printed cottons, printing of imported white cotton, and wearing of printed cottons. Indigo, too, was officially banned in France between 1598 and 1737.

Nonetheless, the French East Indies Company continued to import Indian cottons. A tangle of conflicting policies or egregious exemptions from policies enabled smuggling, and some economists applauded entrepreneurial piracy. Smuggling flouted the economic and judicial authority of the Crown with its unlicensed, daring, cutthroat, and occasionally wildly profitable practice of protocapitalism.

Although the ban against cotton prohibited its importation to mainland France, the immediate resale of cotton by French merchants to foreign destinations or to the French colonies was allowed—hence the Indian cotton in the Antilles. False claims of resale abroad could hide domestic business. Though Indian weavers, who knew cotton so well, routinely used cotton for both the warp and the weft of their fabrics, European weavers often resorted to using the silk, linen, or wool thread they were more familiar with for the long warp threads, and therefore many fabrics could pretend to be something other than cotton.

The French Crown itself had actually created the biggest loophole of all: the entire port of Marseilles on the Mediterranean coast. Colbert,

Louis XIV's finance minister, had granted the city's chamber of commerce the privilege to trade with the Levant. Somehow that privilege was not revoked when the cotton ban was imposed in 1686. More cotton passed through Marseilles than all the cotton traded by the French East Indies Company from India. Cotton was coming through Marseilles from Cairo, Rosetta, and Alexandria in Egypt, from Seyde/ Sidon, Tripoli, and Acre (now Akko) in what are now Libya, Israel, and Lebanon, from Cyprus, from Greece, and especially from Aleppo, in what is now Syria.

Nonetheless, cotton really only became a normal feature of daily life in 1759, when the French ban on imported cottons was officially lifted. Some people said Louis XV's official mistress, Madame de Pompadour, had lobbied him because she liked wearing cotton so much. More likely, the lifting of the ban had been one among many economic tactics during the mid-century military struggle over India between France and Britain. Because silk had not been supplanted as the fabric choice of aristocracy by 1785, when Térézia came to Paris, cotton was still an insurgent material.

By 1785, cotton had also had another sort of effect, political rather than economic. Everywhere Térézia looked in Paris, she saw people of all social classes dressing just a bit more alike than a Spaniard would expect. Laundresses and duchesses, coachmen and counts were wearing the same fabric. Although quite expensive cottons were used for formal silk-gown look-alikes, on the whole cotton had put decent clothes within reach of all but the most destitute. Cotton had an increasingly prominent place in the wardrobes of the entire professional and skilled labor classes, as well as in those of the established or newly rich. Followers of fashion like Térézia and her mother gave their barely used outfits to their servants, who often resold them quickly in secondhand markets. Women of modest means could adopt the latest fashions more and more rapidly.

Térézia must have noticed that people who were better dressed had more confidence in themselves. Enlightenment ideas about natural equality and representative government made more sense to people in neat, clean, stylish cotton clothes than to people in rags. By the 1780s, erstwhile subservient subjects of the king were starting to feel like individuals with rights.

One single cotton garment had more lingering political repercussions than any other. Memories of the scandal revived every time a customer, like Térézia and her mother, encountered the garment's look-alikes in all the *marchande de modes* boutiques. It was a dress that cost as little as 60 livres, depending on the quality of the cotton. For ordinary women to wear the dress was fashionable. For titled women, risky. For the queen, represented to the public in a portrait, a disaster.

The queen had made her big fashion mistake in 1783, only two years before Térézia and her mother started their Paris shopping.

Queen Marie Antoinette made a catastrophic fashion mistake when in 1783 she posed for a portrait in a cotton dress, which undermined her royal status.

Marie Antoinette's subjects expected her to appear in public attired in sumptuary regalia, including when she appeared in formal portraits. Instead, she had chosen a loose, light, one-piece, white cotton dress, ruffled around the gathered scoop neck and sleeve edges, called a chemise dress. At best, the clueless queen had abandoned all courtly decorum in favor of flighty Paris fashion. At worst, as the name of the dress implied, the queen had appeared in public in her underwear. Inconceivably worse, the dress emitted a whiff of Creole to those who knew the Antilles, though such a terrible *lèse-majesté* thought would have been repressed. In any case, the dress was not the ermine, the gold-embroidered brocade silks, and the abstracted body

shapes that signaled true monarchy. Why respect a queen who did not look like a queen?

The painter of the portrait, Elisabeth Vigée Lebrun, was immediately ordered to create another version, in the hope that if the mistake was promptly and plausibly corrected, it would be forgotten. Vigée Lebrun rapidly replaced the offending portrait with one that did what it had been supposed to do all along. She adjusted the original portrait's viewpoint to diminish intimacy and increase grandeur. She adjusted the facial expression and hand gesture so they would be less personally engaging and more impersonally aloof. Mostly, Vigée Lebrun changed the clothes. Too late. The political damage had been done.

How had such a fashion calamity befallen the kingdom? The queen was all too vulnerable. She had been sent from home in 1770 when not much more than a child to be married (like Joséphine and Térézia). She arrived from Austria at the royal French court of Versailles, where etiquette was punitively enforced. Dozens of appointed noblewomen and hundreds of servants closely surrounded the future queen. Once she became queen in 1774, court etiquette required that "ornaments of royalty" be placed on her during excruciatingly long and absurdly regulated dressing ceremonies. The point of the ceremonies was less to get clothing on a person's body than for the ladies-in-waiting to have their rank recognized. Actual dressing would be interrupted by any violation of etiquette, no matter how infinitesimal. No one was thinking about covering a naked woman. They were calculating whose great-grandmother's cousin's brother-in-law had inherited which title from which duke, how that was modified by last week's court intrigue—and does the equation Rank divided by Gossip mean it's me or you who has the privilege of putting underwear on the queen?

Marie Antoinette's marriage was not consummated for years, so she could not deliver a royal heir. Desperate for an identity, she turned instead to *la mode*. "I am me" (*je suis moi*), she explained, not in the main Versailles palace, but only in the (comparatively) small Versailles palace called the Trianon. There she retreated from all court etiquette, including sumptuary etiquette. Her "me," the modern self she yearned for, could not be comfortable in stiff, bulky royal regalia. When she was pregnant four times, correct court costume must have felt unbearable, rendering the Trianon all the more attractive. Her mother, wise in the ways of statecraft, warned her to look like a queen: "All eyes will be fixed on you." By 1775, Maria Teresa feared her daughter was "hurtling toward an abyss." Hoping counsel delivered in person would be more effective than her many letters, Maria Teresa sent Marie Antoinette's brother to Versailles; he tried and failed to make his sister listen. With a vivid verb, a courtier recalled that by 1778, the queen regularly appeared in noble company "stripped of all the ornaments of royalty."

Imagine, therefore, the horror at Versailles when Marie Antoinette invited a common *marchande de modes* to the palace to discuss clothing purchases tête-à-tête at least once a week—maybe daily, some courtiers believed. The queen and Rose Bertin withdrew together from public palace chambers into small, private rooms to choose clothes on the basis of taste rather than ceremonial function. The queen's entourage sensed the whole monarchic edifice they inhabited had cracked. Some whined that challenges to their etiquette privileges could not be tolerated. The Baronne d'Oberkirch called Bertin an "odd personage, with an inflated sense of her own importance, who treated princesses as if they were her equals," and who had the audacity to call her sessions with the queen "their work." Some, more attentive to the national mood, lamented the bad publicity caused by Marie Antoinette's spending on inappropriate clothing. Others predicted that if socially inferior women copied the results of Marie Antoinette's "work," they might stop believing they were inferior. At court, Bertin was dubbed *Ministre de la Mode*, Minister of Fashion.

Alas for Versailles, there was more truth to the joke than courtiers would have liked. Beneath their decorum lurked a realization that the lowly *marchande de modes* was the sort of successful self-made entrepreneur who heralded a capitalist economy. Rose Bertin worked her way out of the provinces into a traditional apprenticeship in a Paris dressmaker's boutique, and from there, by 1770, set up her own shop, called Le Grand Mogol. Her teeming imagination burbled forth a stream of new accessories and variations on the traditional gown. She was what we call a designer, rather than a craftswoman. Some of her innovations were pleasantly silly: ribbons here, ruffles there, gown jacket tails gathered up once or in three parts, enormous hair poufs topped with trinkets like model ships. Other Rose Bertin innovations tapped into more serious social phenomena.

Bertin probably did not single-handedly introduce the fateful chemise dress to Paris in the late 1770s. The portrait painter Vigée Lebrun took credit decades later, in her memoirs, claiming that she had pioneered a straight white cotton dress at a classical-themed supper party; but her retroactive and self-aggrandizing memory should be considered with skepticism. Actresses may have performed Caribbean-themed roles on stage in a version of the gole before it became acceptable street wear. One prominent impresario, known as La Montansier, had spent years in the Antilles before establishing a theater near Paris and, according to her, gaining the ear of the queen, whom she entertained with theater gossip. No visual proof of a gole onstage before 1783, however, has yet surfaced.

The most likely candidate to have urged Marie Antoinette to wear a chemise dress remains Rose Bertin, if only because the designer sold the queen so many of her clothes. In 1783, the year of the dread fashion mistake, Bertin was paid half of Marie Antoinette's annual clothing expenditures.

Bertin's innovations offered a new and different sort of distinction to her clients, the distinction of being individually stylish. Even a few aristocrats deviated from their sartorial privileges in order to look as fashionable as they looked noble. Bertin was discovered by Marie Adelaïde, duchesse d'Orléans, who had married into a branch of the royal family, and who, with a dowry of 6 million livres, was one of the richest heiresses in France. When this exalted patronage brought Bertin to the attention of the queen, Bertin's career was made. The sumptuary system still guaranteed that whatever the queen wore would be emulated by the nobility and then by the bourgeoisie—in lesser modes. After the portrait scandal, the chemise dress was ominously known as a *chemise à la reine*. A vicious cycle set in. The more Marie Antoinette patronized Bertin, the more style authority Bertin accrued, the more Marie Antoinette spent, and from there to fiscal excess. The queen set the national tone, and the tone turned to shopping at Le Grand Mogol or, failing the Grand Mogol, at its competitors, where Térézia and her mother no doubt shopped from 1785 through 1787.

Their shopping served its purpose. After several overtures that failed because the Cabarrus status was not high enough, a marriage deal was finally negotiated with the senior Marquis de Fontenay, a man who had just barely entered the aristocracy. His father and his wife's father had both been merchants, an activity unfit for nobles. His marquis title was not inherited, but merely attached to property he owned in Fontenay-Aux-Roses, on the outskirts of Paris. The upstart marquis had procured for his son, Jean-Jacques de Fontenay, a government bureaucrat position as *conseiller* to the Paris "Parlement," the law court with jurisdiction lesser than, but parallel to, the legal power of the king, an institution through which many newly minted nobles attempted to improve their status.

Térézia married the twenty-six-year-old Jean-Jacques de Fontenay on February 2, 1788, with a constellation of successful bankers in attendance. From an aristocratic point of view, these bankers made a lot of money, but they were not categorically different from the groom's grocer and draper grandfathers. Trade was still trade. Térézia had just barely accomplished her family's desire to enter the nobility, as a marquise, the Marquise de Fontenay. She had done what she was told to do, at the age of fourteen.

(293)

Costume de Bal.

CHAPTER 3

STRAINED SEAMS

(*Juliette*)

Around the same time Térézia entered by marriage into the French nobility, in 1787–88, a provincial but promising young beauty was called to Paris. The Revolution would make her famous as Madame Récamier. Still named Juliette Bernard, she came from Lyon at the behest of her parents, who had moved from the provincial city to set her stage. Like Joséphine and Térézia, Juliette arrived in the capital to be restyled. Unlike Joséphine's and Térézia's families, however, Juliette's did not count completely on nobility to advance a daughter. As tensions rose in France, the Bernard family hedged its bets. Though their livelihoods depended on the Crown, they socialized with liberals. Some sort of reckoning with absolute monarchy seemed inevitable, but what sort?

Juliette's exceptional destiny was set in motion before her birth. Most children in the late eighteenth century did not have one mother and three fathers. During the 1770s, three close male friends, Jean Bernard, Pierre Simonard, and Jacques-Rose Récamier, all loved the same beautiful woman. It seems to have not mattered to these unusual men whether their love for Marie Julie Matton, called Julie, was sexual, platonic, or marital. They just wanted to be together with her and with one another. According to a mysterious decision of which we have no trace, all four agreed that Julie would legally marry Bernard, and that this arrangement would change nothing in their *ménage à quatre*. Julie gave birth on December 3, 1777, to a baby named Jeanne Françoise Julie Adélaïde Bernard, called Juliette. All three men raised her. She remained their only child.

The four parents were convinced from the moment Juliette was born that their daughter was the most adorable girl in the world. Such a child, they agreed, should be carefully cultivated. Lyon was no Paris, but it was one of France's biggest, most economically dynamic cities, famous for its silk industry. Juliette was educated by Catholic nuns at the convent of La Déserte in Lyon. Her friends later said that from this schooling she retained a gentle submission, resignation to fate, and consolatory piety. The Catholic cult of virginity also made a lasting impression.

But Lyon could serve only as prelude. There was no substitute for Paris style. Juliette was brought to Paris to live in a household presided over by Julie Bernard, Jean Bernard, and Pierre Simonard, with Jacques-Rose Récamier a regular presence.

None of Juliette's four parents were noble. Récamier, for instance, came from a family of hatters, booksellers, and printers. Together, the three fathers nonetheless earned plenty of middle-class money to lavish on Juliette's education. Bernard was named "receveur des finances" to the French crown in Paris in 1784, which meant he collected and administered customs taxes. It was rumored that this lucrative position was obtained from one of the king's ministers by Julie. More important than the truth of the rumor is its indication that Julie was considered very ambitious. Récamier became the most financially successful of Juliette's fathers, in banking. He had strong international connections, notably to Spain, and was comfortable dealing with the aristocrats who scorned his profession.

According to the custom for girls, Juliette's education was primarily in the arts. Under her mother's vigilant supervision, she learned to dance in order to move gracefully, to sing, to play harp and piano. She learned some history, literature, and philosophy. Arranging flowers and perfumes to enhance interiors appealed most to her. Though typically these "accomplishments" were acquired at home, from tutors, and were not intended to lead to a professional career, they could be intellectually rigorous. Juliette was probably better educated than either Joséphine or Térézia.

Her mother, Julie, established a salon upon moving to Paris. Like clubs, salons connected men in a wide variety of cultural, economic, and government fields. They determined reputations and shaped public opinion. Unlike clubs, salons were presided over by women. As soon as Juliette arrived in Paris, Julie put her daughter on display in her salon to teach her child how beauty and style could wield influence. At her mother's side, Juliette learned how to become a salon hostess in her own right, so that a future network of creativity and power could revolve around her.

The Bernard/Simonard/Récamier salon aimed for a progressive but not radical position. Most people in France had come to resent the Crown's chronic mismanagement of national finances, noble tax privileges, and the Third Estate's lack of meaningful political representation. The American Revolution of 1776 had initially been supported by France in order to weaken France's traditional archenemy Britain. Yet the republican principles of the Declaration of Independence had made an impression, along with those of European philosophers such as Locke, Rousseau, Diderot, and Voltaire. In the salons of Paris, men and women discussed constitutional monarchy, reason, science, entrepreneurship, freedom of speech, and freedom of religion.

They also gossiped, followed fashion magazine advice, listened to piano music, wept over romantic novels, praised neoclassical paintings, and admired attractive women. The editor of the prominent magazine *Mercure de France*, Jean-François de La Harpe, accepted a salon invitation from Julie Bernard and added: "For all time, and in every place, my heart belongs to the charming Juliette." Rumors of Juliette's exceptional beauty spread. Her face was round, with small, fine features, "pearly" teeth, "rosy" mouth, dark, naturally curly hair, and an "incomparable brilliancy of complexion." She was what we now call petite or gamine. Everyone agreed that what made Juliette so lovely was a fusion of physical and personality qualities. Words like "tender-hearted," "goodness," "charity," and "virtue" were always used to describe her.

Juliette's dynamic mother, however, did not rely entirely on natural beauty or character for her daughter's success. The artifice of clothing was also essential. Juliette recalled that her mother "attached the highest importance to dress." The person closest to Juliette later in her life transmitted her memory: "Consequently, every time she [Julie Bernard] took her daughter to the play, or into society, occasions which in her maternal vanity she multiplied, the poor child was obliged to pass long hours at the toilette."

On the one hand, the ultimate toilette remained royal. Julie took her daughter one day to the Palace of Versailles on the outskirts of Paris. King Louis XVI and Queen Marie Antoinette sometimes allowed their humbler subjects to watch them dine. The monarchs presented a stunning spectacle in their majestic apparel. Along with others in a long line, Juliette and her mother filed by, filled with reverence for the expanses of thickly brocaded silks, sparkling jewels, lace ruffles, and curled, powdered hair.

On the other hand, in 1787–88, the best place to update one's toilette was the redeveloped Palais Royal in the heart of the city. Such was the luster of this shopping phenomenon that anyone who cared about fashion knew all about it. Not only was it *the* place to actually shop, its message was diffused by countless popular prints. The Palais Royal was a concept as much as a particular shopping destination.

The Palais Royal-gallery's Walk.   *Promenade de la gallerie du Palais Royal*

The name "Palais Royal"—royal palace—reveals the original source of its aura. Serene Highness though he was, Louis-Philippe II, duc d'Orléans—husband of the ultrafashionable Marie Adelaïde, duchesse d'Orléans, who launched the designer Rose Bertin—converted the ground-level arcade of his palace and its gardens into a commercial complex to monetize them. It opened to the public in 1784. This shockingly modern swerve created a shopping center only minutes away from leading *marchande de modes* boutiques like Bertin's Le Grand Mogol on the rue Saint Honoré. The venerable architectural vocabulary of ancient Greece and Rome—columns, arches, capitals, coffered ceilings, and pale blond stone—had been put in the service of Fashion. The arcade and gardens survive, complete with boutiques, so that we too can experience the seductions of the Palais Royal.

Behind its royal surface, the Palais Royal housed a fashion world unto itself. To attract a new sort of shopper like the ambitious middle-

Nowhere in 1780s Paris was it more fashionable to see and be seen than the Palais Royal.

class Julie Bernard, the duc d'Orléans assembled the most novel spectacles alongside fashion boutiques to entice and retain a very mixed social crowd. Julie, with her daughter Juliette in tow, could choose from among 145 boutiques to amuse themselves, among them waxworks, cafés, hair salons, and jewelry shops. The waxworks were thrillingly realistic, the powdered hairstyles piled high, adorned with swaying plumes and miniatures of items such as wheelbarrows. At the north end of the Palais Royal, shoppers could refuel at a new sort of public eating establishment: a restaurant, with priced options on menus, called Le Grand Véfour (still in business in the same place). Unlike shopping at the usual boutiques, which required going in and out of doors and onto city streets, at the Palais Royal no one feared the weather because they were protected by arcades. People lingered. They came to see and be seen in their finery as much as to shop. The crowds themselves became an attraction. It was rumored that prostitutes cruised the Palais Royal day and night. Although the illicit sexuality was decried, prostitutes actually made the crowds more titillating.

The mix of clothing worn in the Palais Royal confounded archaic sumptuary regulations. A few people who frequented the Palais Royal continued to wear silk *robes à la française* and densely embroidered *habits à la française*; some women dared cotton gowns and some men the solid black three-piece suits of the professional class; a few impertinent chemises à la reine might be spotted. But who was wearing what? In the Palais Royal, sumptuary codification failed, and that failure was itself part of the Palais Royal's dangerous appeal. If everyone could look so much alike in the latest fashions, nobility and legitimacy might not be more than appearances. Palais Royal fashion hinted at a possible equality between princesses and whores, princes and intellectuals. To shop there was to flirt with the idea of democracy.

The Palais Royal brought to life the pages of fashion magazines like the *Cabinet de modes* (Fashion cabinet) or the *Journal de la mode et du goût* (Journal of fashion and taste). These magazines, which put fashion in the context of literature, music, and theater, were aimed at women like the Vicomtesse Rose de Beauharnais, the Marquise Térézia de Fontenay, or Madame and Mademoiselle Bernard: women who wanted to be at the forefront of the latest style, and wondered whether they were on a cusp of history. Fashion magazines had their doubts about what they observed. They articulated the mixed feelings most people had about the speed with which fashion was changing society. "One could propose, without being contradicted, that it is no longer normal today for women to wear the most formal gowns (*grande Parure*), any more than for men to wear the most formal suits (*habits à la Françoise*), with hats under their arms and swords by their sides." "Was not our century, or rather our actual era, destined to be prodigious?"

Pundits designated two phenomena as the most prodigious. One was the chemise à la reine. The other was the adoption by fashionable women of accessories previously worn only by men: "Vests, jackets, curled hair, hats, canes, watches, gloves, shirts, cravats." During the 1780s, the most serious challenge to the three-part gown's hegemony were these quasi-androgynous superficial touches.

Then in summer 1788 a real alternative to ancien régime clothing arrived in Paris. It gripped the imagination of France with a vision of exotic otherness, however, rather than of possible reform. Three ambassadors and a retinue had been sent to the capital by Tipu Sultan, ruler of the southern Indian kingdom of Mysore, who sought an alliance against Britain. The diplomatic stakes were high. Yet, typically for France just before 1789, political logic took second place to spectacle. An observer lamented that the clothes worn by the Indian men were all too fascinating; people were "more struck by the originality of Asiatic costumes than by the importance of our possessions in India."

The ambassadors' attire caused a sensation. Hordes of curious Parisians gawked at the ambassadors in person, and images of the ambassadors circulated widely. "Indomania," as art historian Meredith Martin

Ambassadors from Tipu Sultan were brought to marvel at the glamour of the Palais Royal.

VUE DE L'INTERIEUR DU NOUVEAU CIRQUE DU PALAIS ROYAL
ET DES AMBASSADEURS DU NABAB-TIPOU.

1.er Am. Mahomid Durvisth, &c. 2.e Am. Acbur Ally, &c. 3.e Am. Mahomid Otchman, &c. 4.e Culbe Ally, fils du 2.e Am. 5.e Goolami Saib, gouro du 3.e Am.

Présentés au Roi en une Audience publique tenue à Versailles le 10 Aoust 1788.

À Paris chez Le Vachez, M.d de Tableaux au Palais Royal, sous les Colonnades N.o 258.

has called it, was enhanced by the tour the ambassadors were given of Paris highlights. By picturing the ambassadors in the newest promenades and shopping destinations, prints associated them with the cosmopolitan aura of the capital. Tellingly, a print represented them admiring the Palais Royal.

Style-conscious people like the young Joséphine, Térézia, and Juliette were impressed by the luxury of the fabric, embroidery, and cut of the ambassadors' dresses, as well as the harmonious combination of their dresses with sashes and turbans—without being able to perceive them otherwise than as foreign. Among the Indomaniacs, it was Elisabeth Vigée Lebrun who left a complete visual record of her observations. The same artist who had painted the scandalous chemise portrait of the queen in 1783 once again, in 1788, depicted the fashion craze of the moment.

Vigée Lebrun dedicated most of the portrait's surface area to ambassador Mohammed Darvesh Khan's outfit: a floor-length dress, sashed at the waist, worn under an embroidered jacket, with a turban wrapped around his head. By choosing a slightly low point of view, the artist conveyed the pride of the ambassador, and also the luxurious expanse of what she knew was an exorbitantly expensive fabric. French women already coveted this fabric, a cotton so fine it was like mist. The chemise à la reine Queen Marie Antoinette had worn for her notorious portrait was made of extremely expensive muslin. To cotton connoisseurs, the queen's portrait had been all the more outrageous because they could tell she had squandered an immense sum on her hopelessly inappropriate dress.

This was the sort of cotton elevated to an imperial level by seventeenth-century Mughal rulers. Indian textile specialist Sylvia Houghteling has shown how the emperors Akbar and Jahangir developed the manufacture and Indian market of Bengali muslin, and demanded it as tribute. Portraits of the emperors wearing the fabric, enthroned amid their silk- and fur-clad courtiers, proclaimed Bengali muslin's superiority. Sometimes called *malmal*, or *mulmul*, it was so ethereal it seemed as if it had been made by magic.

The magic was in fact extraordinary Bengali skills. Bengali muslin began with a type of cotton plant, *Phuti karpas*, which grew indigenously in the region, now mostly Bangladesh. The plant is no longer known to exist. Thread spun with the short-staple fibers of *Phuti karpas*

Vigée Lebrun recorded the clothing all Paris raved about in her 1788 *Portrait of Muhammad Dervish Khan, Ambassador to Tipu Sultan.*

was so delicate it could be worked only in the dampest local conditions, and only by young spinners whose eyes were still sharp enough to see the gossamer threads. Today, fine open-weave all-cotton muslins (as opposed to smooth sheet fabric) boast a thread count of up to 200 per inch. Imperial Bengali muslin had a thread count of 800–1,200 per inch. Yet thread count underestimates Bengali muslin, because it is the cellular structure of its raw material and the space between filaments on the loom that made it "*baft-hawa*," woven air, in the words of Mughal poets.

European spinners and weavers simply could not duplicate the most exceptional Bengali techniques, no matter how hard they tried. The differences were visible, and still are. With your eyes within three inches of real fabric, or in a highly magnified photograph, you can see that the matte, tubular, widely spaced threads of muslin look quite different from the thicker, flatter, more lustrous, more closely spaced threads of the finest European linen fabrics. I have handled revolutionary-era muslins in museum costume collections (with gloves). Woven air is no exaggeration.

Early European visitors to the Mughal imperial court quickly noticed Bengali muslin. Merchants found an eager market for fine muslin back home, though little of the imperial best could be obtained. Some may have been given to monarchs as diplomatic gifts. In 1788, the ambassadors from Tipu Sultan gifted Queen Marie Antoinette with lengths of muslin described at the time as "very beautiful." (Had rumors of the queen's penchant for chemises à la reine reached Mysore?) In return the ambassadors received French silks woven in the textile center of Lyons, which shows that by 1788 the French understood the two sorts of fabrics were equivalent. "Very Beautiful" muslin and Lyons silk were both clearly in the same league as the box of pearls, large ruby, and 250-piece set of the finest French porcelain that were also exchanged between the monarchs.

To the surprise of Parisians, the male members of the Indian embassy wore their muslin sewn into a one-piece garment. It had a crossover, sleeved top, and a long, extremely tightly gathered skirt. Paris style connoisseurs could not assimilate the garment, called a *jama*, either to a gown or to a chemise à la reine. Jama muslin was so fine that the body could support the skirt, though the skirt was tightly gathered enough to appear opaque, whereas European gown skirts were so bulky they had to be mounted separately onto a sturdy waistband. A jama resembled a chemise à la reine inasmuch as it was a sleeved floor-length item made of white muslin, but a jama had a tight, fitted body and sleeves. All the parts of a jama were nearly rectangular and assembled, whereas the complexly shaped pieces of gowns were distributed into separate gown parts. Jama simply wrapped and tied, whereas European clothing featured multiple fastenings: laces, stiffeners, padding, serried rows of buttons, and a concealed bristle of pins.

Jama, like Bengali muslins, had been remarked on by early European visitors to Mughal imperial courts. A French traveler in the middle of the seventeenth century, Jean Thevenot, exclaimed: "I cannot tell how to express the manner of it more intelligibly, than by saying it is a kind of gown, with a long Jerkin fastened to it, open being too clutterly." The "manner" of the jama, in other words its construction, was not immediately "intelligible" to Europeans because their "gowns" were constructed differently. By being sewn into one simple garment, jama avoided being "clutterly."

Vigée Lebrun reveled in the simplicity of the jama by painting it as if it were pure solid white. In real life, the most precious jama were embellished with gold embroidery, as surviving examples demonstrate. Just as the most valuable European embroidery was stitched with gold or silver thread, so the most lavish Indian embroidery had perfected the use of sequins, called *tikki*, often in conjunction with *kalabattun*—threads wrapped with silver or silver-gilt *badla*, flattened strips of metal wire—and *gota*, trim or ribbons made with *badla*.

Many less precious muslins, which looked solid at a distance, were

Detail of incomparable Kashmiri shawl technique.

actually embellished with white-on-white embroidery. *Jamdani*, done mostly in the Bengal region, wove supplementary threads directly into the muslin on the loom. *Jamdani* designs, accordingly, tend to be regular and geometric, in keeping with the mechanics of a loom. At very close range, you can see the loom threads going up and over the design threads. Even on a moderately fine muslin, the design thread, which in other situations would look very fine, looks like a gross white rope in comparison with the weave threads. Another major white-on-white technique, which offered more design latitude, was called *chikandari*, or *chikan* work. *Chikandari* motifs were stitched in dozens of ways onto muslin, including long smooth stitches close together, chain stitches, and pulled-thread openwork. *Chikandari* created fields of flowers, vines, and complex foliage that meandered across expanses of white muslin. *Jamdani* and *chikandari* both resembled European lace.

To Parisian eyes, the Indian visitors wore a fascinating combination of sewn one-piece jama muslin dress and wrapped flat rectangles of cloth. Europeans had been accustomed to garments made with intricately cut and tailored pieces for hundreds of years. Yet the ambassadors and their retinues had simply wound fabric around their heads into turbans, and around their waists into sashes. Vigée Lebrun's portrait of Mohammed Darvesh Khan clearly displays her interest in the lavishly embroidered sash, called a *patka*, by emphasizing its breadth, which made the jama waistline seem very high. The other important wrapped flat rectangular element of Indian men's apparel is conspicuously absent from Vigée Lebrun's portrait, as it is from other images of the ambassadors' visit. Many courtiers at the imperial Mughal courts are shown by seventeenth-century miniature paintings wearing a quarto formula of jama, turban, patka, and Kashmiri shawl. Not all, however. Presumably, the marvelously warm shawls were not required in hotter weather. The visit of Tipu Sultan's ambassadors to Paris took place during the summer months, and many an eighteenth-century picture drifting into Europe from colonized parts of India showed men without shawls. The Kashmiri shawl remained a mysterious clothing item in 1788.

Tipu Sultan's ambassadors returned to India. The memory of their clothing receded. Too much was happening too fast in 1788. The art world felt political and economic crisis escalating. High on the list of art topics discussed in the salons ranked the meteoric career of Jacques-Louis David, who threatened the Royal Academy with a style of painting that expressed his angry politics. David's sharp-edged, illusionistically detailed style, which breathed new life into moralistic scenes from antiquity, rebelled against an academy of art beholden to the Crown. His style and career were the antitheses of Elisabeth Vigée Lebrun's flattering pastel tones and dependence on royal patronage. Yet he was not above painting portraits, as she did, to make money and spread word of his skill. In 1788, his most stylish portrait was of a couple: Antoine Lavoisier and his wife, born Marie Anne Pierrette Paulze. David was so acutely aware of fashion that at first he represented Madame Lavoisier wearing the latest fashion-plate hat, though he then painted out the hat, and added scientific instruments, to shift the balance of the portrait from femininity toward Monsieur Lavoisier's masculine endeavors.

Monsieur and Madame Lavoisier occupied the same social position as Julie Bernard and her three consorts. Antoine Lavoisier, like Juliette's fathers Jacques-Rose Récamier and Jean Bernard, earned an income by serving the Crown's finances, in Lavoisier's case as a tax collector. At the same time, Lavoisier conducted experiments leading to crucial discoveries about oxygen and the composition of water, which made

David, the most ambitious painter in France, showcased the latest fashion and deportment in his double portrait of the famous scientist Lavoisier and his artist wife.

him a prominent Enlightenment intellectual. He did not perceive the two aspects of his work as the contradictions they had become. He remained confident that Enlightenment would lead smoothly to necessary reform of the monarchy.

Nor did the Lavoisiers understand the contradictions inherent in the clothing they so proudly chose for their grand portrait. Like their queen, they blithely posed for posterity dressed in what they thought were merely the latest fashions, rather than signs of a monarchy hurtling toward its doom. He wears a solid black three-piece suit, devoid of any embroidery, whose high cost is discretely proclaimed only by the painter David's representation of a silken gleam at the knee of his *culotte* breeches. Monsieur Lavoisier had no idea the black suit's challenge to the sumptuary hierarchy of French nobility signaled the advent of a radical democracy, the execution of the king, a reign of terror, and his own execution by the guillotine within six years. Madame Lavoisier boasts with subtle understatement a muslin chemise à la reine, tied at the waist with blue silk satin. She had no idea a *Declaration of the Rights of Man and of the Citizen* was going to lead the enslaved in France's colonies to demand their freedom and women to claim equal rights.

Madame Lavoisier may have been deluded because the way she wore the novel chemise à la reine conformed fundamentally to rules of women's clothing centuries old. Fashion magazines instructed her: "Under this transparent dress, she wears a petticoat and stays." Rumors circulated that in private, dangerous women wore the chemise à la reine without stays—maybe even Queen Marie Antoinette at her Trianon retreat within the grounds of Versailles. But as David emphasized in his portrait, with the cant of Madame Lavoisier's torso and the huge bell of her skirts, a chemise à la reine was no excuse for abandoning the essential foundations of feminine respectability in public.

This was 1788, the year Bernardin de Saint-Pierre's *Paul et Virginie* became the best-selling novel of France. If Joséphine, Térézia, and Juliette did not read the book themselves, they knew someone who did. The salons of Paris discussed with fervid admiration the novel's primeval island setting and its romantic faith in true love. Readers gasped at the horrible, unforgettable, sublime culmination of the novel's plot. The heroine is shipwrecked within sight of her home and her lover. Virginie faces a life-and-death choice. Either she sheds her petticoats and swims to salvation, or the sodden "bouffant" mass drags her to the deeps. "And Virginie, seeing death was inevitable, placed one hand on her clothing, the other on her heart, and raising her serene eyes on high, seemed like an angel who takes flight toward heaven."

Calls for King Louis XVI to make major concessions to the Third Estate were getting louder. Complaints against taxes, fiscal policy, abuse of privileges, the price of bread, and the coldest winter on record were escalating. Women were undermining the medieval clothing guilds by shopping for androgynous accessories or chemises à la reine from *marchandes de modes* and strolling the Palais Royal. Yet Virginie's self-sacrifice—possibly the first "fashion victim" in literature—dramatized the still-conservative demands of Paris style. The magazines all agreed: women would never cease wearing gowns, with shaped, conical bodices and wide skirts over "petticoats." Not ever.

Coeffure en Fichu. Spencer de Velours.

PART II

DURING THE REVOLUTION

1789–1804

Mise d'un Jeune Homme.

CHAPTER 4

OFF WITH THEIR SILKS

1789–1793

THE FRENCH REVOLUTION OF 1789 began in *redingotes*. When this jacket, with its high collar, wide lapels, and big buttons, became the key part of the three-piece suit, it led revolutionary men to dismantle the royal sumptuary apparatus. For men in suits, a masculine fashion revolution was stitched into systemic legal, economic, and labor reforms. They did not intend it to lead to a feminine fashion revolution. The one traditional social relationship revolutionaries did not want to disrupt was the gendered relationship between men and women. Feminine fashion hardly changed in any important way during the early, constitutional, years of the Revolution. Yet a masculine fashion revolution cleared away all obstacles to style invention, and set the example for a radical change of clothes.

King Louis XVI was obliged by fiscal crisis to call an assembly of the Estates General, which had authority to raise taxes. The Estates General had not been resorted to for over 150 years. Doing so required the dangerous inclusion of the Third Estate: the unprivileged, highly taxed 99 percent of the French population. The hereditary nobility of

By 1791, Rose de Beauharnais had adopted a curved version of the masculine redingote jacket.

Térézia posed in a redingote bodice and androgynous hat.

the ecclesiastical First and secular Second Estates sent representatives inclined by birth to preserve the status quo. The representatives of the Third Estate, however, were elected, which whetted their appetite for a new form of government. They came to Paris with litanies of local grievances (*cahiers de doléances*) far exceeding what Louis XVI and his nobility had expected the Estates General would deal with. A pamphlet published in January, written by Emmanuel Joseph Sieyès, roared: "What is the Third Estate? Everything. What has it been hitherto in the political order? Nothing. What does it desire to be? Something." The representatives of the Third Estate took action as an elected government. On July 14, 1789, the royal fortress of the Bastille in Paris fell to a mob. Everyone realized a world-historical revolution had begun.

Joséphine and Térézia expressed their support for the early Revolution by posing in redingotes. Fashion magazines throughout the 1780s had trembled at the merest hint of androgyny, when women adopted feminine versions of the jacket in lieu of bodices, despite the uncontested continuation of stays and long full skirts. After summer of 1789, however, the revolutionary resonance of the redingote overrode gender conservatism—just a tiny bit. Joséphine posed for the first portrait of her that survives in a tricolor redingote celebration of the new French nation. Her blue bodice opens alluringly at the neck to reveal edges of red vest and white chemise, while her red-white-and-blue head-dress nods to men's military hats. Térézia posed in a high-buttoned, high-collared example with matching top hat, the masculine severity relieved by plumes and a light full neck bow. In December of 1793, at the start of her relationship with the militant Tallien, she gave a public speech in support of the Revolution looking "stunningly beautiful" in a redingote-inspired gown with contrasting lapels and buttons—the earliest verbal description we have of an outfit worn by her. It sounds similar to Joséphine's portrait apparel.

Térézia and Joséphine had personal reasons to express their enthu-siasm for the Revolution. Their transactional marriages into mainland aristocracy failed so catastrophically that their illusions about the insti-tutions of the ancien régime were destroyed.

DESPITE Joséphine's Paris makeover, her husband Alexandre de Beau-harnais was never satisfied with her. She hadn't read enough books, didn't sparkle in salon gatherings, didn't write him often enough, demanded too much attention, didn't understand him sufficiently. We know this from pedantic letters he sent her while he was off on military adventures and with his several mistresses. If only she would apply her-self the way he told her to, she could improve, he intoned. "I am ready to choose domestic happiness and peace before the riotous pleasures of society. However, behaving as I did, I fancied that my wife—had she felt genuine friendship toward me—would strive to draw me closer to her and to acquire those qualities which I admire and which would hold me in check. Not so!"

Whatever his disdain, the family transaction that had married Joséphine—then still called Rose—to Alexandre de Beauharnais required an heir. He breezed through Paris between dalliances and nine months later Joséphine gave birth to a boy, Eugène, in September 1781. She was seventeen years old. Alexandre was pleased at the birth of an heir, but by November 1781 he had gone off gallivanting again. Joséphine began to build her own alliances through her in-laws' social networks, notably with members of the powerful secret society of Free-masons, who favored Enlightenment philosophy and political theory. When Alexandre returned, she immediately became pregnant again. Left behind in Paris, she gave birth to a daughter, Hortense, in April 1783. Joséphine wrote to an aunt on Martinique that she had learned to "correct herself of the very strong feeling" that her husband had "inspired in her."

Instead, Joséphine reoriented her plans around her children. Biog-raphers have emphasized her subordination of herself to men, espe-cially Napoléon, because he was, well, Napoléon; but the pattern of her decisions can also be interpreted as tactics to protect and advance her children.

When Alexandre de Beauharnais received news of his daughter's birth in Paris, he wrote Joséphine in a rage. The baby, he stormed, was not his. Alexandre wrote from her native island of Martinique, where he had gone with yet another mistress—ironically, because Joséphine's family was there. Alexandre's mistress, in the hope of detaching him from his wife, had bribed an enslaved servant to tell an extravagant tale about Joséphine's premarital sex life on Martinique. Family and friends on the island said the tale was ridiculous, but it suited Alexan-dre to believe it. He was within his marital rights to order his wife into a convent.

> Make your arrangements; never, never will I allow myself to be so abused again, and since you are the sort of woman who would fool people if we lived under the same roof, be so good as to get yourself to a nunnery, as soon as you receive my letter. . . . You will continue to deny, because from your earliest age, you have made falsehood a habit.

Alexandre stormed back to France to enforce his decision. A nineteen-year-old Joséphine temporized, hired a lawyer, fought back, and won a 6,000-livre pension and custody of her children, though she did have to concede that their son, Eugène, would be returned to his father when he turned five. Of their daughter, Hortense, Joséphine wrote to her father: "She is my consolation; she is delightful in face and character."

Alexandre's order to join a convent backfired. At the Pentemont Abbey, run by Bernardian nuns, social networking was practiced better than piety, and Joséphine made well-connected friends. Though some women retired to convents permanently, others, like Joséphine, resided there temporarily and provisionally during difficult phases of their lives. When Alexandre's furor subsided, she moved in with his family, which implies they were not entirely on his side of the marital argument. She had trouble getting Alexandre to pay her pension. In 1788, taking Hortense with her, she retreated to Martinique, from which Alexandre had returned to France. Against the odds, Joséphine had broken free of her abusive marriage and, together with her daughter, begun to manage her own life.

Away from mainland France, Joséphine missed the start of the French Revolution. She stayed on Martinique till 1791, alternately reconnecting with family in her childhood home, and amusing herself in the capital, Port-Royal. From Port-Royal, she wrote home for a dozen fans and "a casual fine linen ball dress"—our earliest indication that the fabrics commonly worn in the humid heat of Martinique inclined her against formal silk. In Port-Royal, a lifetime of insinuations against her moral integrity also began, in contrast to the island's earlier defense of her when Hortense was born. An army officer who met her in 1789 remembered more judiciously than many acquaintances:

> This woman, without being exactly pretty, pleased with her figure, her cheerfulness, and the goodness of her heart. Preoccupied with procuring the pleasures to which her age and charms entitled her,

she quite publicly challenged the more or less flattering opinions one might have had about her. But as her funds were extremely limited and she liked to spend, she found herself frequently obliged to dip into the purse of her admirers.

Joséphine had not grown prettier with adulthood. She minimized her bad teeth by smiling and talking with her lips as closed as possible. Nonetheless, men were strongly attracted to her body. She was the sort of slender that gets called willowy, because she swayed easily and gently. Her limbs, hands, and feet were all delicately fine. Sources disagree about her height, but it is possible that she was even taller than Térézia. (Of the three pairs of shoes belonging to the revolutionary fashion trio and preserved in the French national costume collection, the longest and narrowest is Joséphine's, while the smallest by far is Juliette's.) For the rest of her life, descriptions of her tended to include the sexual effect of her body, even as they pointed out the imperfections of her face. Observers also tended to emphasize that her sexuality was not threatening, but charming instead.

What exactly Joséphine charmingly suggested to men is almost never clear. For the rest of her life, and for two centuries afterward, rumors circulated that she traded sex for financial gain, whether money, investment tips, or valuable gifts. Yet it is so easy to condemn women with this sort of accusation that one has to be skeptical. She may have gently solicited direct gifts of money. She probably gracefully suggested giving political or financial favors to other men, from whom she equally gracefully asked for money in return. These are the sorts of exchanges that are most effectively accomplished in person, without leaving paper traces.

Women had few if any alternatives, even within a legal marriage, even when titled *vicomtesse*, Joséphine had discovered to her chagrin. Monarchic legitimacy had failed her. The approved ways for women to obtain financial support she had experienced entailed subordination, entrapment, and arbitrary punishment. Besides fighting Alexandre in court for financial support, Joséphine turned to marginally illegitimate means of supporting herself, her son, Eugène, and her daughter, Hortense. After her marriage to Alexandre de Beauharnais disillusioned her, Joséphine took financial support only from men she could walk away from. (Even when Napoléon divorced her, she negotiated a terrific settlement.) Already by the time the Revolution started in 1789, she operated beyond the pale of feminine respectability because there was no independence anywhere else. Joséphine couldn't care less what people said about her afterward, as long as she and her children thrived. Let them talk. She was willing to suffer insinuations or outright accusations of impropriety.

Joséphine left Martinique in 1791 in fear of revolutionary revolts brewing in Port-Royal. She returned to Paris, not realizing she was headed into graver danger. On the mainland, Alexandre had become a political personality. He was among the nobles who supported constitutional government, and was elected president of the governing National Constituent Assembly. In his case there was not much privilege to give up, since his nobility was of such dubious and recent vintage. He went with the national army in 1792 to fight France's enemies. In January 1793 he voted for the execution of King Louis XVI. He and Joséphine reconciled at a distance for the sake of their children. She leveraged Alexandre's revolutionary positions to make friends among several political factions, including the Marquis de Lafayette, who supported a constitutional republic, and Jean-Lambert Tallien, a rising radical.

TÉRÉZIA'S marriage also fell apart as soon as it began. Her wedding night horrified her. Later, her daughter wrote as delicately as was then allowed:

> My mother, then 14 years old, a little naïve, lively and trusting
> to excess, had married without joy, and without sorrow, the man

presented to her and who she hardly knew. Her good and tender spirit would nonetheless have attached her to her husband if he, with his revolting acts, his unfaithful and profound immorality, had not saddened from the first moment this heart which asked only to give itself.

What were the "revolting" acts? People didn't tend to name them in those days. We do know that the Vicomte de Fontenay soon installed a lower-class shopgirl in the marital home as his mistress. The newlyweds agreed to live separate lives, and when Térézia gave birth to a son, called Théodore, on May 2, 1789, some people doubted who the real father was. Yet the Fontenay family accepted the baby as the heir to the (recently acquired) family title. After becoming a mother at fifteen years old, Térézia began to cultivate a social life separate from her husband's, turning away from the marital role expected of her, toward independence.

Among the many men and women who remarked on her exceptional beauty was the painter Elisabeth Vigée Lebrun, author of the scandalous 1783 chemise portrait of Queen Marie Antoinette as well as of the 1788 portrait in Indian apparel of the ambassador Mohammed Darvesh Khan. The portraitist had seen many a face over the course of her career, but none, she said, more lovely than Térézia's. "She was both beautiful and pretty. . . . Her smile, her gaze had something ravishing about them, and her figure, her arms, her shoulders were gorgeous."

Several sources later claimed it was in a gathering at Vigée Lebrun's studio that Térézia first met Jean-Lambert Tallien, a rising young revolutionary politician, who knew Joséphine and her husband well. Advocates of major ideological reform like Tallien ceaselessly built political alliances and honed their ideologies in public, notably in salons and in artists' studios. They swirled around Térézia, captivated by her beauty and her personality.

Everyone who ever met Térézia agreed, not only on the final verdict, but also on the details. Vigée Lebrun astutely pinpointed a union of the eternal and the singular, of perfection and character. Words like "goddess" and "sublime" alternated with more erotic vocabulary. When people described Joséphine, they talked about her silhouette as a whole and about how she moved. Yet when both women and men described Térézia, including Vigée Lebrun, they catalogued a long list of her body parts: her limbs, her torso, her breasts. Every feature, they gushed, was gently rounded and divinely proportioned. Many people added that her unusual height gave her exceptional presence, or that the intense contrast between her extremely black hair and her extremely white skin was exquisitely Spanish.

Not only was Térézia beautiful, people rhapsodized, she was good. It was like what people said about Juliette Bernard (later Madame Récamier) but more surprising, for the time, because Térézia was so erotically attractive. She elicited the French word "*bonne*," which means at once kind, generous, and sweet. It is always easy to guess which descriptions of Térézia are by people who actually met her, and which are not; invariably, the people who said she was astoundingly *bonne* turn out to be the eyewitnesses.

The social circles Joséphine and Térézia joined in the early, constitutional years of the Revolution believed with palpable fervor that they could start society all over again. The French Revolution of 1789 aimed not only to overthrow King Louis XVI but to change the mentality on which monarchy was predicated. Revolutionaries attempted to secure the freedom of thought they knew was fundamental to their vision of the future by reforming every aspect of daily life. Which is why they started their Revolution with a men's fashion revolution. The men around Térézia and Joséphine (still then named Rose) began to put their political convictions into action by wearing them.

The men's fashion revolution had been prepared for decades by the evolution of the three-piece suit. Named "the Great Renunciation" by early twentieth-century psychologist J. C. Flügel, the movement began in Britain, arguably at a precise moment. On October 7, 1666, the great diarist Samuel Pepys noted that King Charles II had announced his ordinary subjects should wear three-piece neutral wool suits in public.

The British suit came from the countryside, though it was sometimes worn in town to mark disapproval of fancier masculine attire. When the solid-color, high-collared, widely lapelled long-tailed "riding coat" migrated to France in the next decades, where its name was deformed into *redingote*, it was widely acknowledged to have originated in Britain, from whence came its practical utility. The redingote was described in 1725 by a French magazine as "clothing come from the English . . . very common now for the cold, the rain, and especially to ride horses." The next year a leading French journal pessimistically called it "an outfit very little flattering, and which according to all signs will have more success in the country than in the city." In 1786, a French fashion magazine was still identifying the new style from across the Channel with riding gear, in particular "buck-skin" breeches, "English Boots," and a long flexible cane, yet conceded it brought "grace, bearing, and ease" to menswear.

By the 1780s, the suit was also identified with British liberal politics. Gouverneur Morris, ambassador to France from the republican United States, mused: "Everything is *à l'anglaise*, and the desire to imitate the English prevails alike in the cut of a coat, and the form of a constitution."

The liberal suit had by no means eliminated what it reacted against. Throughout Europe, men of high rank who could afford sumptuous clothing switched back and forth between suits and magnificence depending on the occasion. Court clothing etiquette remained what it had been. The British invented the material object that is the suit; the French Revolution invested the material object with democratic principle.

Before the Estates General destined to launch the revolution convened, on April 24, 1789, representatives of the Third Estate asked the Crown's "Grand Master of Ceremonies" whether "particular" costumes would differentiate the representatives. "Particular" was the key word, shorthand for "particular to hereditary rank." The Grand Master swiftly responded that representatives of the First and Second Estates would wear feathers in their hats and robes in "magnificent" fabric. Representatives of the Third Estate would wear black suits. The Crown's first attempt to maintain monarchy hoped to quell sartorial rebellion. To the Crown's dismay, its proclamation was not obeyed.

It took only three days for the Third Estate to resist on behalf of equal clothes for equal men. By April 27, a Third Estate deputy retorted that "distinction in garments" might lead to all sorts of other nefarious distinctions. It was necessary and just for all deputies to appear "only as Frenchmen." A united nation meant united suits. The suit unified men, in theory, by being the same for men of every class: it unified them economically by being made of accessibly priced fabrics, and visually by its solid color and standard shape. In its purest form, its three pieces were made of the same fabric, notably black wool.

Arguments shot back and forth in pamphlets, letters, speeches, and newspaper articles, initiating all the themes that would come to characterize the constitutional Revolution. On the defense, a deputy of the clergy, both a prince of a religious chapter and a secular baron, announced he would retain his privileged purple apparel. On the offense, a deputy of the Third Estate accused the Grand Master of Ceremonies' order of "caprices" and noble attire of "imbecile arrogance," maintaining that a uniform dark suit would foster "union" and "virtue." The prominent representative Honoré Gabriel Victor de Riqueti, comte de Mirabeau, who would soon play a major role in the Revolution, endorsed a fiery public letter in favor of dark suits for all representatives. The letter opened with a salvo: Who did the Grand Master of Ceremonies think he was? The stakes of the suit controversy were no less than freedom itself. When the Crown imposed "arbitrary," "despotic" clothing rules, the letter thundered, it was a "symptom" that there was "nothing left to lose." "To give a different costume to the deputies of the different estates, is it not to reinforce the evil distinction among the estates, which we can consider the original sin of our nation, and from which we absolutely must be purified if we intend to be regenerated?"

"It is the funeral of the monarchy," observed Germaine de Staël when she watched the Third Estate representatives assemble in Paris on May 5, 1789, all dressed in dark suits. As a brilliant political analyst, she understood that the dark suits were not just themselves funereal; they spelled the death of monarchic values. The representatives of the Third Estate had acted preemptively on their demand that all representatives wear black suits, regardless of the rank into which they had been born.

An accurate and expressive painting was made in 1839 of the fateful assembly. With the advantage of hindsight, the painting visualizes what Germaine de Staël foretold. Members of the Versailles court sit high above, around the enthroned king, flanked below by the clerical First Estate representatives in purple or red and by the noble Second Estate representatives wearing gold-faced cloaks and holding feathered hats in their laps. (Also prominent—standing next to a table covered with gold fleurs-de-lis embroidered on blue—is Jacques Necker, Germaine de Staël's commoner father, who in 1789 was vainly trying to reform the monarchy's finances.) The solid black mass of the Third Estate representatives, however, dominates the painting's foreground space and from it rise Sieyès and Mirabeau. The Third Estate, closest to the painting's viewers, represents France's future.

On May 25, 1789, one of the revolutionaries among the representatives moved that the representatives of all estates must attend assemblies in dark suits. By June 11, a leading figure, Jean Sylvain Bailly, mayor of Paris from 1789 to 1791, noted that all representatives were indeed wearing the requisite dark suit, and that thenceforward only

Representatives of the three Estates are each shown as a group: the First, clerical and noble, Estate in the left foreground; the Third, common, Estate in the right foreground; and behind them, the Second, noble, Estate.

men in black would be allowed into the government's assemblies. And on October 15, a decree officially banned any clothing distinctions according to rank among representatives. The representatives of the noble First and Second Estates gave up their colors and ornaments, with all their shine and glitter. Thenceforward dark or neutral matte solids were worn by revolutionary men of every rank, on all occasions, informal and formal.

The masculine fashion world issued its manifesto against the ancien régime by denouncing the "luxury" on which fashion had previously depended. On July 5, 1790, a leading Paris fashion magazine, the *Journal de la mode et du goût* (Journal of fashion and taste), announced: "Luxury declines, the merchants cry; already gold and silver are no longer used for adornment; only solid colors are worn." The magazine applauded, calling the use of precious metals in clothing "barbaric," which was a code word for counterrevolutionary. In place of barbarism, the magazine proposed "taste." Anyone could be born with taste. Taste was an expression of individuality. (The magazine also asserted there would always be more "taste" in France than anywhere else.)

No Renunciation so Great could escape resistance. Some opposition came expectedly from conservatives, Catholic prelates for example, who have not yet to this day given up their cardinal red vestments. Objections also came from within the revolutionary government. Some of its most radical leaders turned to their ally David, painter of the double Lavoisier portrait. Revolutionary authority, David volunteered, required attire more artistically elevated than plain suits, something more like what the ancient Greeks and Romans had worn. In 1794, he made a proposal for official uniforms involving tights, tunics, and decorated cloaks. It was ignored. In 1795, David's persistent artistic admirers suggested he try again, and a few of the most pompous members of the government did sometimes wear his design for gigantic feathered hats and sweeping cloaks over sashed tunics, but not ordinarily. A member of the government tactfully chided in 1797: "We must stay closer to our customs [usages] instead of wanting to dress the representatives of the French people like Romans or priests." The three-piece suit had become "our customs" within eight years.

Middle-class men had found an ideal expression of their values. Equal yet competitive, the suit rendered all men alike, while accommodating individual detail. Skilled tailors corrected paunches, stoops, scrawny limbs, or awkward proportions according to a common upright, streamlined tubular ideal, with a hint of muscular strength across the (padded) shoulders. Assertions of personal taste and wealth were confined to the punctuation marks of hats, lapels, cravats, vest materials, or watches. Even trendy fashion magazines suggested only minor alterations to the suit. Over time, ankle-length pants replaced breeches, jacket tails lengthened or shortened, and vests alternated between single-breasted and double-breasted, yet men kept on wearing tailored pants, jackets, and vests coordinated into suits, season after season, decade after decade.

Countless portraits of men from these years confirm the potential of the suit for subtle affirmations of a new masculinity. For example, the 1793–94 portrait of Bertrand Barère de Vieuzac, who met the young Juliette while attending her mother's pre-revolutionary salon, and who went on to become an important member of several revolutionary governments. To convey his authority, Barère leans on official documents, but relies more on the suit, which abstracts his body into an impersonal silhouette. His dark jacket and pants conform to sober anonymity. He treated himself, however, to a flash of double-breasted, multibuttoned red vest and an exuberant plaid madras cravat.

These men in suits were capitalists. They believed in clothing markets regulated only by supply and demand. In 1791, the government abolished guilds. Two laws, passed within four months of each other, and named after representatives, eradicated labor organizations that had endured for more than five hundred years. The d'Allarde law, passed in March 1791, responded to a crescendo of complaints against guilds for constituting barriers to the "freedom" (*liberté*) of the individual. It granted workers freedom *from* guild authority. Guilds could no longer oblige workers to stay within a guild for their whole working lives, or set their wages. The Le Chapelier law, passed in June 1791, granted freedom *to* employers to hire and fire at will. Whereas the guilds had bonded masters and workers, the Le Chapelier law pitted the owners of property and workers against each other. Workers were denied the right to

Barère, extreme revolutionary, posed for a 1793–94 portrait in the newly egalitarian dark wool suit, accented by a bright vest and cravat.

an 9.   *Costume Parisien.*   *(268)*

Costume du Matin.

form what we call labor unions. Many historians mark the Le Chapelier law as the origin of the modern middle and working classes. From the capitalist perspective of employers, it was every man for himself. From the nascent socialist perspective of laborers, an organic system of mutual obligations had been replaced by conflict between a dominant middle class and an exploited working class.

The design, production, and marketing of French clothing had been unbound. In principle, after June 1791, anyone who wanted to set up a fashion boutique was free to, and could offer anything for sale they dreamt up. Anyone who wanted new clothes was free to choose whatever they wanted to wear from whatever store appealed to them. Nothing much actually happened, though, because by summer 1791 the French economy went into a tailspin. Money for new businesses or new clothes vanished.

Regardless of financial reality, the revolutionary government pursued its legal destruction of the old clothing order to its logical conclusion. In October 1793, the government decreed a law whose crucial passage reads: "No person of one sex or the other may constrain any male citizen [*citoyen*] or female citizen [*citoyenne*] to dress in any particular way, everyone being free to wear whatever garment and style of their sex they please." The word "particular" meant "according to inherited rank," just as it had when the representatives of the Third Estate first rebelled against the dictates of the Crown in April 1789. The start of the constitutional fashion revolution was fought by and for the elected representatives of the French people. Four years later, those elected representatives granted clothing liberty to everyone they represented.

Fashion historians have lamented the abolition of the guilds. Guild specialization in particular materials or techniques, and their years of disciplined training, had indeed fostered supreme levels of skill. Many have said that Parisian clothing crafts went into an inevitable and irreversible decline. Well over a century after the abolition of the guilds, a prominent French fashion historian expostulated: "One of the great crimes committed by the Revolution was to abolish the corporations and their privileges. It was an unforgiveable fault from which we suffer still today." Arguably, this type of opinion is somewhat nostalgic. Paris crafts limped along through sheer force of habit, and were revived in the nick of time by the development of haute couture for women in the middle of the nineteenth century. Moreover, tailoring too was a craft, more visible and coveted than ever, since men's tailoring no longer hid behind embroidery or lace.

After opening the Revolution with a clothing salvo, the revolutionaries proceeded to replace the absolute monarchy with a constitutional monarchy led by an elected government. In August of 1789 the government drafted the *Declaration of the Rights of Man and of the Citizen*. The *Declaration* announced the principle that all men have equal, natural, and universal rights; it formed the preamble of France's first written constitution, adopted by the revolutionary government in September 1791. A sequence of revolutionary governments—National Constituent Assembly, National Legislative Assembly, National Convention (usually referred to by abbreviations of those official names)—pursued the debate about how and why the *Declaration* would be put into practice. On September 27, 1791, the government declared "that it be declared relative to the Jews that they will be able to become active citizens, like all the peoples of the world, by fulfilling the conditions prescribed by the Constitution." After passionate disagreements, on February 4, 1794, the government declared the abolition of slavery: "It decrees that all men, without distinction of color, residing in the colonies, are French citizens, and will enjoy all the rights assured by the Constitution." The abolition of slavery occasioned the circulation of prints showing women of color in Antilles headscarves and jewelry, which must have reminded Joséphine of her childhood—though not in the most dignified goles.

Alongside these momentous legal proclamations, the Revolution's reform of daily life continued. A revolutionary calendar altered time itself. History was started all over again with the September 1792 declaration of the First French Republic, which became the start of Year I (not the January starts of either 1792 or 1793, which complicates translating between calendars). New weeks had ten days, and new months had names based on nature, such as Germinal for a germinating month in spring, or Thermidor for the thermal extremes of midsummer. Space was rationalized by a decimal system that standardized and coordinated the measurements of length, surface, volume, and temperature. France's geography was remapped by dividing the nation into eighty-three administrative regions (*départements*) roughly equal in size and numbered in alphabetical order. Town squares and streets were renamed. Grammar was adjusted so that all French people could address each other as equals.

Yet amid all these reforms, women's clothing remained essentially the same as it had been before the Revolution. When the October 1793 clothing law decreed, "No person of one sex or the other may constrain any male citizen [*citoyen*] or female citizen [*citoyenne*] to dress in any particular way, everyone being free to wear whatever garment and style of their sex they please," "of their sex" was a major limiting condition. Only men were full citizens of the new revolutionary Nation, and thus entitled to its full clothing rights. Nothing more needed to be explicitly stated in the law because male revolutionaries correctly assumed that the superior status of men would automatically keep men from wanting to dress like women.

They also counted on a hatred of women in pants that was common to all classes. Prints picturing the most radical women revolutionaries, with captions like "Françaises devenues libres" (French women become free), showed them in top hats and redingote bodices—bodices clearly worn over stays, and in skirts over full petticoats, though the skirt mass was raised a bit off the ground. The ankle-length pants that gave the most radical popular faction of the Revolution its name, *sans-culottes* ("without knee-breeches"), were obviously forbidden to women because they were,

Though revolutionary men had overthrown sumptuary laws for themselves, revolutionary women before the Terror were still confined by stays and petticoats.

after all, pants. (On November 7, 1800, the city government of Paris officially outlawed pants on women. The law was not revoked until 2013.)

French women had not become sartorially free at all. By 1793, the tectonic plates of men's style had created a new masculine sartorial landscape, while women's style had hardly budged. Feminine clothing habits did not yield even when time, space, and monarchy did. The same styles in vogue before the Revolution merely appeared in red-white-and-blue versions. Revolution in women's clothing was all surface and no substance, so far.

Women as well as men wore the most decorative sign of the Revolution: the *cocarde*. A small but visible red-white-and-blue circle, often gathered or pleated, the cockade was originally masculine and military. It began to be worn as a token of allegiance to the Revolution on the very day the Bastille fell, the fourteenth of July, 1789 (still today the French national holiday). At first men were expected to wear tricolor cockades, then were obliged to by law. Finally, on September 16, 1793 (30 Fructidor I), women were also obliged by law to wear cockades. Cockades, however, were only political ornaments. A business owner could pin a cockade to his middle-class suit just as well as a militant Jacobin could to his Phrygian cap. A woman could pin a cockade to her bodice over the same stays that the ancien régime had ordained. The clothing that had achieved deep, lasting, true political change among men was the revolutionary suit of 1789, not cockades.

A legal frenzy to oblige more and more people to wear cockades did not signal an increasing acceptance of the revolution. On the contrary, it signaled an increasingly unstable government frantically trying to enforce political virtue. By fall of 1793, the government was attempting to impose its authority with decrees, and with the guillotine. France was headed toward cataclysm. Only a violent national trauma would shake society enough to permit a women's clothing revolution. And only the personal experience of that trauma would cause Joséphine, Térézia, and Juliette to lead fashion where it had never been before.

(209.)

Costume du Matin.

Cheveux à la Titus. Tunique Courte,
garnie d'Agrémens en Chenille.

Tivoli.

CHAPTER 5

CUT TO NOTHING

1794

I N OCTOBER 1793, Queen Marie Antoinette was spuriously tried
and sentenced to death. David remorselessly drew the *ci-devant*
queen on her way to the guillotine. She had saved one last clean chemise in which to die.

The revolutionary government of France sank into authoritarian
violence, dragging Joséphine, Térézia, and Juliette toward disaster.
They did not cut their pasts out from under themselves. The Terror did
that for them.

The National Convention government was faced in 1793 with military threats from abroad, dissension within its ranks, and rioting in
the streets. In April, an extreme faction called the Committee of Public
Safety gained control; in late May, the Committee of Public Safety's
supporters expelled the moderate Girondins from the National Convention; in September, a Revolutionary Tribunal was given the power
of arbitrary pseudo-trials and immediate death sentences. On September 5, Barère—the habitué of Juliette's mother's pre-revolutionary salon
who posed for his portrait in a suit—now a member of the Committee

David drew the *ci-devant* queen Marie Antoinette on her way to the guillotine punitively dressed in a chemise.

of Public Safety, proclaimed: "Let us make terror the order of the day!"

By spring 1794, the law was whatever the Committee of Public Safety said it was. A counterrevolutionary traitor was whoever the committee feared, on the left or on the right. Denunciations settled factual, frivolous, or imaginary scores. Paris jails filled with supposed enemies of the nation, and so did those of provincial cities like Bordeaux. No one dared oppose Robespierre; he controlled the police, the politically doctrinaire Jacobin Clubs, and the loosely organized, easily enraged Paris Commune of militant workers.

Unfortunately for her, Joséphine was legally named Rose, vicomtesse de Beauharnais. Signing herself "Citoyenne Beauharnais" did not help. She was among those rounded up on the orders of the Committee of Public Safety and accused of various counterrevolutionary tendencies. Mostly she was guilty of being married to a noble. Alexandre de Beauharnais was accused of not fighting the enemies of France with enough enthusiasm, but above all he was guilty of being a vicomte. The title, too shallow to be acknowledged by France's ancient nobility, sufficed to incriminate him. Joséphine, still married to Alexandre despite their separation, was condemned to the same Les Carmes prison as her husband. Every morning after her incarceration on April 2, 1794, Rose was assembled with her fellow prisoners to hear whether she would die. Not just die. Would she, like Marie Antoinette, be reduced to a chemise, loaded onto an open cart, and paraded through the streets of Paris, while surging mobs screamed imprecations? Would she climb the steps of the guillotine to the shrieks of enough maddened revolutionaries to fill the Place de la Révolution, and be thrust beneath the blood-stained angle of the blade?

Many of Joséphine's fellow prisoners made it a sport to meet their fate with noble calm, just to annoy their jailors. Not her. Day after day, she wept. Nonetheless, she started a sexual affair with a tall, strong, handsome Republican general, also a prisoner, Lazare Hoche. Many prisoners during the Terror, expecting death daily, affirmed life in this way. Hoche himself later said the affair was not personally about Joséphine.

From prison Joséphine wrote to her daughter, Hortense: "It's so hard to be separated from you and my darling Eugène, I think constantly about my two little children who I love and hug with all my heart." The children, left in the care of a servant, sent petitions to the government and pleaded for their parents' release. In vain. Bribery obtained for them only the sight of their parents in a prison window at an appointed time. They waved from across the street. Alexandre and Joséphine waved back. It was the last the children would see of their father. On the twenty-third of July, 1794, at the age of thirty-four, Alexandre de Beauharnais was guillotined. Just before his execution, he wrote a dignified farewell letter to his wife and children, reminding Joséphine of his "fraternal attachment" to her, entrusting their children to her care, and affirming his patriotism. Four days later, the Terror ended. Joséphine was released from Les Carmes on August 6.

As for Térézia, she sensed political danger in Paris by the beginning of 1793, and sought refuge in Bordeaux, taking her son, Théodore, with her. Some of her relatives lived there. In Bordeaux, Térézia met Tallien again. He had been elected to the governing National Legislative Assembly of the newly declared French Republic in September 1792, then sent to Bordeaux in August 1793 by the Committee of

Public Safety to extirpate counterrevolution. Opponents of the Revolution who wanted to escape mainland France and reach the Caribbean French Antilles, where they had heard they would be safe, clustered in the port city. Térézia and Tallien became lovers. He was young and rather good-looking, with curly blond hair and a longish nose turned up at the end. More important, he held life-and-death power over the city of Bordeaux. He could protect her and her son.

Térézia had a terrible scare when she was accused of counterrevolutionary tendencies and condemned to a Bordeaux jail in early December 1793. In the absence of due-process trials or defined sentences, she could have stayed there for a very long time, or been executed. Tallien, however, was able to spring her after a few days.

Heedless of this dire warning, Térézia stayed in Bordeaux, where she devoted her leisure to intellectual pursuits: reading, playing music, and painting miniatures, to judge from a contemporary visitor's description of her Bordeaux apartment furnishings. She did make a show of loyalty to the Revolution. To participate actively in a revolutionary "national festival," she wrote a speech on the topic of education, pleading in favor of sympathetic and gentle pedagogy. She urged mothers to devote themselves scrupulously to their children, because a "careless and guilty" mother was a "monster" and a "public calamity." Her determination to keep her own son, Théodore, with her in Bordeaux despite the dangers of the Terror argues for her sincerity. To make her relationship to Tallien completely public, perhaps to fend off another arrest, she asked him to stand at her side in front of the crowd and read her speech for her. What people remembered was not the speech, however, but her appearance on the dais. This was the occasion on which she wore the redingote gown, which lingered in the memory of a witness.

At the time, Térézia's behavior, living with no shame in what was conventionally considered wanton debauchery, was shocking. She maintained her own apartment, where Tallien came and went. In the absence of a legitimate marriage, or an obvious legitimate income, detractors assumed she turned the sexual spell she cast on Tallien into cash. To compound her offenses, they alleged the money he paid her came from abuse of his government position.

Stories circulated of her sordid mercenary wiles. One repeated by most of her biographers features a watch: Among the first victims of the Terror in Bordeaux was a former mayor of the city named Saige, who was rich, and owned a wonderful watch. So wonderful that its brand, price, and technology are always detailed in the story—it was a Breguet watch, worth between 7,000 and 8,000 livres, and automatic. Abraham-Louis Breguet was the leading watchmaker in a golden age of watchmaking, appointed to the king, and collected by Marie Antoinette. The Breguet company is still in business, and makes new wrist versions of their luxurious 1780s pocket invention, one of which sells, as of this writing, for more than $189,000. When Tallien and his henchmen condemned Saige to the guillotine in October 1793, Saige coolly put the watch on the table at which his judges sat. Although Saige was ostensibly keeping the watch from being stolen by his future executioner, he was symbolically indicting Tallien as his true executioner. Tallien immediately indicted himself too, as a thief. He brazenly took the watch off the table and put it in his pocket. Later, witnesses saw him hand the watch to Térézia, who accepted it, though she knew where the watch came from.

Térézia, however, gave valuables away as fast as she acquired them, and often to counterrevolutionaries at risk. Supplicants received money, connections, or information, simply because they asked. Historians who work with primary sources now agree that Térézia used her influence over Tallien whenever she could to keep victims out of prison or help them escape the country. She was a real-life version of the Scarlet Pimpernel character of nineteenth-century romance novels, who cleverly saves the lives of nobles doomed to the guillotine.

She even rescued her first, abusive husband, Jean-Jacques de Fontenay. When Fontenay decided to flee mainland France for Martinique

in February of 1794, less than a year after their divorce, it was to Térézia he came begging for money to pay his passage. According to an
eyewitness—present because she herself was begging for counter-
feit passports—Térézia opened a casket, removed handfuls of jewels,
wrapped them in a kerchief, and told him, "Take it all, it's for you."

Such acts astonished critics who knew her only by reputation. Many
years later, one noblewoman remembered her surprise. Being noble—at
that time the comtesse de Gouvernet—she was in mortal danger in Bordeaux, when "Providence" sent her a "special protection" in the form of
a woman she had heard "used and abused her liberty," "Mme de Fontenay, then named *citoyenne* Cabarrus." In her desperation, Gouvernet
pleaded for help on the flimsy basis of having met Citoyenne Cabarrus
once in Paris. To the amazement of the comtesse, Térézia responded
immediately that she would convince Tallien to save her and her children. In keeping with every other reaction to Térézia, Gouvernet could
not refrain from exclaiming in her memoir: "No being had ever come
so beautiful from the hands of the Creator. She was a perfect woman."
Térézia's features, hair, skin, smile, height, grace, and voice were all
ideal. Alas, "one was penetrated by painful feelings when one considered that so much youth, beauty, grace, and spirit were abandoned to a
man who, every morning, signed the death of several innocents."

Like most of her contemporaries, the comtesse de Gouvernet was
convinced Tallien's toleration of, or collusion in, Térézia's actions could
be explained only by her sexual control over him. The Parisian leaders
of the Terror agreed. Térézia's counterrevolutionary critics believed she
served the Committee of Public Safety, but the Committee of Public Safety believed she was a counterrevolutionary. When complaints
against Tallien's leniency were lodged in Paris, they were attributed to
his "intimate liaison" with the "wife of the ex-noble Fontenelle [Fonte-
nay] . . . protector of her caste, nobles, financiers and profiteers."

At the end of May 1794 came the order of arrest signed by Robespierre himself. Condemned by the Committee of Public Safety, Térézia

was incarcerated in La Force. Of all the Paris prisons, La Force most horribly evoked how constitutional government had first turned toward Terror. It was where hundreds of prisoners had been massacred in September 1792.

One atrocity in particular stood for the violence into which revolution had descended. The princesse de Lamballe, lady-in-waiting to Queen Marie Antoinette in her Trianon palace enclave, was summarily tried inside La Force on the third of September. The princess was alleged to have engaged in lesbian sex with the queen, among other crimes against the people of France. After the foregone conviction, the princess was dragged outside the prison, where she was beaten and slashed to death by a mob. Her head was hacked from her body and paraded through the city on a pike to the Tuileries Palace. The mob demanded to see the king and queen. When Marie Antoinette appeared, furious cries from the mob demanded she kiss the mauled face of her friend.

Those are the confirmed parts of the princess's tragedy. At the time, rumors circulated of worse, rumors believed by both revolutionaries and counterrevolutionaries, each side according to its own paranoia: the princess's heart had been eaten by the mob, and her genitals hacked off to be paraded along with her head. This was the vortex of associations that whipped around La Force, the nightmare that haunted the women condemned to its cells.

By July 1794, Tallien and several other leaders of the Terror resented Robespierre's tyranny, and feared for their own lives. They plotted a coup d'état. Térézia got word she was about to be executed. Aided by a bribed jailor, she smuggled a message on July 25 to Tallien that has remained famous in the annals of French history.

> The police chief has just left here, he announced that tomorrow I
> will go before the tribunal, which is to say to the scaffold. The dream
> I had last night was so different. Robespierre no longer existed and
> the prisons were opened. A courageous man might be able to make

the dream come true, but thanks to your unworthy cowardice, no one will be left to enjoy such a good deed. Adieu.

Tallien managed to send her a reply: he would free her, or go to the guillotine with her. Two days after Térézia sent her ultimatum from inside La Force, Tallien rose to his feet in a full assembly of the governing National Convention and denounced Robespierre. Robespierre tried to retort. He was shouted down. Support for the Committee of Public Safety by the Jacobin Clubs and the Commune collapsed that same day. Térézia was released from prison on July 30 (19 Thermidor, Year II). Soon after Robespierre's execution, the Committee of Public Safety, the Montagne party of the far left, the radical Jacobin clubs, and the working-class *sans-culottes* Commune were disbanded. Ever since, the overthrow of the Terror in 1794, in the heat of that sixth revolutionary summer, has been called "Thermidor."

After the Terror ended, survivors were left to cope with its long-term consequences. Many women had been stripped of what defined them socially: their husbands, fortunes, and noble titles. Joséphine and Térézia had also lost their illusions about the French Revolution. Bartered as girls by their families in exchange for the slightest entry into nobility, they had been abandoned by their husbands, left outside the protection of Catholic marriage and French monarchy. No sooner had they begun to fend for themselves by allying outside of wedlock with constitutional revolutionaries than the Terror arbitrarily imprisoned them. To what social institutions did they owe debts? None.

AMONG the long-term victims of the Terror was also, not so obviously, Juliette Bernard. Whatever plans Jean Bernard, Pierre Simonard, Jacques-Rose Récamier, and Julie Matton may have had for their exquisite daughter, the Terror brutally interrupted them. By spring 1793, no one in France knew if they would survive the next week. No one knew how long the Terror would last. Any idea that Juliette might marry into the aristocracy, or into the wealthiest banking circles, had been rendered ludicrous by the mass emigration of aristocrats and the concealment of all valuables. Anyone previously associated with the monarchy and anyone in high finance anticipated death by guillotine. Bernard and Récamier qualified on both counts. Juliette's two fathers had served the monarchy, the one administering taxes, the other in finance. Récamier said he went to witness the beheadings of King Louis XVI and of Queen Marie Antoinette in order to prepare himself for his own execution.

The four parents must have panicked. How could they protect their wealth? If Récamier, the most affluent of the three fathers, were executed, how would Juliette's future be assured, since on paper she was not his child but rather Bernard's, who might also be executed? Their solution was to make Juliette Bernard the legal heir of Récamier—by marrying him. On the twenty-fourth of April, 1793, Juliette Bernard and Jacques-Rose Récamier were very quietly wed. He retained the remarkable good looks of his youth, and he was rich. Still, he was forty-two and she was fifteen. He was also her father.

Récamier had been openly raising Juliette all her life, so there is no question whatsoever that he was her emotional father. That he was also her biological father raises the issue of literal incest. The four parents probably did not expect to deal with this issue. They must have assumed that the Terror would end with Récamier dead, ideally before anyone fully realized his marriage to Juliette had occurred.

Privately, Récamier left a tactful explanation, written to a relative just after his engagement to Juliette. He alluded to a passionate youthful relationship with Juliette's mother Julie and declared his steadfast loyalty to Julie. He wanted to respect Julie's wish for her daughter's security. About Juliette he plainly wrote: "I am not in love with her." He felt a "genuine and tender attachment to her." He believed she would "ensure the happiness of my whole life" and that "the benefit will be reciprocal." He would have the satisfaction of doing his financial duty by his daughter, and would prove his everlasting devotion to her mother. At the moment he wrote the letter, Récamier could plausibly assume he would not outlive the Terror and Juliette would inherit his money.

At the end of the Terror, however, Récamier was alive, and Juliette was married to him. If the married couple had resorted to the radically new option of divorce, the divorce itself would have provoked the malicious gossip they dreaded. Instead, Juliette's family and friends protected their reputations, as much as hers, with a public relations campaign that paradoxically combined whispers with pronouncements. They openly proclaimed that Juliette's marriage was not sexually consummated. Year after year after year. People who didn't know the family well or who didn't care took this unlikely tale of perpetual virginity at face value. After all, on paper Juliette was the legal daughter of Jean Bernard. Those who knew more understood why the marriage hadn't been consummated, and quietly accepted the marital fait accompli. Of course their acceptance seems weird to us. But in a way the loud story of virginity must have made people feel better about accepting the Récamier marriage. They must have told themselves that at least father and daughter were not having sex with each other. Those who lived through the Terror understood that many strange decisions had been made under mental duress. They granted each other emotional amnesty and moved on. After amnesty came amnesia.

Juliette's niece, the person closest to her at the end of her life (technically Récamier's niece), explained in print that Juliette willingly consented to all the conditions of her "astonishing" marriage. Juliette gave consent to her mother Julie, after a "long conversation." In light of the story told so consistently afterward of Juliette's virginity, we can guess that a prime "condition" was to refrain from sex with anyone (including her father)—an arrangement no doubt sincerely presented to her as a temporary expedient. A Catholic girl of fifteen who had been educated by nuns may have believed that remaining a virgin could be saintly. Regardless, it would have been difficult for a girl of fifteen to refuse consent to her beloved mother, especially when her mother was backed by all three of the men who had acted as her fathers.

Unlike Joséphine and Térézia, Juliette survived the Terror with plenty of money and a husband. But her marriage was its own kind of judiciary verdict, and a lie. In an age that forbade extramarital sex to respectable women, it meant she was condemned to virginity for the rest of her husband's life, which meant her entire youth. At first her submission to her parents enforced her fate. Then, in 1816, women's revolutionary right to divorce was repealed. In a way, Juliette had been as betrayed by obedience to her family and to the institution of Catholic marriage as Joséphine and Térézia had been.

All three women had nothing left to lose after the Terror. Desperation opened their minds. They would not be defeated. They would do more than survive. They would make the most of what history had dealt them, whether colonial origins, damaged reputations, incarceration, or exclusion from normal marriage. It was time for the inconceivable alternatives.

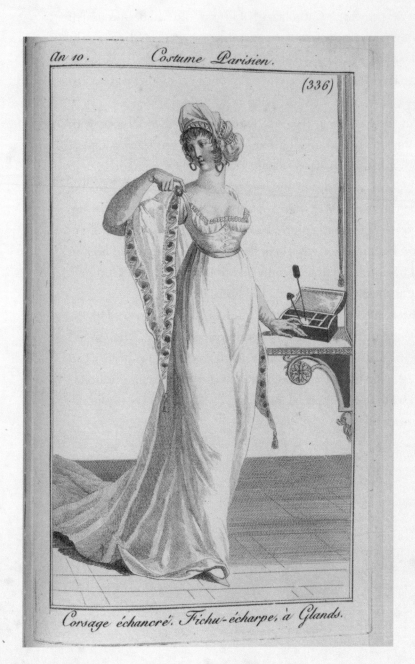

(336)

Corsage échancré. Fichu-écharpe, à Glands.

CHAPTER 6

DESPERATE MEASURES

(Térézia & Joséphine)

1794–1796

IN FALL 1794, Térézia and Joséphine appeared together in public
wearing dresses so slender and mobile no one could believe their
eyes. The contrast with what had been in style only months before
was incredible. Some aspects of the marvelous dresses seemed vaguely
familiar—the translucent muslin maybe, the phenomenal simplicity of
the cut—but the whole design was shockingly, delightfully fresh. And
the brazen confidence with which the two women wore their outfits!
Everyone in Paris wanted to see. The capital of fashion was conquered
within months. It was the fastest, most total change of clothes in history. Térézia and Joséphine resurrected into fashion paradise the same
garment in which Marie Antoinette had died.

How does any fashion change? Leaders always turn out to be crucial, but the conditions of fashion leadership are so various that many
academic disciplines contribute vital perspectives, including art history, economics, labor history, legal history, psychology, semiotics, and

sociology. In the usual cases, formal, individual, financial, technical, legal, sexual, rhetorical, and group factors each operate at different velocities, with overlaps and balances.

In the extraordinary case of the French Revolution, all factors interacted at gale force. Novel fabrics, embellishments, cuts, and silhouettes were immediately available from France's colonies. Traditional social structures could offer no resistance. An entire sumptuary court culture had vanished. The medieval guilds that controlled the making and selling of clothes had been abolished. Everyone in France suddenly had a legal right to make individual clothing choices.

It was a perfect fashion storm. One person found herself in the eye of the storm, in a unique position of influence at a single moment.

Citoyenne Térézia Cabarrus started a new life for herself on Thermidor, July 27, 1794. Far from breaking her spirit, the dread La Force had increased her resilience. Allowed after twenty-five days of solitary confinement to join the other prisoners in La Force, Térézia confronted death every morning. As she recalled, "executioners drunk with blood" assembled prisoners with a "frightening bell-toll of their enormous keys, and the rattling of their appalling locks" and read them the list of who would be guillotined that day. For the rest of her life, social scandals were laughable by comparison. Robespierre tried to bribe her into betraying Tallien, who he (correctly) feared was plotting against him. He sent a messenger to Térézia's cell: "Put it in writing that you knew Tallien was a disloyal counterrevolutionary [*mauvais citoyen*] and that he betrayed the Republic in Bordeaux, and we will give you your freedom and a passport to foreign countries." She answered: "I am twenty years old, but I would rather die twenty times." Her loyalty to Tallien became the romance that launched her legend. Robespierre had added insult to the injury of her incarceration: "Let her be given a mirror, once a day!" She turned her prison mirror image into the height of fashion when she was released.

France fixated on Térézia's story. When Tallien freed her from La

Force two days after Robespierre's execution, a crowd gathered at the gates to watch the lovers embrace in tears, then parted to let them walk toward a waiting carriage. The message she had sent to Tallien on July 25 inciting him to resist Robespierre was memorized and recited. Soon after, Tallien was wounded in an attempt on his life, possibly in revenge for Robespierre's fall. His first public appearance after his recovery, with Térézia, in the audience of the Odéon Theater, was announced ahead of time by newspapers. Every seat in the theater was filled, and more people packed the stairways. The crowd rose in a standing ovation to the couple. "*Vive Tallien! Vive Notre-Dame de Thermidor!*" Long Live Our Lady of Thermidor!

Térézia became the face of liberation from terror.

Our Lady of Thermidor was selected by the new government to lock shut the Paris Jacobin Club on November 11, 1794 (accompanied by a male member of the government), an act that symbolized the end to the power of the Jacobin faction that had supported Robespierre and the Terror. The prime minister of Britain, William Pitt, exclaimed, "This woman could close the gates of Hell." Térézia said she wanted peace, not revenge. To a woman friend back in Bordeaux, Térézia wrote: "Long Live, Long Live Forever the Republic! May factions and intriguers perish, such is the vow of one of their victims." She used her influence on the press. One idealistic young journalist remembered her urging him to support reconciliation by forgiving and forgetting: "Madame Tallien, who at the time seemed to us humanity incarnated in its most ravishing form wanted to see me and often indicated to me the most clever means to arrive at her saintly ambition." He added that the whole post-Terror régime was under the beneficial influence of women like Térézia.

Térézia, however, could not afford to live on adulation. She assessed her financial situation a month after her release from prison. It was disastrous. Her first husband had absconded with much of her dowry, and she had debts to pay for her prison expenses. (In those days, prisoners would bribe guards for necessities like edible food.) She was in an illegitimate liaison with a man who had no money, and who already she suspected was never going to earn any money. She wrote to a friend back in Bordeaux, asking her to sell anything of value she had left there, and send basic supplies: wine, oil, sugar, coffee, tea, candles. Such staples had become expensive to buy in Paris. Her cherished guitar, she hoped, would fetch a decent price, but her clothes, she lamented, wouldn't sell at all. Already by fall of 1794 her pre-Terror clothes were too old-fashioned to be worth much. She had a child to support, and soon realized she was expecting another. To satisfy social expectations, she might have to marry Tallien, even though that would solve none of her financial problems. In January 1795, Tallien wrote to a Paris newspaper that, contrary to rumors, "la citoyenne Cabarrus" owned no money in foreign banks and "much less" wealth in France than was whispered.

Térézia needed to profit from the social situation in which she found herself. Two waves of upheaval in rapid succession—the constitutional revolution followed by the Terror—had offered her unprecedented opportunities to maneuver into the heart of power. A provisional government was hastily constituted after Robespierre's execution, called the Comité du Salut Public, led by Paul Barras, with Tallien a key member. The government continued to feel precarious after its official establishment in 1795 as the Directory. Unscrupulous civilian and military officials mingled with financial speculators. Confiscated noble and church properties were traded in hasty, covert deals. Corrupt contracts with the Directory government, especially to provision the army, enriched commoners from one month to the next. The volatility of the official currency, *assignats*, enabled those with insider information to reap windfall profits. At their highest levels, these financial schemes were France's banking system. They were brokered during parties and in a new generation of salons hosted by ambitious women.

Released from the nightmare of the Terror, the whole nation partied. Inhibitions disappeared. People danced in the streets, cavorted with lovers, flocked to the theater, and flitted from salon to salon. "It was embraces in all the streets, in all the theaters, reciprocal surprise at being alive, which redoubled and rendered almost crazy the joy of this resurrection."

The revelers included unrepentant royalists, intent on causing trouble, who caricatured the new feminine and masculine clothing styles. In order to be fashionable, and at the same time show disdain for the Revolution, men in these gangs exaggerated the cravats and lapels of the new suit, while women took the brims of their hats and the trains of their dresses to ludicrous extremes. They were labeled Lady Marvels (*Merveilleuses*) and Incredibles (*Incroyables*), pronounced something like "mayvayers" and "anquoyables" in the lisping speech they affected to go along with their clothing.

What some interpreted as moral debacle or orgiastic frenzy was only the surface turbulence caused by profound and irrevocable social forces. Old noble elites had been executed, disgraced, or distanced by self-exile. Landed wealth had been confiscated, monarchic offices abolished. Into the void rushed young talent and entrepreneurial capitalism, so fast it felt like a hurricane.

Into that void also rushed a new clothing style. For a woman in Térézia's position to win a share of Directory power, no avenue was available other than the seduction of men. To attract and retain men's attention, the most visible lure would be a spectacular way of clothing her body. Térézia needed something on the order of the French Revolution: individual, free, and radically different from the past, something on the order of turning prison underwear into fashionable outerwear. For someone with her audacity, the wilder the gamble, the better.

All by herself, Térézia might not have translated a style concept into real garments. She had a new best friend, however, with an unconventional design imagination, and a knack for combinations. It does often take two minds in dialogue with each other to achieve a creative breakthrough. According to a proverb, "two heads are better than one." In fall 1794, the second head belonged to Joséphine, then still named Rose de Beauharnais.

Rose was freed from prison shortly after Térézia, to similarly dire prospects. Alexandre de Beauharnais had been guillotined days before; her dowry, his money, and his real estate had all been confiscated on the grounds of counterrevolutionary treachery, and the social privilege of his title had been abolished. People like her were contemptuously called *ci-devant* aristocrats. Her reunion with Eugène and Hortense de Beauharnais was joyful, but caused more financial worries. Rose wrote to her mother on November 20, 1794. "You will no doubt have learned of the tragedy that has befallen me: I have been a widow these four months past. The only consolation and support that are left to me are my children and yourself, mother dear." How was she going to survive, let alone feed, clothe, educate, and launch her children?

Rose still had contacts. She turned to the people she had met and cultivated after her marriage collapsed, during the first constitutional phase of the Revolution. She counted on the seduction skills she had deployed even in prison, during her fling with General Lazare Hoche, when she was already thirty—middle-aged by the standards of the eighteenth century. Rose got back in touch with Hoche. He was as tall, strong, and handsome as ever. Their affair may have revived, though not for long; his wife was more of an impediment than when they had been hidden in jail. But with his military career back on track, at least Hoche could reconnect her to the men who had organized the Thermidor coup against the Committee of Public Safety and seized government power.

Among those men, Tallien was a likely ally. Tallien had met Rose's husband while Beauharnais was a member of the pre-Terror National Constituent Assembly government. The two men became close enough that when both Rose and Alexandre de Beauharnais languished in Les Carmes, Tallien helped watch over their children, Eugène and Hortense de Beauharnais, while he shuttled back and forth between Paris and Bordeaux. Moreover, Rose had met Térézia in Paris, before Térézia and Tallien became a famous couple in Bordeaux during the Terror.

After the Terror, Joséphine and Térézia realized they shared the same determination to remake themselves. The two became best friends. Rose wrote to an aunt in fall 1794: "Madame Tallien is infinitely beautiful and good; she uses her immense credit to do favors for all the unlucky people who petition her, and she gives everything with such an expression of happiness that it was as if she were the one who should be doing the thanking."

Consider the friendship from their perspective. (History has so far looked at their friendship from the perspective of the men who led the Revolution.) Térézia and Joséphine left no written traces of their style collaboration. It takes only common sense and a little empathy, however, to find motive and result. Put their past prison experiences together with their sudden public appearances in a dramatically new style. What do best friends do when they share a desperate situation? They assess challenges, exchange ideas, build on each other's assets, come up with a plan, urge each other to be bold, and then support each other in public.

Contemplating their style options as they dressed to dominate Directory society in fall 1794, Térézia and Joséphine knew anything they chose had to work within the parameters of neoclassicism. Since the 1770s, a reaction against the pastel tendrils of earlier eighteenth-century rococo style had set in all over Europe. David was the most

"Morning dresses" in the *Journal des dames et des modes.*

prominent among a generation of artists whose sharp edges and primary colors invoked ancient Greece and Rome. Pure white became the artistic color of clothing choice, in the mistaken belief that marble sculpture had always been white. (In fact, the sculpture had lost its original paint.) Women danced with veils to perform classicism in salons, and posed for stylized portraits or *tableaux vivants* in long, shapeless white drapery. Such drapery was only costume make-believe, but it did have the approval of artistic authority, including David's.

Shapeless, however, was not what two women intent on seduction had in mind. The more accurate the classical costume, the less flattering it actually was. Genuine ancient Greek and Roman women's clothing had consisted of two wool rectangles as wide as an arm-span, each folded over and belted at the waist according to the wearer's height, the two widths pinned at intervals along the shoulders and arms. Every bit of painstakingly woven textile was preserved. That the cumbersome wool folds impeded movement was hardly a problem, because wealthy women who could afford to be richly dressed were supposed to spend most of their time sitting indoors—spinning thread or weaving more fabric.

How could a modern Parisienne, however, hop into a carriage loaded with such voluminous mantles, whirl around a ballroom, or gambol with her children? In the fall, winter, or spring she would shiver with her arms exposed, and drafts coming in from all sides. How could she fit the tailored redingote jackets and coats fashionable since the 1780s over wool rectangles bunched far beyond her shoulders? Authentic antiquity was out of the question for functional daily northern European attire.

One absolutely critical classical lesson had to be retained. Beneath their pinned wool rectangles, the women of antiquity had not worn anything—no stays, no petticoats. To eradicate stays and petticoats for daily wear would be a truly revolutionary move. The staple of every elite woman's wardrobe, the gown, was materially predicated on stays and petticoats to support its fifteen to twenty-five yards of opaque skirt. The gown's separate jacket was cut to fit exactly over stays.

The 1788 bestseller *Paul et Virginie*, the novel whose heroine chose to be dragged to a watery grave by her petticoats rather than shed them, had only become more popular in the 1790s. All it would take to shock society profoundly would be to appear on normal occasions (as opposed to onstage art events) free from under-armor.

Térézia could look back on her La Force incarceration and know what it was like to live for weeks without the foundation garments of femininity. Amazingly, it was possible. Though Rose had not been as sartorially deprived in Les Carmes, her own prison experience allowed her to imagine her friend's. The punitive chemise shift provided an idea. Exactly how its poor, rough linen and sack shape could be made glamorous, however, was not immediately obvious.

By winter 1795–96, when Térézia commissioned the famous portrait of herself in prison, the transformation had occurred. Though she had herself explicitly pictured in a horrible La Force dungeon cell (with a sentimental profile drawing of Tallien on the wall behind her), the rough linen chemise her jailors had mocked her with was reimagined as a pristine, fine white muslin dress, jauntily cinched with a plaid madras scarf. The raven hair that the jailors had hacked off with knives appeared in the portrait to be artfully styled in symmetrical layers. Humiliation had been elevated to jail chic.

What happened between early fall 1794 and winter 1796? Of all the styles in fashion before fall 1794, only the chemise à la reine could even hypothetically be worn without stays and petticoats. But in mainland France, fashionable, affluent women simply didn't dress that way. Drapery playacting in arty salons or theater did not translate into daily dress, as fashion magazines right up until the Terror attest. Joséphine (still called Rose), however, had been raised on Martinique, where women of color did wear the gole predecessor of the chemise à la reine for daily wear, in public, without stays or petticoats. Moreover, she had spent a long stretch of time on the island only three years earlier. (There is also a chance that the actress Julie Candeille wore something like a gole when she played the role of an enslaved woman in the explosive 1789 abolitionist play *Black Slavery, or, the Happy Shipwreck*, staged in Paris.)

Goles as they were worn on Martinique formed an overall straight white silhouette that could pass for classical. Goles had also evolved from coarse linens toward fine Indian cottons to subvert the sumptuary laws that forbade silk. Even the most luxurious muslin goles, the ones worn by the lightest women of color, were practical, with long fitted sleeves set into high armholes, unlike the puffy chemise confections worn by Queen Marie Antoinette and her acolytes.

That left the technical problem of fit around the bust and waist. Antilles goles were sometimes slightly nipped in at the waist, and French chemises had been sashed at the waist. It would be ideal, from the perspective of women like Térézia and Joséphine who needed to showcase their bodies—and who, after all, had grown up with pre-revolutionary clothing habits—for garments to be anatomically shaped. Nor were they or any women likely eager to switch to plain cotton surfaces. They were used to decoration. Those problems were both solved by following the commercial trail of Antilles gole fabrics right back to India.

The fine white cotton available to women of color in the Antilles could be found in finer, lavishly embroidered, versions in India. And in India, the finer, embellished grades of muslin were already being made into garments with fitted tops and long gathered skirts: men's jama. French colonists in India knew jama on a daily basis, and Paris had been fascinated by them in 1788 when Tipu Sultan's ambas-

"Gauze kerchief on a cherry-red velvet base. Priestess-style chemise. Sleeves in silk knit," in the *Journal des dames et des modes.*

1798.   *Costume Parisien*

(20.)

Fichu de gauze sur un fond de Velours Cerise.
Chemise à la Prêtresse, Manches en Tricot de Soie.

sadors arrived on their diplomatic mission. Though the transparency of jama could have been considered awkward, it corresponded to a fantasy that normal classical clothing had also been transparent. Not only did jama have waists, they were habitually worn with wide patka sashes that cinched waists intriguingly high.

Sashed jama solved every problem posed by genuine classical clothing. The columnar silhouette of antiquity had relied on belts slung low on the hips, which in real life looked lumpy to modern Parisiennes. But a high tight waist reconciled the ideal of a column with the desire for fit. A dress based on a jama would be light, compact, fitted where it counted, easy to layer over for warmth, and practical for active ordinary wear.

A dress worn without stays or petticoats was sure to be outrageous. A dress modeled on the clothing of people Europeans considered racially inferior was inconceivable. A garment borrowed from men would be illegal. But this was where the rage for classicism covered a multitude of sins. Europeans were so convinced of the natural superiority of their classicism that they were not going to identify the true origins of revolutionary dresses. They would see the Bengali muslin, the humbler indienne cottons, the Antilles gole, the jamdani and chikandari embroidery, the jama cut, the patka location of a waistline, and all they would recognize was their own classicism. The elimination of stays and petticoats would be impossible to ignore, but it would be mitigated by classicism, with just enough outrage left over to attract the attention Térézia and Joséphine hoped for.

The classicism already prevalent before 1789 cannot explain the speed with which fashion changed between 1794 and 1796. The sudden rupture of the Terror explains it, coupled with the immediate availabil-

Chapeau-Capote, orné de Fleurs et d'Épis.

"Turkish-style hat. Hood-hat," in the *Journal des dames et des modes.*

ity of ready-made models from France's colonies. Térézia and Joséphine were jolted into what might be called either appropriation or appreciation. In a wild moment when nothing was normal, they were able to introduce a radically new style to Paris at lightning speed because its elements existed already elsewhere.

Nonetheless, the dresses Térézia and Joséphine championed were not exactly identical to Indian jama or Caribbean goles. Sometime between fall 1794 and winter 1796 they adapted their models.

And then, the adaptation caught on like wildfire. After being sifted for accuracy, countless contemporary and retrospective accounts converge on those critical months as well as on Térézia's and Joséphine's leadership. The single most useful was written by a reporter from Britain, under the pen name "Lady of Fashion." This one source has it all: dates, names, locations, and outcome, all of which are separately confirmed by many other sources.

In 1796, the Lady of Fashion was first alerted to an astonishing revolution in Paris by a prolific commentator named Louis-Sébastien Mercier. According to the grumpy fifty-six-year-old Mercier, lascivious women had wrought a straight, unstructured dress malediction on the city. Upon further inquiry, the reporter heard that "females (though surely not the most virtuous) have actually appeared in public thus equipped." When the Lady of Fashion arrived on the spot, however, the turpitude did not seem so abominable, though the degree of the transformation since 1794 was indeed extraordinary: fashion was "wonderfully changed within these two years." The Lady of Fashion knew right where to get to the heart of the matter: a Paris theater. There she met a regular theatergoer, a Frenchwoman who was eager to talk. The Frenchwoman immediately singled out "Madame Tallien, asking 'whether I did not think her extremely handsome, and her dress charming?'—and then, before I could possibly answer,—'It matters not, however, what she wears,' added the French lady, 'for she sets everything off to the greatest advantage; yet, as you appear to be a stranger, I would recommend to you to notice her dress, it being the newest taste, and called *robe ronde à la Flore*; surely nothing can be more becoming.'" The French informant proceeded to boast that the Parisian style led by Madame Tallien was so superior that the rest of the world would soon imitate it: "We have such a variety, and all so elegant, that you will be puzzled which to admire most—a circumstance, of course, you will not be surprised at—because since forever, French ladies have made themselves famous for their fashions, and all the nations of the globe rush to follow them, and copy us." To show the reporter copying in action, the French informant pointed to two women in an adjacent box, dressed in outfits like Térézia's. She reassured the reporter that the two women were "*femmes comme-il-faut*," respectable women. Curmudgeons like Mercier wanted to believe that the fashion revolution was confined to immoral women, but the British Lady of Fashion saw that Térézia had influenced all ladies of fashion.

STAGE 1 Traditional three-part gowns began to change into radical one-piece dresses when bodices were attached to skirts.

If only the Lady of Fashion reporter had illustrated her letter. Unfortunately, no visual evidence records exactly how the two fashion leaders went from gowns to dresses between fall 1794 and winter 1796. Maybe their audacity and imagination allowed them to switch their entire wardrobes in one fell swoop. And perhaps their entire wardrobes had been confiscated or lost while they were in prison.

We can, however, see the process of change during these crucial months thanks to a few very precisely dated paintings of other women. (There are no fashion magazines to help us here, because the Terror halted the publication of all Paris fashion magazines, and the great post-Terror fashion magazine, the *Journal des dames et des modes*, didn't launch

STAGE 2 Waistlines rose and skirts deflated.

Waistlines settled right under the bust and petticoats vanished.

STAGE 3

A newly married Joséphine celebrates the fully developed columnar dress.

STAGE 4

until 1797.) These detailed paintings chart fashion revolution in four stages. Early fashion adopters could have taken the process one, two, three, or four steps at a time.

In **Stage 1**, the multipart gown was abandoned in favor of the single-part dress. Union was achieved between the bodice and the skirt, at the natural waist. This dramatic junction was concealed by a narrow sash, usually in a contrasting color. From the pre-Terror jacket, the Stage 1 bodice inherited a back fitted by a diamond-shaped piece, and inset, long fitted sleeves. Venturing into novel construction experiment, the Stage 1 bodice was fit in front by being gathered at the throat on a drawstring. The crossover front flaps of the Indian jama top hid beneath this gathered front. In Stage 1, the skirt started to deflate over residual petticoats.

In **Stage 2**, sashes crept upward from the waist, whether they got wider or were doubled. Skirts continued to diminish. At this critical point, stays were no longer necessary because the waist was freed, and petticoats dwindled.

In **Stage 3**, the dress silhouette reached dramatically new proportions of very small top to very long skirt. Sashes crept up right under the bust, and any remaining petticoat looked more like a gathered lining.

In **Stage 4**, Stages 1–2–3 arrived at their logical conclusion. The skirt was so pared down that the white cotton dress looked columnar, though it was in fact a skirt gathered and mounted to a bodice with a seam. The seam continued to be concealed by a sash. In Stage 4, stays and gathered petticoats were banished completely, and the dress was worn over a straight slip. Whether long or short, its sleeves were inset.

At Stage 4, we finally have a visual testimonial to Joséphine's leading role in the launch of the revolutionary dress. For a full-length portrait painted in spring 1796, she posed as confidently and dynamically as if she had been wearing this brand-new dress concept all her life, as if she hadn't just broken barriers in women's clothing history five hundred years old. She twisted backward in a way no stays would have allowed, her skirt hanging between her knees and wrapping around her calf, free from all petticoats.

The four stages mark a clear, linear path away from the traditional gown toward the revolutionary dress. Most people probably went through messier fashion adoptions, which turned leading examples into a social movement. What if in 1794 your wardrobe was stocked with gowns made out of valuable fabrics? Or if the new style both attracted and scared you? Or if the materials and techniques appropriated from colonial sources were so alien to your European sensibility that you were confused about how you would cut and sew your next dress? Or if you lived far from Paris, and fashion news reached you slowly or unreliably?

Dressmakers and wearers rarely leave written answers to such questions. An unusual journal entry provides rare insights. When Maria Nugent, across the Atlantic in Jamaica, was presented with a new-style dress from Paris, designed for balls, she puzzled over its strange cut. Though she lived in the Caribbean, she could not recognize the gole. She wrote that her new ball-dress had "sleeves" though "scarcely any," and she was especially surprised that it was all in one piece, for which she used a British word, "frock." Nugent proclaimed the straight-line, one-piece muslin dress "the admiration of all the world over." The style change was so dramatic it made her ponder the future of fashion, wondering if "fifty years hence," it would "be laughed at and considered as ridiculous as our grandmother's hoops and tissures [metal-thread silk brocades] appear to us now."

Costume de bal.

an 11.   Costume Parisien.   (467)

Bonnet du Matin, Corset Élastique.

Surviving dresses in museum collections mutely but vividly echo Nugent's doubts. A sudden, radical style change certainly posed thrift and design challenges to most women. The material traces of those challenges are signs from the past for us to decipher in the present.

It was worth cutting the most precious fabric you had invested in or inherited; but how to make a skirt substantially longer so it could start under the bust? Solutions abounded. To recycle as much valuable silk as possible, you could slice into your big old skirt and add pieces to the bottom of a narrowed skirt. The longer and wider the pattern repeat, the trickier it was to execute that solution, but with care the expensive patterns could be matched at the new seams. Adapting old bodices was easier. With a few deft snips, you could remove trim from around the waist, shorten the bodice, then sew the trim back on at its new, higher level. Timid? Not sure this radical new style will last? Hedge your bets by keeping your longer bodice intact and just attach the skirt higher up and leave the lower bodice folded inside. Not sure a bodice can stand the weight of attached skirts? Add a lining made of the sturdy native linen you are used to. Take a deep breath and try those crossed front bodice lining flaps you've heard about. You can hide them beneath the outer cotton of your new bodice, or its recycled silk. Still not sure any bodice can hold up gathered skirts? Fake it. Attach shoulder straps to the skirt concealed by a separate but matching short bodice. Your entourage will be fooled into believing you have divined the secrets of the genuine one-piece dress. Do what you have to do, because this new style is "the admiration of all the world over."

An 6. Costume Parisien. (42)

Chapeau de Paille blanche, garni de son Fichu et lancé sur le côté. Schall de Soie en Telle.

An 7. Costume Parisien. (84)

Chapeau de Velours Soucé, orné de ganses d'argent. Schall Pinceau à Bordures Noires.

An 9. Costume Parisien. (285)

Coeffure à l'Antique. Schall de Soie.

An 10. Costume Parisien. (344)

Turban en Pyramide. Schall foulard.

Turban posé sur un Bandeau.

CHAPTER 7

AT EASE

(Térézia)

1794—1799

FASHION REVOLUTION meant sexual liberation to Térézia. After she helped topple the Committee of Public Safety and Robespierre in July 1794, freed from prison, she shed all remaining feminine inhibitions, including her ancien régime costumes. Citoyenne Cabarrus, soon to become Madame Tallien, famously the most beautiful woman in Europe, put style in the service of eros. She clothed an astounding self-possession in radically new Parisian elegance.

The spectacle Térézia created of herself comes down visually to us across the centuries in the form of portraits. One of those portraits, though by an artist not now well known, Jean-Bernard Duvivier, has the merit of observing Térézia's style closely. Posed casually, she lounges, with one leg stretched out on the yielding red velvet cushions of a sofa, the other flexed. A satin-slippered foot rests on a hassock. Absentmindedly toying with a triple-strand pearl bracelet she can't even bother to put on, she looks dreamily out of the picture, with a gentle smile at some passing thought. The softly draped curtains above

No matter how formal the portrait, Térézia could lounge in the total, liberated, comfort of the new style.

her, together with her black shawl carelessly tossed over the back of the sofa, and the billowing background clouds illuminated by a golden light, convey both comfort and glamour. This woman is in charge of her dress, not the other way around. Her skirt adjusts to the bend of her knee. Folds of fabric cascade between her legs and over the edge of the sofa to accommodate her body; the subtle twist of her torso emphasizes that she is not wearing boned stays. Notre Dame de Thermidor shrugs her slip sleeve off her shoulder.

We do need to be careful with the evidence of formal oil portraits. They were slow to be commissioned and painted, and often retroactively recorded styles a sitter had perfected after many live experiments that made the style famous, so the dates of paintings can be misleading. Unlike the live performances, however, portraits endure. Talented artists were able to record how bodies inhabited total ensembles, in complete spatial settings. Moreover, the usual struggles between a patron and an artist over control of a portrait tended to be resolved in favor of the patron—especially when her style celebrity was as ultimately advantageous to an artist's reputation as Térézia's, Joséphine's, or Juliette's.

Portraits also publicized. Major portrait commissions were often intended to communicate with an audience larger than the sitter could meet personally. Publicity during the revolutionary era began before a portrait's release, in the artist's studio, where influential people would gather to comment. The most prestigious regular public exhibitions of paintings during the period, called Salons (confusingly, the same word used for club-like private social gatherings, but capitalized), were attended by as many as five hundred thousand people during their eight-week runs. People talked about striking portraits as cultural events long after they had seen them, and wrote about them to far-flung correspondents. Some portraits were popularized by prints made after them.

Normally, a style as startling as Térézia's might not have caught on, or not so quickly. But Paris during the Directory was not normal. The way her clothing referenced the violence of the Terror resonated with quite a few other French women. In 1795 a "Victim Ball" was held in Paris to honor those slain by the guillotine. A particular shade of blood red, called "amaranth," became the signature color of the Directory. Women wore amaranth "victim ribbons" around their necks to commemorate the cut of the guillotine's blade. Ghoulish amaranth victim ribbons were also worn crossed over bodices or sleeves, down the sides of dresses, or twined into hairdos.

Fashion news spread rapidly through Paris during gatherings so public they brought together members of previously segregated social classes. Ever after, Talleyrand, the diplomat and wit, would call any event that mixed social classes "a Directory dinner." Térézia was among those who appeared at several events a day. She was part of a social set known to rise at ten o'clock in the morning, make the rounds of the salons, dine at five o'clock in the afternoon, dance at five or six outdoor balls in warm weather or attend three theaters when it was cold, and finish partying only at midnight. From parties, balls, parks, and dance halls, news of Térézia's style rippled outward, carried by word of mouth, by letters, by newspaper reports. Térézia was reported to have danced at a public ball in the trendy Frascati dance hall dressed as "a savage in flesh-colored tights and a lawn tunic, with gold rings round her legs." Royalists were appalled.

But to others, Térézia was still Notre Dame de Thermidor. Normally, it would have been a problem to associate anyone who presented herself so provocatively with Notre-Dame, the Virgin Mary, mother of Jesus Christ, especially when she was a divorced single mother. In fall 1794, as Térézia was first making her fashion mark, she was clearly not Tallien's wife. She was not named Térézia Tallien, but rather Térézia Cabarrus, or Citoyenne Cabarrus. She was not even living with Tallien. He was living at his mother's, while she was living in an apartment in the Chausée d'Antin neighborhood. She married Tallien only on the sixth of Nivôse, Year II (December 26, 1794) in a small, quiet civil ceremony. She had taken the precaution of a notarized contract—what we would call a prenup—to separate all her belongings from Tallien's: those that she possessed at the time, and any she might accumulate in the future. Their daughter was born five months later. Rose de Beauharnais was present at the birth, and became the girl's godmother. The baby was named Rose Thermidor after her godmother and after the coup d'état that had made her mother famous.

Exaggerated rumors of how much Térézia owned stemmed from public knowledge that her father had been the banker of a king, the king of Spain. Though her father had not been born a noble, funding monarchy was dangerously unpopular in revolutionary France. Tallien's fellow government representatives attacked his personal life in the assembly hall of the National Convention: "Let him tell us what he's doing with the wife of an exiled noble who happens to be the daughter of the Treasurer of the King of Spain." Tallien did not back down, but defended Térézia. He was challenged again on the floor of the National Convention five days after he and she were married. Harassed about "the Cabarrus treasures," he decided to refute calumny by announcing their wedding, as if it were a matter of state. "A woman has been spoken about in this assembly. . . . I wouldn't have thought she would occupy the deliberations of the National Convention. The daughter of Cabarrus has been spoken about. Well then! I declare, in the midst of my colleagues, in the midst of the People who hear me, that woman is my wife." He and Térézia had been such notorious lovers in Bordeaux that he added: "As for the woman who some have wanted to occupy the assembly with, I've known her for eighteen months; I knew her in Bordeaux; her misfortunes, her virtues made me esteem and cherish her. When she arrived in Paris, in the time of tyranny and oppression, she was persecuted and thrown into prison. . . . *Voilà, citoyens,* the one who is my wife."

Husband and wife lived in a new home called the Cottage (La Chaumière), which began to become a famously chic rendezvous during a celebration on the evening of their wedding. Térézia had seized a small one-story house from her ex-husband, who owned it, by simply occupying it, taking advantage of his absence and disgrace as a *ci-devant émigré* noble. It was located in an almost rural enclave within the city of Paris, amid poplar trees and lilac bushes, located near the Champs-Elysées, which really were fields (*champs*) then, close to what is now the Avenue Montaigne. A contrast between rustic exterior and sophisticated interior gave the Cottage that *je ne sais quoi.* Every detail of its décor was luxurious. Her porcelain set, for instance, came from the great manufactory of Sèvres. According to contemporaries, the entrance hall was organized around a basin in neoclassical style surmounted by a figure of Neptune, armed with a trident, around whom played cupids. Erotic themes continued in the lavish bedroom, where around a monumental bed suggestive sculptures occupied the four corners of the room. At the center of the bedroom was a sculpture ostensibly of Diana, goddess of the hunt. It surprised no one that the goddess resembled Térézia.

Térézia became famous for taking off clothing as much as for putting it on. Talleyrand quipped: "No one could be more expensively undressed." For some, Térézia's clothing reduction was admirably spare. One woman who met her during the Directory described her wearing only a pink crêpe tunic over a white dress with short sleeves, no ornament in her black curls, and a single strand of pearls.

The theatrical exception that proves the fashion rule: A dancer at the Parisian Ballet, Théâtre de l'Opéra, illustrated in *Journal des dames et des modes*, July 18, 1798.

She commented favorably: "Madame Tallien had more severity than levity in her manners." Another woman, Laure Junot, duchesse d'Abrantès, approved of a simplicity she associated with antiquity: "She had adopted a semi-Greek costume that looked great on her, and which she wore with supreme grace; it was simple and even severe. It contradicted the common assumption that a pretty woman is even prettier when adorned."

Less admiring stories also evoked undress. As many observers noted, she replaced stays and petticoats with a knit base-layer in flesh shades, which seemed tantamount to no underwear at all. The duc de Broglie remembered Térézia appearing on the Champ de Mars "dressed like Diana, her bust half-naked, wearing sandals, and clothed, if the word can be used, in a tunic no lower than the knee." Commentators were fascinated by her sandals because they exposed her feet. A tale circulated of a party during which Térézia wagered that everything she wore, including her sandals, weighed less than two livres (about two pounds). She took off all her clothes, they were weighed, and she won her bet.

Moral or immoral, Térézia's style fascinated the people who rose to prominence after Thermidor. These power brokers met, mingled, and made deals in the Paris salons, which regained their influence after a hiatus during the Terror. Directory and Consulate salons included men and women who would never have had the opportunity to mix before the Revolution. By comparison with pre-revolutionary salons, the new Paris salons bred young talent and prized ambition over refinement. Each of the half dozen most prominent salons was well known for its characteristic tone, and style of costume.

Térézia's salon specialized in money and political influence. The most noticeable woman among her guests was her best friend, Rose de Beauharnais. Other hyperfashionable women attended too, among them the charismatic Fortunée Hamelin, who became a good friend. Germaine de Staël frequently attended Térézia's salon for a change of tone from her own more intellectual one. The political theorist and novelist acted as the "muse," "grave, majestic, solemn," of Térézia's salon. She was entrusted by her hostess with the guests talking diplomacy, but liked to drift into the circle talking sex. Generals Lazare Hoche (formerly Rose's lover) and Jean Bernadotte (future king of Sweden) attended. So did artists, among them the anglophile Carle Vernet and Jean-Baptiste Isabey, who was probably giving Térézia art lessons at the time, and certainly taught the *ci-devant* vicomtesse de Beauharnais's daughter, Hortense de Beauharnais. Musicians attended, as well as actors, poets, and singers. The two regulars soon to play the biggest roles in Térézia's life were Paul Barras, at the helm of the post-Terror Directory government, and Gabriel-Julien Ouvrard, one of the Directory's most successful financial entrepreneurs. Ouvrard recalled that Napoléon met his future wife in Térézia's salon before anyone took him seriously: "He was perhaps of all those she entertained the least in evidence and the least favored by fortune."

News of Térézia's style spread most rapidly and effectively through her appearances at Paris theaters. Fashionable men and women commonly went to the theater every night during the Parisian winter social season. They sometimes hopped from one theater to another in a single night, the way we hop from one bar or nightclub to another. Theaters in the age of Revolution were much smaller than ours today. Spectators with cheap tickets stood packed on the floor within feet of the stage, and almost as close to the more expensive box seats above and behind them. A stack of the most expensive boxes immediately flanked the stage, oriented so that their occupants were as much on view as the plays.

Audiences did not observe either the plays or other members of the

Art and fashion news spread through prints.

Detail of an evening fan featuring a Térézia look-alike.

audience passively. Newspapers told readers in advance which politically charged lines of plays to cheer or boo, more vociferously than ever once the Revolution began. Theater performances functioned as political arenas, in which rival factions voiced their opinions, under cover of reacting to what was being performed on stage. You went to the theater to gauge which way the political winds blew. On the night of Thermidor, for instance, people flocked to the theaters to figure out whether Tallien and Barras's revolt against the Terror was going to succeed, or whether Robespierre would hold on to power.

Similarly, people went to the theater to pick up fashion tips at close range. Actors and actresses on stage occasionally wore something noteworthy, but the brightest stars were in the audience. While plays were being performed, other dramas and plots unfolded in the motions of the fans women carried, their mother-of-pearl mounts gleaming in the theater darkness, ornaments glittering, waving, winking. On one especially charming Directory-era fan preserved in the Paris museum of fashion, a painted figure sparkling in bright pink bodice, sequined skirt (with real sequins attached to the fan!), triple-strand necklace with ruby centerpiece, and dark natural curls wafting from a ruby-studded tiara might well be Térézia herself.

TALLIEN was elected to the provisional post-Thermidor Committee of Public Safety (Comité du Salut Public) government, and when the permanent Directory government was elected in 1795, he was the youngest member of its legislative body, the Council of the Five Hundred (Conseil des Cinq-Cents). But as the months went by, Térézia noticed her husband was outtalked and out-maneuvered by the other men in her salon; he was not going to make the most of his role in the Thermidor coup either politically or financially. In May of 1798, Tallien lost political office, and never regained it.

Capote de Florence. Tunique de Mousseline brochée.

Térézia's children later said she became disillusioned with Tallien by October 1795. She was sincerely shocked by his participation in a summary mass execution of some 750 royalists in the province of Brittany. A friend remembered her saying: "Too much blood on the hands of that man, I was disgusted forever by him." She wrote with hindsight, in 1826, that "when you are crossing a tempest, you can't always choose your life-line." Looking back later on Térézia's early salon, the financier Ouvrard recalled that "in her home," "Tallien reigned without realizing that General Barras dominated."

Barras's cynical moral flexibility had served him well so far. A soldier from way back, he had been stationed before the Revolution in France's colonial Indian trading post, Pondicherry. Though he came from a noble family, he had become a staunch revolutionary, elected to the National Convention government from 1792 to 1795. He was among those who voted for the death of King Louis XVI. Wily and self-satisfied, thick-set, with coiffed dark curls and small calculating eyes, he led a life that mingled public administration with personal gain.

At the head of the Directory government, Barras preserved the crucial tenets of revolutionary principles by compromising with most factions. He was willing, for instance, to let self-exiled nobles back into the country, provided they would support him. It was he who summoned a young and obscure Napoléon Bonaparte to rally a military force to defend the Directory government from a coup d'état. Like

An 10.   Costume Parisien.

(414)

Coeffure à Chignon Relevé. Épingle en Cuvrecée.

other men milling around Térézia, he sanctioned deals that speculated on the value difference between revolutionary paper assignats and gold, often involving dubious army contracts. Talleyrand, who himself set out to amass what he called "an immense fortune" during the Directory, said that "financiers only do their business well when states do them badly." Many French citizens were ruined, but Barras kept foreign enemies at bay, a republican government alive, and his inner circle in luxury.

Térézia Tallien gravitated toward Barras during the fall of 1795. She began to act as his consort at the Luxembourg Palace, where he installed himself and entertained like a monarch of yore, at state expense. With a palatial setting and a vast budget, Térézia consolidated her international celebrity. During parties, she moved from one group to another, speaking gently with everyone. At a time when women were expected to ornament social gatherings with their artistic accomplishments, she played the harp as well as the piano, and declaimed verse. Her reputation for music, beauty, and style continued to be matched only by her reputation for generosity. A witness remembered her as a perfect foil for Barras: "Gentle, good, sympathetic and helpful. From the moment she had any influence, she used it to aid and defend the unhappy."

Many years later, Barras wrote his memoirs and turned out to be remarkably spiteful. He slandered everyone, except Térézia. She had left an indelible and unalterable impression on him. Time and political reversals of fortune could not dim the memory of her radiant charm.

> Amid all these gentlewomen, one whose charms undoubtedly entitled her to be classed in the first rank of objects worthy of attention, attracted universal attention. This was Mme. Tallien, who, since the 9th Thermidor, had shown herself in all the public places, even at

the theatres, winning undisputed supremacy over her sex. She was the feminine dictator of beauty.

What he appreciated most about her was her erotic self-assurance. She had sex with men, Barras wrote (though he was writing in a prudish era), simply because she enjoyed sex. She was great in bed, he remembered, playful and relaxed in addition to being incredibly beautiful. She reveled in pleasure for its own sake, without second-guessing. She never traded sex for money, he said, because she was above mercenary calculations.

Beauty leveraged by courage and style seduced Europe in the aftermath of the Terror. Térézia achieved international celebrity. Her aura was so overwhelming that it cast shade on her style partner. But Joséphine's turn was next. As chaos subsided and Directory leaders attempted to stabilize elected government, the French Revolution entered yet another phase. Both friends were about to succeed beyond their wildest dreams.

(356)

Bonnet garni en Tulle. Fichu sur l'épaule.

CHAPTER 8

ALTERED FORTUNE

(Joséphine & Napoléon)

1794–1796

THE DIRECTORY SEDUCTION destined to change the course of history was not Térézia's of Barras, leader of the government, but Rose de Beauharnais's of an unknown, awkward, lowly army officer. Just as Rose had intuited the potential for Paris fashion of what was worn in France's colonies, so she sensed something imperial in a young man named Napoléone Buonaparte from the provincial French island of Corsica. When they met, and even when they renamed themselves Joséphine and Napoléon on their marriage certificate, she was a Paris fashion star and he was obscure. Without her style, and her friendship with Térézia, he might not have risen to power.

Rose had met Barras before the Terror, when she was still married to Alexandre de Beauharnais. As part of her campaign to remake her life after her losses during the Terror, Rose wrote to Barras flirtatiously. "It has been a long time since I have had the pleasure of seeing you. It is remiss of you to forsake an old acquaintance like this. I trust you will respond to this reprimand. I now reside at No. 371, rue de l'Université."

Joséphine Bonaparte pictured by her friend and style ally Isabey in 1798.

He did respond. No one seems to have much liked or trusted Barras, but he helped people, in exchange for something he wanted. Barras insisted in his memoirs that he had a sexual affair with Joséphine, and historians have agreed, though close scrutiny of evidence makes her latest biographer think the affair was extremely brief. Joséphine attended the stream of parties that eddied around him, most importantly Térézia's.

Napoléone Buonaparte (the Corsican spelling of his name) is supposed to have first tried to seduce Térézia. This is not proven. In any case, she was not interested, but did take pity on the poor condition of his uniform. She gave him a note to the appropriate authority, asking on his behalf for some new wool cloth. When he reappeared, she is said to have jested to her whole salon: "Well, my friend, you've got your breeches at last." Some biographers have said Napoléon resented this demeaning sexual innuendo so much that he turned to Joséphine. Others have said that Barras dumped Joséphine for Térézia, and gave Napoléon to Joséphine as her consolation prize. If so, it was impressively urbane of Napoléon to write a very nice note to Térézia on the twenty-ninth of Floréal, Year IV (eighteenth of May, 1796). Calling her "*belle citoyenne*," he sighed: "I have a feeling that when I tell you I miss the happy moments I spent in your company, I'm only repeating what everyone tells you. To have met you is to be unable to forget you." He added a postscript for her husband: "A thousand and a thousand greetings to Tallien."

Retroactively, Napoléon's destiny loomed large over everyone's memories of Joséphine, including Barras's. When he wrote his memoirs many years after Napoléon had fallen from power, Barras was still nursing grudges. Like many of Napoléon's detractors, he thought he scored points against the emperor by maligning his empress. It must have galled Barras that he had been the first to take notice of Napoléon and promote him, way back in 1793, when the unknown Corsican defended a fort during the siege of Toulon, a vital port city.

Barras made a direct, intimate comparison between Joséphine and Térézia.

> [Joséphine] derived none of her attractions from nature, but everything from art. Madame Beauharnais believed she could make up for and surpass what she lacked in actual advantages in comparison with Madame Tallien by consummate cunning and artifice. In this respect they seemed, so to speak, to be waging a mutual war, even when they were actually sharing each other's triumphs.

At least Barras was conceding that Joséphine and Térézia "were actually sharing in each other's triumphs," and that in Joséphine's case some "art" was involved. Though he used the word "art" pejoratively, we can interpret his comment positively. Of the two friends who flaunted their dress inventions together, it was probably Joséphine who did more of the designing.

Everyone who knew Joséphine during the Directory years of 1794–99 remarked on her love of clothes and style surprises, among them Claire Elisabeth Jeanne Gravier de Vergennes, comtesse de Rémusat.

> Being a friend of the beautiful Madame Tallien, she was introduced into the society of the Directory, and was especially favoured by Barras. . . . Madame de Beauharnais had very little fortune, and her taste for clothes and luxury rendered her dependent on those who could help her indulge it. . . . She dressed with perfect taste, enhancing the beauty of what she wore. With these advantages and the constant care she bestowed on her attire, she contrived not to be eclipsed by the youth and beauty of many of the women by whom she was surrounded.

Joséphine and Térézia made the most of what they had, inventing a style they could afford and which flattered them. Yet they did not quite get away with turning colonial rags into fashion riches. Instead of tracing the sources of Joséphine's artful clothing inventions back to her childhood on Martinique, and recognizing them as design influences, people twisted her background into racist accusations against her sexuality.

When she was only fourteen, a man recalled, "her figure was that of a nymph; her entire person bore the mark of the vivacity, the freedom, the abandon that only Creole women know how to combine in their movements, their manners, their tone of voice, even their silences." Looking back on Joséphine's whole career, one of her imperial ladies-in-waiting wrote: "She was not a person of remarkable intellect. A Creole, and frivolous, her education had been a good deal neglected." Napoléon invoked her "Créole" headscarf in an erotic context.

> I would be so happy if I could be there when you get dressed adorably, little shoulder, little white breast, elastic, nice and firm; above that, a little face with the Creole kerchief, to nibble. Of course I haven't forgotten the little visits; you know, the little black forest. I give it a thousand kisses and I can't wait for the moment I'm there.

Years after he had divorced her, from exile, he equated the Trois Islets location of her childhood home with her genitalia: "She had the prettiest possible cunt. The Trois Islets of Martinique were there."

When Barras compared Térézia with Joséphine in his sour memoirs, he purported to recall that Joséphine's "libertinism sprang merely from the mind, while her heart played no part in the pleasures of the body. . . . The lewd Creole . . . had sacrificed all to sordid interests." He claimed she traded sex for money or favors with many men. "It was even said that the infidelities of the Creole had overstepped the bounds of propriety, and that, rising superior to the prejudice existing against a dark skin, she had had intercourse with negroes."

The slurs aimed at Joséphine reached Térézia too. It was yet another of the challenges they faced together during the Directory and Consulate. Both of them were accused of not being sexually White enough,

Térézia and Joséphine accused of dancing naked for Directory leader Barras by the hostile British caricaturist Gillray.

especially when it came to the (probably) false rumor of their having three-way sex with Barras.

"Madame Talian and the Empress Josephine dancing Naked before Barrass in the Winter of 1797—A Fact!" announced the caption of a vicious caricature by the artist Gillray. His image catered to British fantasies by picturing Napoléon peeping at Joséphine and Térézia dancing together for Barras. Gillray represented the two women naked except for hairstyles and jewelry associated at the time with the Caribbean or with Africa. Both are given extremely curly long black hair, too exuberant for White hairstyle norms. Huge hoop earrings hang from Joséphine's ears, while both women's arms are encircled by stacked bracelets. Térézia's nose has been flattened and broadened.

In another caricature, Gillray pictured Térézia with dark brown skin, a huge head of tight black curls, and voluptuous, possibly pregnant, curves—all messages of physical excess. He used the French word *doublure* in his caption to insinuate an African secret behind Térézia's Spanish birth. The word *doublure* ostensibly means a lining, but to British ears sounds like "double" or "duplicity."

La Belle Espagnole, —ou— la Doublure de Madame Tallien.

A caricature racializes Térézia.

To be fair, Napoléon also identified with both Joséphine's outsider origins and her ambitions. By birth, he, like Joséphine, Térézia, and Juliette, had started life tantalizingly close to the edge of mainland aristocratic power. The island of Corsica became French only just before his birth. He too had been given an unprecedented opportunity by the social upheavals of the Revolution. When all the French army's most highly ranked officers were killed or went into self-exile because they were aristocrats, someone had to take their places. The government was obliged to recruit and promote extraordinarily young men at top speed. Napoléon calculated that Rose de

Beauharnais, with all her salon connections, could accelerate his ascension even more. Not only did they have a lot in common, she offered him an immediately enchanting experience. From the first time they met, she wrapped him in the triple delights of sex, children, and style.

A sexually naïve Napoléon Bonaparte was ushered into erotic heaven by a skilled and sophisticated lover. He wrote to her: "I awake all filled with you. Your image, and the intoxicating pleasures of last night, allow my senses no rest. . . . How can I rest any more, when I yield to the feeling that masters my inmost self, when I quaff from your lips and from your heart a scorching flame?"

Yet Joséphine simultaneously produced a ready-made nuclear family for Napoléon. She made him feel at once selfishly like a complete man, and selflessly like a complete father. Eugène de Beauharnais and Hortense de Beauharnais, her children by her first husband, the guillotined Alexandre de Beauharnais, took to Napoléon immediately, and he to them. They remained loyal to him throughout his rise to and fall from power. They tolerated the marriages he arranged more for his own benefit than for them; they weathered his repudiation of their mother. And he remained loyal to them, in his way. He made them rich and he made them royal.

Both Eugène and Hortense told stories that approved Napoléon's entry into their lives. Eugène recalled—or imagined, we aren't sure which—a symbolic relay of paternal authority from his biological father to his stepfather. According to Eugène, Alexandre de Beauharnais's sword had been confiscated, and somehow Napoléon had it in his keeping. Eugène supposedly decided to ask Napoléon for the sword. "The following day he came in person to bring me the authorization I had so ardently wished for. He asked if he might visit again, and seemed to enjoy my mother's company more and more." Hortense fondly exaggerated Napoléon's looks and rank and emphasized his fascination with her mother when she recalled her first meeting with him at a dinner hosted by Barras on January 21, 1796.

> At the table I sat between my mother and a general who, in order to talk to her, annoyed me by lunging forward with such excitement and perseverance that I had to sit back. I could thus observe, in spite of myself, that he was handsome, with a very expressive countenance, but strikingly pale. His tone was fiery, and he seemed interested only in my mother. It was General Bonaparte.

The décor into which the still-barely Rose introduced her ardent young lover immersed him in her style innovations. Like Térézia, Rose had created a showcase for herself. She too had chosen a small house, in her case more a pavilion than a villa, which she rented in 1795, on the rue Chantereine, right near Térézia, and the Récamiers.

In this quiet, verdant part of the city, trees and a garden sheltered the two-story pavilion. It had been built of buff stone almost two decades earlier, in 1776–78, with a mansard roof and gray shutters. Just small enough to be cozy, it easily accommodated two adults whose children attended boarding schools (the normal way to raise children in an era before public schools). The pavilion included a five-sided enclosed dining porch, a living room with French doors leading to the garden, an office on the first floor, and bedrooms on the second floor. The rue Chantereine pavilion may not have been fully furnished when Napoléon first slept there as Rose de Beauharnais's lover, because she was still scrambling for money, but it was undoubtedly more elegantly decorated than any place he had lived in before. In comparison with the stodgy style of his provincial Corsican childhood, the army barracks of his school days and early military postings, or the squalid Paris lodgings he could afford, the rue Chantereine pavilion was sensuously exquisite. Joséphine's taste in décor echoed her serenely spare and refreshingly novel taste in fashion.

Rose began pulling strings for Napoléon. He had acquitted himself well several times, notably when he defended the Directory government from royalists during the "13 Vendémiaire" coup. Only the influence of the woman who had agreed to marry him, however, explained to their contemporaries why, soon after their marriage banns were posted on the eighteenth of February, 1796, he was suddenly named commander of the army in Italy by Barras on March 2. A general noted: "The public saw in this posting favour for Madame Bonaparte rather than wisdom and concern for France's interests." Or in the words of Napoléon's own brother Lucien: "Barras has taken charge of Joséphine's dowry, which is the chief command of the army in Italy." The wedding took place on March 9. Witnesses included Barras for the groom and Tallien for the bride. To make their ages come out the same at twenty-eight, on their marriage contract she subtracted five years and he added two. That he was six hours late for the wedding was one sign he intended to control her. Another was his insistence that she cease calling herself Rose and instead use the nickname Joséphine he had devised out of one of her middle names, Josèphe.

Rose was now Joséphine Bonaparte, and began to dress accordingly. Her horizons expanded as Napoléon's defense of revolutionary France took its battles abroad.

An 10   Costume Parisien.   *(349)*

Coeffure en Cheveux, ornée d'un Bandeau de Perles.

"Hairstyle wrapped in headband ornamented with pearls," from *Journal des dames et des modes.*

Cheveux à la Titus. Tunique à la Mameluck.

CHAPTER 9

MINIMALIST PRINCIPLES

(Juliette)

1794–1799

M EANWHILE, A THIRD fashion star rose to fame. Térézia and
Joséphine had taken Paris by storm, and storms frighten most
people. Their style was irrevocably, if thrillingly, associated with prof-
ligate sexuality and ruthless ambition, as well as with Parisian excess.
Most women would have hesitated to imitate them if they had not been
balanced by another celebrity, whose reputation was as pure as theirs
was wild. For such a radically new style to sweep Europe so totally and
rapidly, complementary style personalities had to be in play. Juliette
legitimated fashion revolution.

During the 1794–99 years of the Directory, any new entrant into
the fashion lists was sure to be compared with the dominant Térézia Tallien. When she and Juliette Récamier met sometime between
1794 and 1796, their entourages anticipated they would clash. Térézia
had the advantage of total confidence. She never appeared threatened
by anyone. As an eyewitness described it: "When she appeared in a
salon, it was like night and day: she made the day and put the others

Marguerite Gérard's double portrait of the supposedly rival beauties Térézia and Juliette acknowledges their close friendship.

in the shade." Only Juliette came close to attracting as much adulation, and even she didn't stand a chance. Judgment was quickly delivered. According to the tastes of the revolutionary era, Térézia's "fine figure, her bare arms, her grace, the beauties of every kind" ranked above Juliette's admirable "lithest figure," "most elegant simplicity," and "quiet dress and simple grace."

At the same time, partisans agreed the rival beauties were equally good and kind, both of them exceptionally *bonne*. So they should not have been surprised when the two women instantly struck up a friendship, which flourished as Juliette's star rose. An artist even made a double portrait of the two of them confiding in each other. The petite Juliette is at home, dressed in a private morning wrapper and bonnet. Contrary to some of the more indignant rumors about Térézia's clothing, she wears a demure long-sleeved white satin dress paired with a scoop-necked slip, which extends above the dress at the throat and below its hem; she has laid her outdoor straw hat aside to join Juliette for a cozy chat over a letter and a miniature portrait.

Without creating any conflict, Juliette astutely adjusted the style Térézia and Joséphine had introduced with such abandon. The Terror had left Térézia and Joséphine with a sexual problem in 1794. They were obliged to forfeit sexual respectability in order to obtain the most essential support for themselves and their children. The Terror also left Juliette with a sexual problem in 1794, though of a different sort: she had to remain a virgin in order to avoid committing either adultery or incest. Her genius was to realize that the same dramatically new style that solved Térézia's and Joséphine's problem could also solve hers. Perhaps she understood that their situations, though seemingly opposite, were symmetrical. She too could take control over her sexual fate and achieve her own fame. The new style could turn her virginity into celebrity.

Had Juliette been an ordinary person, she would have obeyed the incest taboo invisibly. She would have lived a lie in secrecy, quietly hiding her true relationship to her husband. Juliette may have reasoned that this solution would not work anyway. Though people outside a close circle might only suspect Récamier was her biological father, everyone knew for a fact that he had been among the three men who raised her.

Instead, she said nothing, and turned virginity into a spectacular style. White signals virginity. Touch white, and you leave a mark. Juliette trademarked absolute whiteness. She appeared in radiant white every day, morning, afternoon, and evening: white cotton in public for day, white satin for formal wear and evening. (Someone once saw her at an evening event in a black dress and was shocked.) She chose white accessories whenever possible: white gloves, white slippers; pearls, not diamonds, because pearls gleam whiter than diamonds sparkle. White clothing was her artistic medium, her media brand. It was a brilliantly successful tactic. Juliette Récamier turned the worst thing about her life into her best asset. The alchemy of fashion transformed a shameful secret into glorious fame.

Her version of revolutionary style was chaste enough to spread fast, from Paris to the virtuous housewives of the provinces, to the cosmopolitan cities of the rest of Europe, across the Atlantic to the stalwart democratic ladies of the new United States, and all the way to Lima, Peru, where the most stylish women in Latin America congregated.

Juliette's tactic tapped into the Revolution's most exalted ambitions. Among the many great intellectuals she inspired, the literary celebrity René de Chateaubriand wrote: "Her beauty merges her ideal existence with the material facts of our history: serene light illuminating a storm picture." Juliette's contemporaries described her with the word "pure." Germaine de Staël exclaimed: "In the midst of all this success, what you are and what you will remain is an angel of purity and beauty."

Madame de Genlis, tutor of royal children and best-selling novelist, hoped (in vain) to write an authorized biography of Juliette because: "From your earliest youth, you were thrown, with a gorgeous face, a refined and probing mind, into the heart of swirling errors and follies; because you have witnessed everything, and were able to retain, through these storms, religious feeling, a pure soul, a life without stain, an open heart to faithful friendship, without envy or passionate hate."

The great novelist and political theorist Benjamin Constant, the most important of Germaine de Staël's lovers, was sure Juliette, Térézia, and Joséphine were the most famous feminine celebrities of his time. He would not deign to write about Térézia because she was famous for "love affairs without delicacy," or Joséphine because she was famous for "guilty concessions to successive tyrannies." He wanted to praise only Juliette. "The one I speak of emerges shining and pure from this atmosphere which damaged what it did not corrupt."

Seducing with virginity was perverse, to be sure. The perversity was precisely what made Juliette Récamier's tactic work. In the Latin from which the word "perverse" comes, *per* means away, and *vertere* means to turn, to transform, to translate, to change. Juliette's fashion tactic turned her virginity away from the ordinary and transformed, translated, changed it. She twisted it. And everyone who works with thread knows that twisted threads are the strongest ones.

Juliette mesmerized great painters as well as writers and political theorists. One of David's star students, François Gérard, perfectly captured her perverse appeal. Gérard became the most successful portraitist of the revolutionary and Napoleonic periods, from the 1790s through the 1810s. David remained the acknowledged master of history painting, and continued to paint remarkably observant portraits, but Gérard cornered the fashionable portrait market. His portraits of Juliette, Joséphine, and Térézia count among his most memorable images.

For her portrait by Gérard, Juliette poured herself deliciously into a sugar-white dress and a caramel shawl. Their fabrics animate every turn her body takes. We want to roll into the cashmere around her hips, to ripple like muslin or cashmere from her hand and knee. We wish our breath would flutter the aerial ruffle of her minuscule bodice, across her luminous breasts and shoulders. This fairy entices without succumbing. Though the fabric of her dress describes every swell, its opacity refuses us the sight of anything beneath. A hard, stone edge in the portrait separates her from us, and puts her on a cool, straight-lined stage from which we admire her at a safe distance. She has literally put herself on a pedestal.

Juliette preferred to pose from a distance. Rather than appear in person constantly all over Paris, she appeared strategically. She encouraged public whispers, rumors, and anticipation. To be admitted into her presence became a privilege, something to write about and remember.

The exception that proved her rule was a trip abroad to London in 1802. There, she allowed herself to be constantly seen in person (chaperoned by her mother). Chateaubriand said she amazed the English with her "foreign" and "novel" appearance. A contemporary witness described her triumph.

Juliette deployed all her seductive charms for her life-size portrait by Gérard.

Madame Récamier was, not the most beautiful woman in Paris, but the most fashionable woman. Her bizarre coiffure, her rare and almost mysterious appearances at the theater and in public places had given her, even reaching to the working people of Paris, a celebrity no other woman of her era had. All the English newspapers announced her arrival, and people came from the Three Kingdoms [England, Scotland, and Wales] to see the *fashionable beauty*. . . . In the streets, at the theater, on the promenades, crowds thronged around Madame Récamier. Women of the highest rank, the most eminent men of England had themselves introduced to her by the Prince of Wales. She was at almost all his soirées. Her portrait was sold everywhere.

The portrait in question may be a print based on a drawing by the fashionable British artist Richard Cosway. It was widely reproduced. In it, Juliette coyly plays the part of an ancient Roman vestal virgin. Standing safely behind four steps of stone, she is barely veiled from head to toe in white gauze. When the print was copied in the leading Parisian fashion magazine, it was explicitly captioned "Vestal." Juliette's commitment to all-white lent itself to costume performances of classicism. For a portrait by Eulalie Morin, Juliette draped herself in an unusually accurate, if wispy, imitation of ancient Greece. Neoclassicism justified Térézia's and Joséphine's style, and it justified Juliette's.

Yet Juliette's success was a distinctly contemporary, revolutionary Paris phenomenon. For the portraits she considered major, the ones by artists like Gérard, she did not wear classical costume, but rather the same radical chic Térézia and Joséphine had cobbled together from colonial sources.

The command center of Juliette's celebrity was her ultrafashionable Paris town house. Juliette's husband, Récamier, bought the 1777 building in 1798, from Jacques Necker,

Juliette's trademark virginal white style.

father of Germaine de Staël and one-time finance minister of Louis XVI. It was during the course of the sale that Juliette first met Germaine. The town house, on the rue du Mont-Blanc (now named the Chausée d'Antin), was in a neighborhood that attracted new revolutionary elites, who left the previously fashionable Faubourg Saint-Germain neighborhood to old aristocrats. The location could not have been more professionally convenient for Monsieur Récamier, being right near the town houses of his banking partners Jean Frédéric Perrégaux and Jean Jacques Mallet, with whom he managed the public treasury (Trésor Public) during the Directory and Consulate and with whom he would become a regent of the Bank of France when it was founded in

The consistent principle of Juliette's white attire earned her the acclaim of intellectuals.

1800. The financier and banker Ouvrard also lived in the neighborhood. Térézia Tallien's Chaumière home and Joséphine Bonaparte's pavilion on the rue Chantereine were in the vicinity.

Monsieur and Madame Récamier entrusted the interior redecoration of their town house to a leading Paris architect, Louis Berthault. Berthault exceeded their expectations by hiring Charles Percier, who went on to become the most fashionable decorator of the entire era. Berthault and Percier attended to every detail. The décor had to be superb. Juliette was intended to be the crown jewel of a salon whose setting would show her off to best advantage.

At the start of the Directory, in late 1794, Térézia's deceptively rural Chaumière introduced the period's sophisticated salon tone. Juliette perfected it with her Monday salons, starting in 1799. The halls of the Palace of Versailles, once thronged with courtiers, had been emptied by the Revolution. A new generation of urbane Parisian salon interiors harbored the highest ambitions of a revolutionary elite, which included hosts, guests, and designers. Térézia's model helped Juliette calculate correctly that the more fashionable her interiors were, the better they would attract a rising cohort of young men. Percier understood her ambition, being himself one of those young men. He was the perfect person to design the sort of loping curves, sensuous silk hangings, erotic wall-paintings, sculptures of nudes, and flaming torchères that would put guests in the mood for power, all dizzyingly reflected in mirrors.

Isabey models casual masculine chic in his 1796 life-size portrait by Gérard.

To get the ineffable tone of a salon exactly right, the Directoire relied on Jean-Baptiste Isabey's perfect taste. Térézia, to whom he gave art lessons, and Joséphine, to whose daughter he gave art lessons, must have appreciated how his aesthetic revolved around his own personal elegance. Isabey found his calling not so much in academic high art, but rather in what we recognize as the ephemeral art of lifestyle consulting, which he pioneered. Among his close friends were all the artists who designed the interiors and painted the portraits of the Directory and Consulate, as well as all its most fashionable women.

One look at a portrait of Isabey explains why. Gérard's full-length oil does justice to his friend's revolutionary style, the paradigmatic masculine model of a new nonchalance. Why not renounce silks, lace, and embroidery when you could look so good

Boilly's 1798 art world who's who, set in Isabey's studio. All the men wear revolutionary suits and have abandoned wigs.

in shapely breeches, leather boots, and a high white neck-cravat? Why not renounce the glittering carapace of the old court *habit à la française* when you could hire a new kind of tailor who trimmed, padded, interfaced, proportioned, and stitched wool so that you looked like yourself, only better? Why fuss with a powdered, symmetrical wig when you could toss a mop of natural dark curls across your brow?

Isabey's studio became an ultimate masculine style rendezvous. Its interior decoration was designed—of course—by Percier, complete with painted garlands and draped allegories of the arts. Luckily for us, another fashion connoisseur, the painter Boilly, set a group portrait of artists there. Each man in Boilly's image wears a more perfectly tailored suit and knotted white cravat than the next, while Isabey leans jauntily toward an easel in a dashing red jacket. Boilly's painting is the closest we can get to a collective picture of the aspiring young men who clustered in Juliette's salon. A (self-serving) comment by Benjamin Constant defines them: "An instinct for beauty caused her to love in advance, before knowing them, men distinguished by a reputation for talent and genius."

Though no painting of Juliette's whole rue du Mont-Blanc salon survives, her salon furniture does. The sofa, chairs, side tables, and stools pioneered the very latest neo-Greek style, and evinced the supreme woodworking craft of Jacob Frères. Patron, design, and craft have together earned the set a place in the collection of the Louvre Museum. Juliette must have imagined in advance how the bright solid blue wool of the set's upholstery would contrast arrestingly with the diaphanous white cotton of her dresses, as well as how the alternating blond and dark natural woods carved into smoothly swooping frames would harmonize with her bare arms, throat, and face. Her guests would feel they belonged with her while they occupied matching seats. Picture Juliette twisting toward you in one of the chairs the way she does in her portrait

Juliette's legendary bedroom in 1802.

by Gérard. Her eyes, Benjamin Constant wrote, could "reach the depths of every soul."

The room for which the Jacob furniture set was commissioned, in which Juliette hosted her intellectual salon gatherings, was not the only room to which visitors were granted access. Her whole house was famously fashionable. Parisians and foreigners came to gawk, and sent reports all over Europe.

Visitors could see public rooms, like the salon living room and the dining room, and also private rooms. Juliette gave tours, which culminated with her bedroom. A visitor noted that whenever a woman arrived, Juliette would take her by the arm and say, "Would you like to see my bedroom?" Men crowded around. "A parade of *cavaliers* would hasten their steps to the sanctuary." The bedroom was high-ceilinged, with luminous rich dark mahogany wood and lavish bronze ornaments, hung with glistening violet silk and sheer white muslin. A canopied bed was raised by two steps on a platform and flanked by swans, associated in ancient myths with eros. Behind the bed—"the ethereal bed of the place's goddess: a cloud of muslin, a white vapor!"—the wall was a mirror. "Madame Récamier's bed is supposed to be the most beautiful in Paris."

Like Juliette's clothing, her bedroom was spectacularly virginal, at once an erotic vision and a refusal of sex. Just as she made actual appearances, and ensured images of her appearance circulated, so she personally showed visitors her bedroom, and encouraged reports, creating an ever-widening gyre of celebrity. Descriptions and drawings of her bedroom survive precisely because it was famous. Like Juliette's salon furniture, and for the same reasons, her bedroom furniture—including the bed—is on display at the Louvre Museum.

Those who saw Juliette's bed sometimes called it an altar, sometimes a throne. Every visitor could imagine worshipping her body in bed, because they could see themselves in the mirror behind the bed. But no one was ever actually allowed to. She exerted a force field that held people close but not too close. A letter from her to an overeager suitor gives the flavor of her defense tactics.

> My friendship for you cannot change, but you disturb and will entirely spoil one of the friendships which I value most, by trying to find in it? what can never be there. Think of me as a sister and you may be sure of all my friendship and of all my confidence. This poor life of ours is so sad, and your friendship might be very sweet to me and useful, and I cannot tell you how painful it is to me to feel embarrassed with you and to be obliged to talk of indifferent things.

René de Chateaubriand told a fellow admirer: "One finds in her, by some extraordinary combination, the double enchantment of the Virgin and the lover. She seduces like Venus, and inspires like a muse. One falls in love at her feet, and is chained there by respect." In his memoirs, which have become a classic work of French Romantic literature, Chateaubriand summed up her spell.

> Nearing my end, it seems to me that everything I have loved, I loved it in Madame Récamier, and that she was the hidden source of my emotions. My memories of various times, those of my dreams, like those of my realities, have been kneaded, mixed, melted into a composite of delights and sweet sufferings, of which she has become the visible form.

Juliette Récamier offered men romance with none of its dangers, the thrill of pursuit with none of its sexual consequences. She remained enigmatically silent while they sang her fame. She protected them, and herself, by reserving all her eloquence for her appearance.

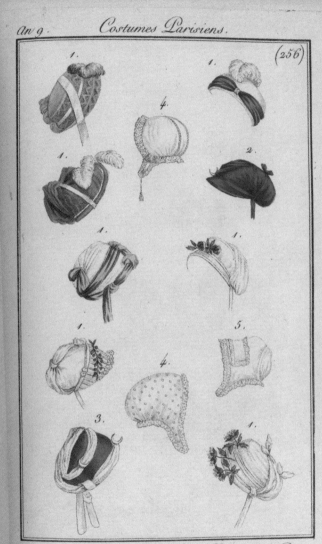

1, *Demi-Capotes.* 2, *Chapeau de Velours.* 3, *Demi-Turban.* 4, *Coquets.* 5, *Coquet-Cornette.*

Chapeau de Paille, garni d'un Large Ruban.

CHAPTER 10

A DIRECTORY OF
ACCESSORIES

1794–1804

YOU GET READY TO GO out the door. You run your fingers through your cropped hair. Depending on the weather and the occasion, you slip on the right jacket, maybe a hat and gloves, and stash your keys, glasses, and money into your handbag. On the street, you stride confidently in your flat shoes. Bonjour, Paris, it's 1794.

If the difference between humans and animals is truly that humans accessorize, then fashion revolution pushed humanity to the next stage of evolution. History has fixated on the columnar white cotton dress, the centerpiece of formal portraits. Yet in daily life the dress was only a fashion core around which whirled an array of marvelously novel and practical accessories. If we look aside from the most formal oil portraits to prints about daily life—correctly ignoring caricatures because they are caricatures—we find everyday conveniences. Revolution put individual choice at the heart of fashion, and equipped women for public life.

The first modern fashion magazine told women so. A magazine began to be published in 1797 that instantly caught the mood of the new style. The *Journal des dames et des modes* (Journal of women and fashions) pushed the fashion revolution into high gear. Between April 1793, when the last of the important ancien régime fashion magazines, the *Journal de la mode et du goût*, folded, and March 1797, when the *Journal des dames et des modes* first appeared, European fashion outside of Paris— including European settlers in North and South America—had held its breath. Only a Paris magazine could credibly dictate anything new. British, German, and Italian magazines relied on filched copies of Paris fashion plates. Though Térézia, Joséphine, and Juliette and their Paris followers made style news between fall 1794 and 1797 through portraits, parties, salons, and especially their appearances at theaters, the news was still not being published or disseminated by a compelling magazine.

The *Journal des dames et des modes* was founded by a visionary editor named Jean-Baptiste Sellèque, probably together with Pierre de La Mésengère. Their career plans, as, respectively, a professor and a priest, had been upset by the Revolution, and they turned to publishing. (Both men and women were allowed to renege on unwilling vows to the Catholic Church.) Sellèque, who lived around the corner from the Palais Royal, ran a bookstore from which the fledgling magazine was sold. It was also available from other shops, by subscription, and from street hawkers. Pro-woman, borderline-feminist positions dominated editorial pieces. The fiery women's rights author Albertine Clément-Hémery, notably, was on the editorial board. On the very first page of the first issue, the *Journal* announced: "The degree of civilization to which a people has arrived can only be judged by the respect it gives to its women. This thermometer is infallible." Sellèque and La Mésengère were coeditors until late December 1799, when Sellèque, an innocent bystander, was killed by a bomb meant to assassinate Napoléon.

The small-format periodical appeared every ten days or so, and coupled eight pages of commentary on all aspects of culture with engraved, hand-colored fashion plates. Its initial price, at three livres for three months or ten for a whole year, would have been a big splurge for a skilled worker, but was within the reach of anyone middle-class, considering that issues were shared among family and friends. Unlike the fashion magazines in circulation shortly before the Revolution, the *Journal des dames et des modes* did not hand down reports from royal courts, or defer to noble splendor. Nary a princesse or duchesse was invoked. On the contrary, the editors announced in their first issue that, inspired by the Goddess of Love (*Amour*), they searched for "*la mode*" "at the theater, in theater loges, in theater foyers, backstage," "in boudoirs," "at balls," and on "promenades."

The magazine prided itself on eyewitness journalism and the observed detail. It suggested as many outfits for informal day-wear, including equestrian sport outfits, as for formal evening-wear. Nor were precious materials prescribed. Editors proclaimed the opposite: "What can the genius of *la mode* not accomplish? In the shade of its influence, industrious art gives value to the most vile materials." Fabrics of dresses were rarely specified. The news was all about style: colors, shapes, contrasts, harmonies, silhouettes, proportions. Most of the *Journal* plates showed outfits from head to toe, but some were dedicated to accessories. The first word in the greatest number of all plate captions during the key years 1797–1804 was about an accessory, often *chapeau*, *turban*, *schall*, or *sac*.

The *Journal* addressed an audience able to imitate its contents. The magazine's texts often eased readers into the latest styles by explaining how flattering they could be. Without directly contradicting false rumors of completely see-through Parisian dresses, the magazine instead simply wrote in winter of 1797 that it did not bother with any such style, which would look ridiculous even at a ball, and proposed instead more reassuring "decent dresses with high bodices." Descriptions of plates explained that seemingly light dresses were always to be worn with slips, and sometimes with long gloves.

The scale of the *Journal des dames et des modes* audience became the scale of Térézia's, Joséphine's, and Juliette's impact. The magazine had subscribers all over France, in every provincial city. It had subscribers in Stockholm, Saint Petersburg, Constantinople, and Algiers. The women in the audience of the *Journal* might not want to imitate the extreme degree of Paris salon style, but they could basically identify with the latest Paris fashion.

In the magazine's earliest years, the novice editors kept apologizing for publication or distribution delays, and reminding readers of how reasonable subscription prices were. By treating its audience as individuals who had fashion choices to make, including of the magazine itself, the *Journal* treated readers as consumers. The *Journal des dames et des modes* promoted new values by virtue of its very existence, above and beyond the clothing items it promoted. It was an early instance of mass media by, for, and about middle-class people; it could be emulated by anyone in the skilled working class, albeit with effort.

No wonder the great poet Charles Baudelaire invoked the plates of the *Journal des dames et des modes* at the very start of his immensely influential clarion call to modernity, *Le Peintre de la vie moderne*, published in 1863. He saw in the magazine's fashion plates the germs of modern art. Genius that he was, Baudelaire paid special attention to the *Journal*'s handbags.

Where could women tuck their essentials while wearing the new revolutionary dress? Before the Revolution, in the days of giant skirts over huge petticoats, the problem was solved by pockets attached to a belt worn between the skirts and petticoats. No one noticed a stuffed pocket amid dozens of yards of gathered fabric. The whole line of a revolutionary dress, however, would be spoiled by a bulge. Pockets sewn into the new dress were out of the question. The fabric was too delicate to bear the weight of keys.

Purses, to be sure, had been around since coins. Purses, though, were worn as much by men as by women, often attached to belts. A bag held by the arm, wrist, or hand with a strap (hence "handbag"), and worn by women, was first regularly promoted by the *Journal des dames et des modes*. Ever since, the handbag has been identified with women's fashion. Psychoanalysts pore over handbags; they interpret them as symbols of the womb, and therefore of our first, anatomical, home. According to this theory, when women leave the home, they are still carrying a home on their body. The handbag, private keeper of personal possessions, accompanies women into the public sphere to remind everyone of their domestic femininity. This psychoanalytic theory might explain why handbags are fetish objects, to which women attribute mysterious powers. If handbags weren't magic, why pay those usurious markup prices?

By 1798 the *Journal* called the handbag phenomenon a women's "pockets revolution." "The handbag has definitively replaced pockets. You can leave your lover, never your handbag; it is women's inseparable companion, the faithful depository of their most secret thoughts." Handbags were originally called "reticules" after small ancient Roman mesh purses, but the phonetic similarity between "reticule" and "ridicule" (in English as in French) provided a way to fight back against the new power of fashion by calling handbags "ridicules." The *Journal* occasionally played into this trend with capital letters, and called the handbag a "RIDICULE." Opposition was hopeless, because women obeyed when fashion decreed that handbags were vital elements of a good wardrobe. The *Journal* proposed day handbags, party handbags, and theater handbags, in a multitude of materials and shapes for every public occasion, with embroidered arabesques, beaded patterns, emblems, and even rebus puzzles, which combined signs with pictures. You couldn't take "two steps in Paris" without seeing a different handbag. Any "young lady of social standing" about to be married had to include at least a dozen handbags in her trousseau. Women with handbags to spare were urged to share with less fortunate friends.

Handbags were all the more necessary because not only were dresses

A fashion plate from the pioneering fashion magazine *Le Journal des dames et des modes* promotes handbags, bristling short hair, and the sleeveless Spencer jacket.

A serious intellectual with her steel-blue Spencer jacket and drawing portfolio, by Guillon-Lethière in 1799.

Warm revolutionary clothing for winter months by stylist Isabey in 1795.

too slim for pockets but jackets were too short. The 1780s redingote bodice morphed into the 1790s Spencer jacket. A Spencer jacket was tightly tailored to hug the bust, which it ended right below. A Spencer emphasized the silhouette contrast between a diminutive, detailed top and the rest of the dress. When cut with open, wide, contrasting lapels, the Spencer drew attention to a shapely throat. Yet it added a spice of androgyny to outfits. Legend ascribed the jacket to the British George Spencer, 2nd Earl Spencer, whose jacket tails accidentally caught fire; Spencer kept calm, cut off the tails, and carried on. Spencers in blue and gray shades were perfect for women who wanted to present themselves professionally; they often appear in portraits of women with art tools in hand. A self-respecting professional woman today would be happy to wear such a jacket for her headshot.

Spencers could add perky color notes, or a layer of warmth. For summer, they were made of silks, linens, and cottons, contrasting or matching with a dress, with or without sleeves. In winter wool, they could be padded and quilted. Contrary to persistent stories of women who braved icy blasts in transparent white drapery, the new style offered practical cold-weather accessories from head to toe. A crossed kerchief and high, bow-tied cravat could fill in fetchingly open lapels. For the very coldest winter weather, long padded coats maintained the short-top, long-skirt silhouette by reaching in one line all the way from the bust to the ground. Giant muffs kept hands warm.

We happen to know just how cozy boots could be because Joséphine was prone to chills, and a few of her boots have been preserved. She favored flat ankle-boots, sometimes fur-lined.

Unlike the dainty, heeled footwear of the ancien régime, new-style shoes as well as boots tended to be flat and practical. Fashionable revolutionary footwear unabashedly drew attention to its comfort with pert details and bright colors. Many of the shoes illustrated in the *Journal* are amaranth red with crisscross laces. In fashion plates and paintings, shoes look like delicate slippers, but surviving examples in the Kyoto Institute for Western Costume have solid leather soles and just enough of a heel to keep from slipping.

We can see how quite a few of these *Journal* suggestions looked together in a double portrait of a mother and daughter painted by Gérard in 1799. The mother's ample figure fits easily in her warm brown fur-trimmed dress, which shows off her décolleté. The daughter, who wears a white cotton dress with its slip, twists around at her piano to reveal the leather sole of her laced amaranth shoe.

Everyone could see revolutionary shoes in the streets, along with quite a bit of stockinged ankle and calf, because the trains of day-dresses were not meant to drag outdoors. On the contrary, outdoors, trains were tossed over an arm to raise skirts high off the ground. According to new revolutionary standards, this did not threaten modesty because stockings could be decorative, or part of a functional knit base-layer, the ancestor of our athleisure knit base-layer. The *Journal* consistently showed women walking in flat laced shoes along what the reader was supposed to see as streets or parks. During the early years of the *Journal*, captions often named actual Paris locations, such as the boulevard des Capucines. This was reality fashion, not fantasy fashion.

Ancien régime hats had been useless concoctions perched on top of coiffed-hair edifices. The *Journal* instead suggested hats that actually protected the head outdoors from wind and weather, with func-

Gérard's portrait of a mother and daughter in practical revolutionary dresses, as well as red crisscross laced shoes.

The Journal des dames et des modes proposes radical hairstyles.

tional brims and secure ties under the chin. Nor were women obliged to wear hats at all. The magazine promoted a less formal alternative: "The most elegant coiffure is a turban, surmounted with a rich aigrette, or ornamented with elegantly colored plumes. Its shape can be infinitely varied according to the taste of fashionistas [*modeuses*]." Turbans could be improvised with spare bits of materials, on a whim. However Parisian the variations, the turban's origins were unambiguously labeled "the Levant" or India. Some looked remarkably like the wrapped and tied scarves worn by women of color in the French Caribbean islands. The Revolution's most fashionable headgear was openly derived from the same colonial sources as its dresses.

Casual turbans went perfectly with casual Directory hairstyles. Before the Revolution, women's coiffures had reached gigantic heights of complexity. During the Directory, women cut off their long hair, traditional symbol of femininity, and trimmed it close to the head in asymmetrical, bristling styles. Some radical styles were deferentially named after ancient Rome, like the pixie *coiffure à la Titus*, but even the name "Titus" suggested gender-bending. One haircut was brashly called "hedgehog hair." Instructions about how to style short hair read as if it were the twenty-first century: short cuts, "to be *à la mode*, must be short and without powder, tapered from root to tip, dried with a towel, as soon as they are washed; it gives them an unkempt mood." Women were warned that the shorter the cut, the better the hairdresser had to be, preferably one of the new star hairdressers like Duplan, Hyppolite, or Rey. Joséphine swore by Duplan. Some women alleged they were honoring those whose hair had been chopped off to bare their necks for the blade of the guillotine. Some claimed they had cut off their own hair while they were in prison, just in case they were about to be guillotined, for family to cherish as souvenirs. Some women just copied Térézia's pixie cut.

Whatever the justification, women did what they wanted to do with their hair. Hence the Directory wig mania. Another reason to cut off your hair was to make it easier to wear wigs. Revolutionary wigs were nothing like the ancien régime's curled, white-powdered poufs. Those monarchic wigs declared artifice. Revolutionary wigs allowed women to look natural in whatever way they decided was natural. Wigs came in long and short styles, and in every natural shade, plus blue.

Térézia was rumored to own at least thirty wigs. Whether or not this was actually true, it expressed a perception that she changed her appearance at will. She certainly added fuel to the fire of that rumor by posing for a portrait by Isabey in a long blond wig. Everyone who saw the portrait knew it was a wig because she was so famous for her short jet-black hair. It was a striking portrait,

Térézia provocatively flaunts a blond wig in 1800 for her friend Isabey.

Térézia's notorious pixie cut in 1800.

because she wasn't wearing much else other than the wig, apart from her gold hoop earrings. As she reclines in an improbably sylvan setting, her white dress casually drapes underneath one breast to expose it. This is not a wardrobe malfunction. By flaunting the artifice of her wig along with her bare breast, Térézia asserted her control over her natural sexuality. The wig signals agency.

If handbags, Spencers, and hats had become wardrobe staples, then why do they not appear in more portraits of the period? For the same reason that anything usually worn outdoors does not tend to appear in formal portraits, even today. Formal portraits still customarily feature indoor clothing. (For her formal First Lady portrait by Amy Sherald, for example, Michelle Obama wore an evening gown—with no handbag, jacket, or hat.)

The essential accessories of the fashion revolution were radical precisely because they were not indoor clothing. They helped women get out of the house and into the public sphere. They signaled a woman had left home. A woman wore a handbag on her wrist, a jacket over her dress, and a hat on her head because she was shopping, visiting friends, attending public lectures or scientific demonstrations, contemplating art in the new Louvre Museum, commuting to a workplace, possibly on her way to political meetings. In the Year VI, an accessorized woman even took to the skies. Despite controversy over whether her female organs were too delicate to withstand an aerial journey, up went Citoyenne Henri in a hot-air balloon with balloonist André-Jacques Garnerin, waving the revolutionary tricolor *bleu-blanc-rouge* flag. The *Journal des dames et des modes* celebrated her ascent with a special-insert fashion plate, featuring her charming straw hat, tied with a bow under the chin to keep it

Up, up, and away in a novel balloon for a special insert of the 1798 *Journal des dames et des modes.*

L'Orange.

A dapper young man ponders the Three Graces of the fashion revolution.

from blowing away. Revolutionary accessories announced women were going places.

All of these accessories, along with their implications, decode for us a print that coyly represented Juliette, Joséphine, and Térézia as the leading trio of Paris style. The 1801 print is captioned: "The Orange, or, the Modern Judgment of Paris." A young man in a stylish suit ponders the merits of three equally fashionable women. The audience of the print could immediately identify the women, thanks to its education based on the classics, which connected the "Judgment of Paris" with the European tradition of the Three Graces. In the story of the Trojan War, the Trojan prince Paris makes a fateful judgment among Aphrodite, goddess of love, Hera, queen of Olympus, and Athena, goddess of wisdom and craft. The prize was a fruit, in some versions an apple, in others an orange. According to exegesis of classical myth, these divinities overlapped with the three daughters of Zeus, who represented divine gifts to humanity: Euphrosyne was mirth; Aglaia, elegance; and Thalia, youthful beauty. Sophisticates could play the print's game and identify petite Aphrodite/Euphrosyne all in white as Juliette Récamier; the proud Hera/Aglaia with a tiara as Joséphine; and Athena (Minerva)/Thalia as Térézia, because of the hat she was famous for wearing, called a "Minerva helmet," and the handbag bearing Minerva's Medusa shield emblem. Long before the psychologists' interpretation of the handbag as a womb, Parisians were interpreting it as a kind of shield, carried on the arm at a moment of supreme competition.

Térézia, Joséphine, and Juliette were inevitably hailed as the three contemporary Graces. The well-informed mid-nineteenth-century biographer Arsène Houssaye called them simply "the Graces," and claimed the trio danced together in salons to intentionally evoke the Three Graces theme. We know Joséphine had the theme on her mind later—when she was even more imperially regal—because she set the Three Graces subject herself for a grand marble from the most famous European classical sculptor of the revolutionary era, Antonio Canova.

Canova's version of the Three Graces, like revered versions of the theme by classical sculptors or the Renaissance painter Raphael, offered a time-honored opportunity to compare and contrast naked women. Though naked, Graces were supposed to solicit aesthetic discrimination, rather than mere lust. Beauty was raw, style was cultivated grace. Or as Talleyrand put it, in another of his aphorisms: "Beauty without grace is like bait without a hook." For one short decade, Térézia, Joséphine, and Juliette were thoroughly modern Graces, who, far from being naked, styled themselves into celebrity by using fashion as their hook.

The rise of Juliette as a style alternative to Térézia and Joséphine was itself an exercise in compare and contrast. Moreover, as the 1801 "Judgment of Paris" print demonstrates, after Joséphine married Napoléon in 1796, her style diverged from Térézia's, so fashion offered three leading options: purely minimal, imperially exotic, and boldly free. Each of the revolutionary Graces modeled a variation on independence. Together, as the Three Graces, they modeled freedom of choice.

The 1794–99 Directory was a time of creative fashion invention and contagion. What had begun as individual bids for fame turned into a social phenomenon. The persuasive *Journal des dames et des modes* relayed Paris fashion to the farthest reaches of Europe and beyond. But during the next five years, 1799–1804, even as the Three Graces reached the zenith of their fashion celebrity, their independence was increasingly menaced by the rising political power of Napoléon. The Consulate government he instituted with a coup d'état nominally began as a continuation of the Revolution, but quickly turned into its demise.

Chapeau de Velours. Fichu quadrillé.

CHAPTER 11

FREEDOM FROM CLOTHES

(Térézia)

1797–1804

BY THE TIME Napoléon became a general of the revolutionary army, when he married Joséphine, Europe thought Térézia Tallien had pushed fashion to the furthest possible extremes. She had only begun to shock. Yet the same spirit that freed her style rendered her oblivious to danger.

On the eighteenth of Ventôse, Year V (March 8, 1797), Térézia instituted divorce proceedings against Tallien. It was her second divorce, the repeat exercise of a major revolutionary right granted to women. Though he had been jilted, Tallien remained in love with Térézia, and obtained a court order of temporary reconciliation. Térézia accepted the court ruling to avoid crushing him. Men who fell in love with Térézia stayed in love with her, long after their relationships altered. Tallien wrote to his wife, who was notoriously the mistress of Paul Barras, in spring 1798, after tactfully leaving Paris to accompany Napoléon on a military expedition to Egypt: "The tender memories of your goodness, of our love, the hope of finding you again as lovable, as faithful, of hugging my dear daughter, these alone sustain me in my misery." Tallien feebly tried to stave off the official end of his marriage, and the divorce proceedings lingered until April 1802. He did manage to keep her in name. To this day, in France Térézia is called "Madame Tallien."

On December 20, 1797, Térézia delivered a stillborn baby, in Barras's country château. She had not hidden herself away at all for the previous nine months, any more than she had before the birth of her daughter Rose-Thermidor, in the last four months of 1794 and first five of 1795. Most of Térézia's biographers believe Barras was the father in 1797, but because the birth occurred about nine months after the nominal reconciliation with Tallien, newspapers speculated at the time that she might have had a last fling with Tallien. Some biographers agree with the newspapers. The death of the baby made its paternity a moot issue.

Unabashed by her second pregnancy or public doubts about who she was sleeping with, Térézia embarked on a new relationship. Gabriel Julien Ouvrard had been for years a habitué of her salon. Everyone who met him was struck by his extraordinary intelligence and elegance. His gaze was piercing and his clothing finely tailored. He was reputed to have given generous gifts to several women in Térézia's entourage, among them Joséphine. Ouvrard, like Barras, was married, but everyone expected powerful men to be bored by their wives and amused by their mistresses. Needless to say, women did not usually enjoy the equivalent. Térézia, as usual, was the exception that proves the rule.

Térézia and Ouvrard in effect publicly announced their illegitimate intimate relationship in, of all places, Barras's country château, called Grosbois. Barras himself put them in adjacent rooms, as other guests observed. During a hunt the next day, Térézia rode one of Ouvrard's horses, and the two of them disappeared for a noticeably long time. At dinner, they were seated next to each other. Later that evening, they appeared in the same box at the Paris Opéra theater. This probably happened in the fall 1798, when Térézia was twenty-six and Ouvrard was twenty-nine.

Relatively speaking, Térézia settled down with Ouvrard. His wealth sheltered her and her children with financial security. Once again, as in Bordeaux during the early Terror, she had no qualms about where her lover's money came from. In Bordeaux, however, she had won grudging admiration for her rescue of counterrevolutionaries. During the Consulate years, she was more preoccupied by her private life, and less with public issues. She took the escalation of her fashion celebrity by Ouvrard's wealth for granted.

Just as her husband Tallien stayed perpetually in love with her, the two principal illegitimate men in her life conspired to keep her as happy as possible. In March 1798, Barras bought a villa with a large garden on the rue de Babylone. Ownership of this property passed to Térézia on the twenty-eighth of Pluviôse, Year VII (February 16, 1799), for 50,000 francs, and a few weeks later she bought herself the adjacent gardens; her combined grounds amounted to a private park. Barras may have paid for the Paris property as a farewell gift. Or Ouvrard may have paid for it as a welcome gift. Possibly Ouvrard gave the money to Barras to pay for the property on the condition that he pass the property to Térézia. She herself told her children the property was a gift from Ouvrard.

Whoever it came from, the place was now hers. Térézia lived there, on and off, from 1798 until 1815, and kept possession of it until 1823, long after her relationship with Ouvrard had ended and she was married to yet another man. Today, the seventh arrondissement neighborhood is the most expensive in Paris. A few comparable properties still exist intact in the neighborhood, notably one now open to the public, the Musée Rodin. The back of Térézia's park bordered the park of what is now the Matignon palace, official residence of France's prime minister, whose entrance is on the rue de Varenne. From 1808 to 1811, Térézia's back neighbor was Talleyrand, and from 1811 to 1815 none other than Napoléon.

The real style event here
is the erotic furniture.

The *Journal des dames
et des modes* gave this
image, with its obvious
references, the discreet
caption "interior of an
apartment."

The Paris rue de Babylone villa and park became Térézia's next,
more architecturally sophisticated, Chaumière. She turned it into
a rival of Juliette's Paris rue du Mont-Blanc town house. Térézia's
park was big enough to include a little neo-Greek temple and a mul-
tilevel circular *volière* aviary. In the one-story main house, which
had a symmetrical façade and two perpendicular wings, she reno-
vated an open peristyle at the back into a grand gallery with a lovely
wood parquet floor and views onto the garden. Inside, a little living
room, larger living room, bedroom, boudoir, and bathroom were
hung with lilac, bright blue, bright red, and buff drapery, pleated
and adorned with *passementerie*. The furniture, which Térézia liked
so much she kept it for the rest of her life, was mahogany with gilt-
bronze ornaments, featuring erotic motifs including swans, peli-
cans, and female nudes. One visitor compared Térézia's bedroom with
Juliette's famous bedroom, and found it "more severe" because of
the impressive height of the canopy above the bed, which was a
round, amaranth-red-and-white tent, fringed with gold.

Térézia continued to make the same deep impression on those
who met her. According to the duchesse d'Abrantès, Térézia was so
beautiful that people gasped when they met her. After the gasp, they
were struck by how smart and nice she was. "Her mind was fine and
gentle, her conversation of a sort that made you want it to go on; she
had tact and judgment. Her extraordinary generosity was very far-
reaching, and rarely did she rebuff someone unhappy when she could
help him." Furthermore, "Mme Tallien was extremely elegant. She
set the example, and launched fashions."

At the same time that she entertained on her own in Paris, Térézia also entertained with Ouvrard on a country estate. The verdant
240-hectare Le Raincy, complete with château, forest, and hunting
grounds, was the sort of property that for centuries had been the pre-
rogative of landed aristocracy. Now it was being ostentatiously occupied by a man whose colossal fortune had been vastly expanded in no

time at all through financial speculation. Ouvrard, who came from a common merchant family, was entirely self-made. Before the Terror, he had amassed a considerable fortune in manufacturing and commodities trade with France's colonies (commodities, not human beings, as far as we know). During the Directory and Consulate, he multiplied his fortune through speculation in navy contracts and more commodity trades. He dealt in so many millions of francs (the revolutionary currency equivalent of livres) that a "loan" of 10 million francs to Napoléon—likely extorted as a quid pro quo for the consul's personal coffers—hardly inflicted a dent. Ouvrard's personal relationship with Napoléon was tense, but Napoléon's government and wars allowed Ouvrard to support Térézia with an extravagance beyond anything she could have imagined when she left the prison of La Force in 1794, destitute.

Térézia Tallien and Gabriel Julien Ouvrard did not tactfully hide in Le Raincy. On the contrary, after the main building of the château was torn down, and replaced by a fashionable neoclassical villa, complete with colonnade, the couple threw lavish parties, complete with hunting in well-stocked forests (while the ladies rode behind in carriages) and rich meals, which, by Ouvrard's account, were attended by "kings, princes, lords, all that the nobility, the arts and letters offered best." The entertainments, he boasted, were "so various" and "in vogue." On an especially lavish occasion, guests in one marble-paved room could marvel at bright fish and gold sand in a water-filled basin on a table surrounded by citrus trees. In another room, four fountains gushed four delicious drinks. The wines, liqueurs, crystal glasses, gold and silver tableware were all expensive and abundant. Le Raincy had a stunning bathroom, with a giant marble basin in which many people could bathe at once. Ouvrard sometimes absented himself from the parties he paid for, and left Térézia to be his designated hostess, which highlighted her role as his illegitimate consort. He had not abandoned his wife, and indeed had a child by her during his relationship to Térézia. Madame

Ouvrard did not sparkle, however, and Térézia remained the great love of his life.

Barras's château de Grosbois, Térézia's Paris villa, and Ouvrard's Le Raincy estate had something historically significant in common. They were all properties called *biens nationaux*: real estate confiscated by the revolutionary government from nobles or the Catholic Church and resold. Which goes a long way toward explaining why people who did not know Térézia began to hate her so much.

Already in the Year V (1796), the Royalist paper *Rapsodies du jour* sarcastically reported a note pinned to the hem of Térézia's dress: "RESPECT NATIONAL PROPERTIES." The resonant joke depended on connections between levels of meaning. Literally, the joke pinned Directory real estate deals in nationalized property on her clothing. Metaphorically, the joke labeled her as another sort of property traded in deals among national politicians and financiers. The revolutionary government assignat money in which real estate deals were conducted was grossly debased, and so, by implication, was Térézia.

The economics of the Revolution relied on deals in nationalized real estate. The Grosbois, rue de Babylone, and Le Raincy properties, like noble or church properties throughout France, passed to the sort of bourgeois person who could rarely have aspired to them before the Revolution. To buy such a property was to invest in the Revolution. Subsequent régimes did not dare to dispossess this ascendant bourgeoisie. In effect, the sale of confiscated *biens nationaux* constituted a massive transfer of wealth. In practice as in principle, the Revolution of 1789 broke the landed power of the nobility.

Many of these real estate sales were neither open nor fair. Politicians like Barras, businessmen like Récamier and Ouvrard, and the women in their orbits like Térézia benefited from a dubious combination of insider information and political clout. The bargain sale prices and inflated resale prices of *biens nationaux* real estate could generate windfall profits. Assignats fluctuated erratically in value, which made insider trading information hugely lucrative. Overall, assignats lost most of their value against gold. Someone who had access to gold could therefore buy property priced in assignats for a pittance. It was said, for instance, that Barras bought the château de Grosbois for 300,000 francs when it was worth 3 million. The Directory and Consulate governments turned a blind eye to speculation in *biens nationaux* property, as long as members of the government got a cut. Expectably, these transactions were bitterly resented by those whose property had been confiscated, by those who had been forced to sell due to other financial losses, and by those who believed the nobility had a God-given right to the land of France.

The French Revolution of 1789 was about both ideas and realities. Declarations and symbols change history. They endure long after things turn to dust. The 1789 *Declaration of the Rights of Man and of the Citizen* turned the tide of world politics. But when one class of people lost the land of France and another bought it, the revolution became real. When a woman who wore a symbolic style actually lived her sexual freedom, the revolution became real. When the revolutionary realities of wealth and sex were united in one person, that person was going to arouse some very hostile reactions.

Térézia embodied the revolutionary proposition that women could control their own sexuality. She refused to be confined by marriage, she initiated sexual relationships based on their advantages to her, she had children by different fathers, and she courted a uniquely individual style of celebrity. Opponents of the Revolution interpreted her as diabolical proof of what happens when revolutionary sex meets revolutionary money. Térézia's kindness was interpreted as a lack of principle. Her lovers' loyalty and cooperation were attributed to an evil erotic spell she had cast on them.

Her clothing expressed all the choices she made for herself. Perhaps her one case could have been tolerated, but other women followed suit, at least in the matter of fashion. At first it was the women in her salon,

"An elegant young woman coming back from a walk in her morning neglige," from the *Journal des dames et des modes*, June 2, 1798.

then the fashionable women in other salons like Juliette Récamier's, then all the fashionable women of Paris, then the pictures of women in the *Journal des dames et des modes*, then the fashionable women throughout France, then all over Europe, then across the Americas. What next? When many people looked at the new style, they wondered whether a woman who dressed like Térézia might end up behaving like her. Reaction against Térézia came out of a deep dark place, and it was fierce.

The extent to which women's bodies were freed by the Fashion Revolution threatened an entire established social order. Many theoretical explanations could be given for why European culture since the Renaissance demanded that women's bodies be invisible from the waist down, and that their upper bodies be constrained. Practically speaking, women's clothing simply immobilized them. The wealthier a woman was, the more elaborately her clothing confined her, so any personal power a woman accrued from rank was counteracted by her costume. Revolutionary fashion was resisted not despite its comfort, or despite the mobility it granted women in public. Revolutionary fashion was resisted because of its comfort, and because of the mobility it granted women in public.

A few memoirs make it clear that some men greeted revolutionary style with enthusiasm. Antoine Vincent Arnault, a distinguished politician and poet, fondly recalled the clothing worn in 1795–96. He remembered it being politically progressive, saying it was entirely "republican," as opposed to royalist. He was proud that even nations hostile to republican ideals had adopted the style. He loved how the "shapes" of women's bodies "were covered yet not disguised." It was entrancingly graceful, he remembered, and he explicitly said any reputation for "indecency" came only from women who were "jealous because they could not wear the style well."

Hostile reactions, however, were more frequent, and began immediately. Revolutionary fashion, naysayers asserted, was not at all political, but rather entirely sexual. It was lasciviously, excessively, extravagantly indecent. Women were not covered by their dresses, they alleged, or they wore completely transparent dresses. They were nearly naked. A scurrilous pamphlet was published under the name Belzébuth at the end of the Directory that attacked Térézia with manic repetition, using the same phrases over and over to describe her undress and her power over fashion. "You prescribed for fashionable women to go around with bare asses and to show everything [that] decency orders should be hidden. Your caprices and taste are more closely obeyed than the decrees of the current government."

Térézia's close friendship with Joséphine did not endear her to Napoléon's opponents either. To defame him in 1800, as his authoritarian ambitions became apparent within the Consulate, a nasty, anonymous roman à clef took aim at both friends. The Joséphine character was decried as "never beautiful," "a clever mind," "supple and proud," with "an ardor for pleasure a hundred times greater" than the Térézia character. Though invective hurled at the Térézia character was softened by saying she had "an excellent heart, which wants with eager zeal to help through her influence and even her own money," still she was accused of having "sacrificed on the altar of pleasure," being "all flame and sex," with "a decided inclination to singularity."

The British become hysterical about Paris fashion and its Three Graces.

FULL DRESS

PARISIAN LADIES in their WINTER DRESS for 1800

The British, fighting against Napoléon's army and navy, and whose royal court maintained monarchic sumptuary etiquette, also went on the attack against Térézia and Joséphine together. In a caricature by the imaginative artist Gillray, Three Graces wear completely see-though dresses starting below their naked breasts, with cut-outs around their bums, and amaranth victim-ribbons crisscrossing down to their crotches. In British fantasies, Parisian women traipsed through the winter wearing next to nothing. Rumors started of French women dying in droves of pneumonia or tuberculosis because they wet their dresses to make them cling. Not that these caricatures or rumors stopped British women from adopting a version of Parisian styles. But it was a mild, frilly, padded, cute version.

A myth of transparent dresses has persistently tainted the fashion revolution. As recently as March 2021, the normally sensible British Broadcasting Corporation gave a glib summary inherited from caricatures like Gillray's: "In late 18th-Century Europe, a new fashion led to an international scandal. In fact, an entire social class was accused of appearing in public naked." Confirmation bias hardened into orthodoxy. Clothing historians looked for what they assumed was correct, and filled history books and museum collections with the sheer outer layers of dresses that had actually been worn with linings and scarves. Today, we can best understand this distortion as an effect of gender panic. Threatened by the smallest degree of equality—after all, it was only clothing—opponents used every available trick. They exaggerated, they condemned, they mocked, they forbade. Women were being warned against rebellion. To provide the warning with an anti-heroine, Térézia's independence was recast as depravity.

As the Consulate years passed, the scandal of Térézia's maternity augmented the scandal of her style. She gave birth to healthy babies in rapid succession, one a year for four years in a row: 1800, 1801, 1802, and 1803. At the age of thirty, she was the mother of six living children and had been pregnant seven times, by four different men: Fontenay,

Tallien, Barras, and Ouvrard. Only one of those seven pregnancies had begun within a legal marriage—and that marriage had ended in a divorce. Térézia couldn't have cared less that she committed maternity outside the laws of society. She was a serial offender. To add insult to the injury she inflicted on respectable femininity, she loved all her children and cared for them diligently. No one could relieve their aggravation about her affairs by chortling over how illegitimate mothers were all bad mothers. Térézia, confoundingly, was a good mother.

Fashion, furthermore, helped Térézia refuse shame. The new style cast a cloak of invisibility around her transgressions. Only one description of her during those years mentions pregnancy, and it is the proverbial exception that confirms the rule. Rose Thermidor recounted that her mother was at the Théâtre Feydeau when she went into labor with her in May of 1795. As far as the audience knew, it was just another stylish evening at the theater. No one realized its fashion star was nine months pregnant. Unafraid, Térézia braved the gaze of Paris at its most glaring.

Ancien régime high style had conflicted brutally with pregnancy. If you were fashionable and subject to morning sickness, stays and huge skirts can't have helped with the vomiting. By the fifth month of pregnancy, having your torso laced into a downward-pointing cone must have been excruciating. Some stays had extendable belly flaps, but still . . . In their last trimesters affluent women went into what was actually called "confinement," and stayed at home. Perhaps the clothing problem was so acute that confinement came as a relief. Being lonely, bored, or sedentary may have been preferable to constant pain, not to mention worry that your baby was being damaged. An overactive imagination was not required to worry. Though the dictates of monarchic fashion remained unyielding, plenty of medical tracts

Mother and child a la mode.

warned against the damage tightly laced stays could inflict on babies in utero.

Revolutionary dresses did the opposite. They accommodated pregnancy at every stage. The high waist under the bust required no loosening while a belly expanded. The loose light skirts billowed gradually outward. Revolutionary dresses had drawstrings around the neckline and under the bust that adjusted to allover pregnancy weight gain, as well as any postpartum weight fluctuations. If you were as tall and ample as Térézia, the long silhouette might work right up until delivery.

Rewind to the months of fall 1794 and winter 1795 when Térézia and Joséphine inaugurated the new style. During those months, Térézia was pregnant with her second child, Rose Thermidor. Besides prison chic, besides colonial sources, another factor in the invention of the new style was pregnancy. Térézia liberated herself from the torments clothing imposed on pregnant bodies.

Considering how outraged Térézia's critics have been—ever since her lifetime—at the number of men who fathered her children, it is remarkable that no one has taken into account how long she was pregnant during the Directory and Consulate. Yet all I had to do was multiply nine times the six babies born between 1794 and 1804 (not an especially scholarly feat) to realize she was pregnant for 54 of the 125 or so months in which she reigned over fashion.

Surely we must reevaluate Térézia's reputation as the most beautiful woman in Europe, not to mention the erotic dimension of that reputation. During the time of sexual pleasure Barras fondly recalled, she was pregnant for nine months, and raising two small children. When Ouvrard fell in love with her, she had been pregnant three times. During the most delightful years of Ouvrard's life, while he shared the château of Le Raincy with her, she was constantly pregnant or postpartum. Moreover, she was raising two, three, four, five, and then six children. Who has that kind of physical stamina, let alone erotic magnetism? The comparisons people routinely made between her and goddesses may have been more than trite compliments. She does seem to have been somewhat superhuman.

Térézia modeled a solution to an urgent clothing problem on a daily basis, and she modeled the solution in portraits. Look again at how she posed herself lounging for her portrait by Duvivier. Pregnant or not? The genius was in the ambiguity. Could that raised knee be a decoy, and maybe the position of the arm across the torso too? Térézia was demonstrating how a woman could live in her own body both easily and glamorously, no matter what the moment in her life cycle.

The oil portrait that veers closest to admitting pregnancy was painted by the stylish Boilly, probably sometime between 1794 and 1804. Are Térézia's arms encircling a baby bump or a puff of muslin? Whichever, her dress goes with the two most à la mode items of the moment: her ultrashort haircut and her handbag. Térézia just

Térézia with a trophy handbag, by Boilly.

Térézia with the second of her eleven children by five fathers: Rose-Thermidor, named after her best friend (Rose/Joséphine) and the end of the Terror.

so happens to have dropped the handbag, with its cunning tasseled straps, on the bench next to her, to be sure we notice and covet it.

When Boilly's painting was adapted into a print, the handbag turned into her daughter Rose Thermidor, clinging to her mother's side. It would have been a sentimental cliché, except that everyone who gossiped in Europe knew the child had been conceived out of wedlock, and the mother was moving of her own free will from a sexual relationship with the most powerful man in France to a sexual relationship with one of the richest men in France, neither of whom was the father of the girl. Was the print, destined for circulation (unlike the unique oil painting) daring people to gossip?

Every woman across Europe and North America could feel glamorous while pregnant during the window the French Revolution opened in clothing history. The same artist, Boilly, painted a portrait of his pregnant wife in his studio. She didn't hesitate to pose, and he didn't hesitate to paint the portrait, because she was just as fashionable as ever. Her high-waisted dress is the very latest thing, along with its matching long-sleeved white cotton jacket, deeply ruffled right under the bust.

The great English theorist of women's rights, Mary Wollstonecraft, took advantage of the same revolutionary dispensation. She posed for a portrait by John Opie even though she was pregnant. She wears a trendy dress in the new style with a crossed kerchief at her throat. Within months, Wollstonecraft died from the consequences of giving birth to a

daughter, Mary Godwin. By the time Mary Godwin wrote *Frankenstein*, under her married name,
Mary Shelley, fashion had reneged on pregnancy
comfort. Not until the 1990s did women pick up
where revolutionary fashion left off. Térézia foretold a distant clothing future in which women
would flaunt their baby bumps on social media,
and set new fashion examples because of, not
despite, their swelling bellies. It would be another
two hundred years before style, comfort, and
pregnancy were reconciled again.

Térézia celebrated her body no matter what
the moment, including when she posed for the
most formal and prestigious portrait of her
career. Her grand portrait by Gérard was probably painted at the very end of the Consulate,
in 1804, when she was around thirty-one, after
seven pregnancies. She wears a crown of abundant flowers and lets her bodice slip down a
swelling breast, while the warm red of her shawl
hugs her arm and curving torso, then luxuri-
antly swings down her legs. She is in motion,
climbing a stair, and a breeze blows her skirts
out behind her. Poised and dynamic, strong
and graceful, she looks proudly right at us.

Térézia defied the most fundamental rules
of women's apparel. And she did it with sover-
eign indifference to vicious opposition, kindly,
sweetly, as if it were every woman's natural
right to live easily in her body. She gave history a brief glimpse of clothing freedom for
women, before history took its revenge.

Opposite, top: A portrait
by the painter Boilly of
his very pregnant wife,
dressed in the height of
fashion.

Opposite, bottom: A portrait of the equal rights
advocate Mary Woll-
stonecraft, by John Opie,
stylishly and comfortably
dressed, shortly before
she died from the conse-
quences of childbirth.

Térézia glories in her
body for her most formal
and prestigious portrait,
by Gérard in 1804.

(427)

Chapeau-Turban. Croix entourée de Perles fines.

CHAPTER 12

DRESSED FOR SUCCESS

(Joséphine)

1797–1804

STYLE CAN SUBTRACT, and it can surprise. During the first years of their joint fashion leadership, Joséphine and Térézia surprised by subtracting. After Joséphine's marriage in March 1796, she showed how less could also be more. Simplicity could be synonymous with luxury. At first she dawdled in Paris while Napoléon begged her to join him on his campaign in Italy, where he was fighting against the monarchic enemies of the Revolution. But as soon as she did arrive by his side in June 1797, she translated his military conquests into style triumphs. She had a genius for the unexpected and irresistible pull of treasures from one apparel orbit into another.

Soon after their wedding, Joséphine realized Napoléon might have been a smart choice. She may have felt confident he would get money out of the Italian campaigns. Or she understood she could speculate more profitably on military supply contracts with his insider information. The distinction is important, according to Joséphine's latest biographer, Pierre Branda. Thanks to his knowledge of Napoleonic finances and his research in previously untapped archives, Branda has demonstrated that for several years after her marriage, Joséphine actively invested and made money for herself. She did not merely wait passively for Napoléon to support her. She also traded favors she brokered through contacts, including the favors of information provided to the police. Joséphine summed up her attitude: "My maxim is to always pay in the same currency in which I am paid."

This new reckoning with Joséphine's finances helps explain the acceleration of her style impact. Prior to her marriage in 1796, what she could glean from occasional gifts, small-time graft, and money petitioned from the government as partial restitution of the confiscated Beauharnais fortune was little in comparison with the income Térézia derived from Barras's control of the Directory government. Nor did Joséphine then enjoy an income anything like the banking wealth of Juliette Récamier's husband. In 1796, however, Joséphine started to catch up.

Joséphine decided to complete the decoration of the rue Chantereine pavilion. With her new initials, JNB, she stamped a marital identity on the rigorously proportioned, black-and-white restraint of dishes she and Napoléon would eat from. The dishes' decoration continued to express her earlier lean aesthetic, while her commission of a porcelain set announced its new scope. She wrote to her designer Vautier: "There are funds now and I flatter myself that everything is going well. I desire that my house be furnished with the latest elegance." Among other pieces, she commissioned six chairs and four armchairs in mahogany, six stools and a secretary in lemonwood, two bureaus, a desk chair, and six chandeliers, for a total of 4,490 francs. Unlike with some of the purchases she made entirely for herself, she had the furniture Napoléon was going to enjoy billed to him.

Joséphine tempered a love of luxury with subtle respect for the innate qualities of materials, to an exceptional degree. Several pieces of her furniture have survived from the few years she lived in the rue

Chantereine pavilion. She must have loved them, because she kept them when she moved to a more opulent home. Their spare designs relied on the natural brown of tightly grained mahogany and smoky gray veins of marble, ornamented with delicate vases, sphinxes, lyres, and wreaths. To get an idea of what the pieces looked like, we can still see some of them installed in the museum made from her later Malmaison residence.

Similarly, Joséphine began to upgrade her wardrobe. An inventory made on the occasion of her marriage to Napoléon provides a baseline. In 1796, clothing was still so valuable that every slip was as worth assessing as a Vuitton or Hermès handbag would be today as part of an estate, or a divorce settlement. Joséphine owned eighteen dresses, among them three in domestic imitations of Indian cotton prints, one in linen imitating muslin, and six in real muslin; six real muslin scarves and eighteen imitation muslin scarves in linen; and twenty-four headscarves listed as Indian cotton, which we can assume were Madras plaid. Total value of the wardrobe, including underwear, shoes, and stockings: 729 francs (francs having replaced the denomination of livres in 1795). Cotton was clearly Joséphine's material of choice, at a range of price points.

Joséphine's preferred style of rigorously simple furniture, moved to Napoléon's library in her Malmaison château.

Another inventory was taken of Joséphine's wardrobe two years later. She had acquired 327 francs' worth more clothing, including six embroidered muslin dresses, four imitation muslin dresses in linen, three "*indienne*" "*deshabillés*" and three muslin camisoles. Indian cotton still reigned.

These two inventories allow us to measure how radically the new style had lowered the cost of fashion. Joséphine had been a style leader since 1794, yet the price of her wardrobe was within the budget of a middle-class woman. Remember that Queen Marie Antoinette had a budget of 120,000 livres for clothing in 1783. The difference was indeed revolutionary.

The inventories also allow us to understand how this much more democratic fashion contained the new luxury of fine muslin. Muslin was crucial to all three of the Graces, but in different ways, each characteristic of their individual personalities, and of distinct revolutionary style strands.

Juliette emphasized muslin's minimalism. Her message of purity so completely overrode material realities that we don't know how expensive her muslins actually were. The most enviable clothing of cultures the world over had always been premised on the belief that more was better: more expense, more volume, more detail, more shine. Juliette showed that one perfectly cut white cotton dress sufficed. Fashion was given a new direction. Self-expression through clothing no longer necessarily required a fortune.

A fortune, however, could help, as both Térézia and Joséphine quickly demonstrated. Of the two best friends, it was probably, as usual, Térézia who ventured first. She reinstated Bengali muslin at the height of Paris fashion, no longer as a billowing chemise à la reine but as the dynamic revolutionary sheath. One of Térézia's biographers, claiming eyewitness evidence (though without naming sources), asserts she was the first to wear "muslin" at a public event, by 1796, and cites a price of 40 *louis*, worth about 800 livres. (Which might argue for an event a year earlier, when the franc was declared French currency.) If so, the sum was much larger than what Joséphine's Directory wardrobe inventories suggest she was spending. Perhaps the amount is correct, and indicates how successfully Térézia seduced Directory financiers. Her biographer rhapsodized: "In this kingdom of tulle and muslin, Thérésia is the Queen, the Goddess of this renewed mythology." He named two "ministers" of the "muslin kingdom": a "couturier" who specialized in a Greek look, and Madame Raimbaut, who specialized in a Roman look. The reliable eyewitness the duchesse d'Abrantès wrote that by 1798, Térézia habitually wore "beautiful Indian muslin."

But Joséphine usurped Térézia's muslin "queen" title. Napoléon's valet, Constant, admired on Joséphine "a white muslin dress, with short sleeves, a pearl necklace around her neck, no headdress, curled hair held by a shell comb with a totally charming casualness." The duchesse d'Abrantès specifically named the "Indian muslin" fabric of a dress Joséphine wore, covered with tiny starry openwork, possibly *chikandari*, when she recalled an outfit worn to a morning party: "She was charming attired that way." The duchesse also described another "dress in Indian muslin" in such detail that we can wonder if the trim was *gota*: "A finger-width border in gold lamé looking like a little gold stream." Joséphine did for muslin in Paris what Akbar and Jahangir had done for it in India: made it imperial.

When Joséphine posed in muslin for the fashionable portraitist Gérard (the same artist who painted portraits of Juliette and Térézia), she produced a very different effect than Marie Antoinette had in 1783, when the queen posed in muslin for Vigée Lebrun. No one thought Joséphine undermined her prerogatives. Gérard's fashion skills included his ability to render subtle gradations of textile quality with oil paint. Compare the muslin in his portrait of Juliette with the muslin in his portrait of Joséphine. Juliette's muslin is charmingly delicate, perfect for a fluttering ruffle, but not as magical as Joséphine's. To demonstrate her fabric supremacy, Joséphine arranged the bottom of her dress in a pool at her feet, and Gérard painted it as if it were mist.

According to several memoirs, Joséphine not only wore dresses of

Joséphine wafted the finest muslin around her face, an effect much copied by Isabey for the rest of his career.

Joséphine in a dress whose luxurious fabric pools like mist at her feet, by Gérard in 1801.

finest Bengali muslin but also wafted the precious fabric around her head, neck, and shoulders. The effect was so closely associated with her, and felt so artistic, that her invention was remembered as the origin of a signature Isabey miniature-portrait device. Her friend Isabey did indeed continue to repeat her flattering halo of whirling translucent muslin folds for the rest of his career, including for a portrait of Joséphine herself. Without knowing the technical qualities of the precious fabric, we might doubt the realism of the effect, and attribute it to poetic license.

Like Mughal emperors, Joséphine bejeweled her imperial muslins. Early Directory style had not depended on jewelry. Térézia wore jewelry that was noticed not for itself but because it drew attention to her body. The legendary rings on her toes, bracelets around her arms and ankles, the diamond necklaces sparkling around her breasts—all were more erotic than aesthetic. Juliette wore pearls to emphasize her total abnegation of color. She chose to wear remarkably little jewelry for her portraits, almost none. The jewelry part of the fashion revolution really belonged to Joséphine, and began as the Directory ended.

After Napoléon conquered swathes of the Italian peninsula by fighting battles, he demanded financial tribute in exchange for peace. Most of the money he obtained went back to the Directory government in Paris, where it officially paid the costs of war, while some was siphoned off in secret by political and financial cabals. What wealth in all forms Napoléon could plausibly conceal stayed in his hands, notably the personal "gifts" he was given to assuage his wrath. Joséphine was directly and indirectly the beneficiary. As she reigned over a pop-up court outside Milan until January 1798, she too received plunder, and dealers hastened to offer for purchase their best wares, notably the cameos and engraved gems for which Italy was renowned. Soon after her arrival in Milan, Joséphine also enlisted her brother-in-law Joseph Bonaparte to find her cameos.

Cameos and intaglios had been treasured among media since antiquity. The stones were themselves precious, and they were adorned with tiny but realistic images, usually heads or mythological figures in action, whether carved into bas-relief layers of different colors (cameos) or incised with recessed images (intaglios). Together, stone cameos and intaglios are called glyptic gems. Cameos can also be carved from the relatively softer material of shells. The fascinatingly miniature format, intricate craft, durable materials, and portable convenience of this type of art object combined to make glyptic gems among the most highly prized items in the great cabinet art collections of the Renaissance and Baroque periods. They were kept secure for erudite contemplation in dedicated furniture or small rooms, often together with coins and medals. One fabled cameo in particular passed through the possession of two of the greatest women collectors in history: Isabella d'Este, Marchioness of Mantua, and Queen Christina of Sweden. Named the *Gonzaga Cameo*, it was fluidly carved in precious sardonyx and represented a couple whose exact identity has never been certain. It may have been intended to refer simultaneously to more than one famous pair, associating for instance the Roman emperor Augustus and Livia with the gods Zeus and Hera. The great Baroque artist Peter Paul Rubens, among others, declared the *Gonzaga Cameo* the best he had ever seen.

The Gonzaga Cameo from the third century BCE. Napoléon plundered this legendary gem, with a fabled history of regal women collectors, from the Vatican when he defeated Rome in 1796–98, and gave it to Joséphine. She kept the cameo intact and gave it late in her life to the czar of Russia.

"Headband ornamented with engraved gems. Lace caplet," in *Journal des dames et des modes.*

The gem later passed into the possession of Pope Pius VI, and was thus part of the Vatican collection when Napoléon arrived in Italy. Napoléon added a new chapter to the gem's representation of legendary couples when he seized it from the Vatican in 1797 and gave it to Joséphine.

Joséphine left the *Gonzaga Cameo* as Napoléon gave it to her. He appreciated glyptic stones for their classical historic value, the way collectors since the Renaissance had, and as his art experts did, notably Dominique Vivant Denon, director of his museums. Napoléon instituted a prize for medalists and gem engravers in 1803, and when he reorganized government arts institutions in 1805, he added engraved gems to the roster of fine arts. After Joséphine became empress, she invoked her husband's approval when she nudged a budget gatekeeper for a collection of cameos and turquoises she had asked Denon to assemble for her: "The empress is no more exempt from a little coquetry than any other woman, but in her case it is excusable, given that all she desires is to please the emperor. I therefore beg you to authorize M. Denon to let me have these items as soon as possible."

Joséphine's characterization of herself as a *coquette* reveals what she had actually been doing with "items" since the summer of 1797. Instead of studying one engraved gem at a time as evidence of history, in the context of a sequestered art collection, she had been grouping cameos and intaglios according to her personal taste, and having them set into wearable jewelry. Italy introduced Joséphine to cameos and intaglios, and Joséphine introduced cameos and intaglios to modern fashion. We may never be sure exactly how many of them she collected during the 1797–1804 years of her greatest design originality, or exactly which ones, with the notable exception of the *Gonzaga Cameo*. Already by late 1804, when an inventory of her jewelry was drawn up, which listed her cameos and intaglios as a generic type of possession, she had distributed many pieces to her daughter, ladies-in-waiting, and friends. From a design point of view, the rapid turnover in Joséphine's collection signals why cameos and intaglios are so important to understanding her style. They inspired her to start repurposing old gems into new adornments. Once she started imagining different combinations, she just couldn't stop acquiring, dismantling, exchanging, and resetting. The more of Europe Napoléon conquered, the more gems came her way to experiment with.

Enter the tiara. Joséphine may have been the inventor of this jewelry type, which is now more in favor than ever. She certainly was among the most prominent women to evolve the revolutionary headband into something more permanent than a strip of cloth but much lighter than a crown. Many proponents of revolutionary style had been centering a feather aigrette or jewel above their foreheads on single, double, or triple bands. A miniature portrait by Isabey, ever sympathetic to Joséphine's inventions, shows how she began to put cameos in that position, and attach them to circlets of jewels, in this case five matching strands of small pearls, instead of cloth. The black-and-white cameo and the white pearls pop against her dark curls.

Joséphine mixed rather than matched. She combined old cameos and intaglios with new Italian ones, and glyptic gems with pearls. Multiple coordinated pieces were integrated into total ensembles. For a portrait by the Italian Andrea Appiani, she chose a tiara made of gold and red gems with a cameo at the center and strands of pearls woven into her hair. Around her neck she hung a bold necklace with three brand-new cameos visible: copies of medals struck by Appiani in 1797, allegorically commemorating battles won by Napoléon in Italy. A belt and three armbands of black ribbon sewn with pearls echo the pearls in her hair. Joséphine improvised with the new spots for ornament offered by revolutionary dresses: around the seam between bodice and skirt, at the center-front of the bodice, at the hem of short small sleeves, and in multiple bracelets over the wrists of

Isabey captures his friend Joséphine's jewelry design genius, with a prototype of the tiara.

The cameos around Josephine's throat in this portrait by Andrea Appiani allegorically represent three of Napoléon's victories in Italy.

Joséphine inventively groups three cameos on the new high waistline.

A geometric chest by Biennais held the many treasures of Joséphine's early jewelry collection.

long fitted sleeves. Sets believed to have belonged to her typically include items for several of these spots, often with coordinated earrings. Formal sets included tiaras; more casual sets, ornamented hair-combs. Joséphine's style was too protean for pieces that matched exactly; instead she preferred subtle harmonies.

When she posed for a grand portrait by Gérard, Joséphine orchestrated cameos and pearls with an ethereal muslin dress. Her tiara is rather like the one in her miniature portrait by Isabey, but with two more strands of pearls, seven instead of five, dipping from a central cameo to join a cameo on each side of her brow. Cameos of the same size clasp her short sleeves, at the height of a single round pearl in the middle of her bodice. That central pearl, in turn, repeats the round pearls at the tops of her earrings, from which hang the pear-shaped pearl drops that became her signature earring design. (Eventually she acquired perfectly paired pearl drops in every shade of white, gray, and pink, with a variety of stones at the earlobes, including one pair now owned by the Louvre Museum.)

By 1799, Joséphine was in a supreme position to influence jewelry fashion. That year, as Napoléon took control over the French government as consul, he allowed his wife the use of pearls and precious stones in the national jewelry collection. Six years later, right after the Consulate had ended and the Empire had begun, the *Journal des Dames et des Modes* reported that "a fashionable lady wears cameos on her belt, cameos on her collar, a cameo on each of her bracelets, and a cameo on her tiara."

Having accumulated quite a substantial collection by the end of the Consulate, Joséphine commissioned a beautiful piece of furniture to contain it. Its severe yet graceful mahogany rectangle with fine geometric metal accents was typical of her revolutionary style. In a perfect example of her taste, the piece also functioned cleverly. The box on top, lined in white velvet, could be removed to make it a portable chest. An observant lady-in-waiting, Madame de Rémusat, recalled Joséphine displaying its contents.

> Madame Bonaparte showed us an immense quantity of pearls, diamonds and cameos, which constituted the contents of her jewelcase. Even at that time it might have figured in a tale from the *Arabian Nights*, and it was designed to receive further rich acquisitions. Invaded and grateful Italy had contributed, and so had the Pope.

Later, as empress, Joséphine commissioned a larger, ostentatious piece of furniture to secure her jewelry. It was more a closet than a case, to house a collection whose quantity and cost had reached an imperial scale. Its quality, however, was a legacy of the years before Empire, before Napoléon dictated his propaganda agenda, the years when Joséphine's aesthetic was truly revolutionary.

Our best example of Joséphine's early jewelry taste is an extraordinary watch. It is one of the rare objects from those years that has come down to us documented and intact. Almost all of Joséphine's jewels,

Pendant watch bought by Joséphine on February 18, 1800, for 3,000 francs. The astral design by Breguet allowed her to tell time by touching the diamond arrow, without opening the exquisite watch.

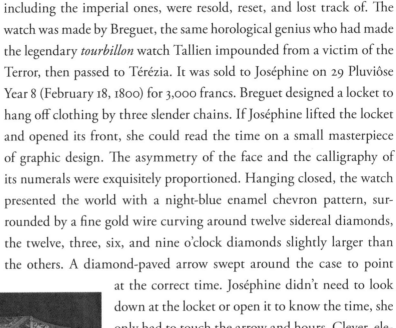

Detail, 1630–37 Windsor *Padshahnama*. Male Mughal courtiers wore *jama* dresses, *patka* sashes, and turbans, some of them with Kashmiri shawls, all tied the same way around their shoulders. Like many images of Indian clothing, this one came to Europe in the late eighteenth century.

including the imperial ones, were resold, reset, and lost track of. The watch was made by Breguet, the same horological genius who had made the legendary *tourbillon* watch Tallien impounded from a victim of the Terror, then passed to Térézia. It was sold to Joséphine on 29 Pluviôse Year 8 (February 18, 1800) for 3,000 francs. Breguet designed a locket to hang off clothing by three slender chains. If Joséphine lifted the locket and opened its front, she could read the time on a small masterpiece of graphic design. The asymmetry of the face and the calligraphy of its numerals were exquisitely proportioned. Hanging closed, the watch presented the world with a night-blue enamel chevron pattern, surrounded by a fine gold wire curving around twelve sidereal diamonds, the twelve, three, six, and nine o'clock diamonds slightly larger than the others. A diamond-paved arrow swept around the case to point at the correct time. Joséphine didn't need to look down at the locket or open it to know the time, she only had to touch the arrow and hours. Clever, elegant, astral, it is quintessentially Joséphine.

Joséphine and Napoléon returned from Italy to Paris. Soon, in May of 1798, Napoléon left again, to fight in Egypt and Syria, nominally on behalf of revolutionary principles. Really, he wanted to get away from the Paris debacles of the Directory and contemplate a coup d'état. He was gone until October of 1799, allowing Joséphine months of Parisian freedom to trade favors, make lucrative deals, buy property, flirt, and launch the accessory that would dominate European fashion for decades. Once again, as with her jewelry, Napoléon's ambitions opened up new style territory for her. From Egypt, he sent her a package of shawls in transit from Kashmir.

All Kashmiri shawls are shawls, but not all

shawls have the same shape, drape, warmth, woven ornament, or fringe as those from Kashmir. Like Bengali muslin, Kashmiri shawls surprised early European visitors to Mughal courts. True Kashmiri shawls were made only in Kashmir, where artisans had developed an unrivaled weaving and finishing process on the basis of a particular local raw material. Wild goats in the foothills of the Himalayas contend with altitude by growing an extremely fine yet warm underfleece (*pashm*) on their bellies. In spring, the goats rub off this fleece on rocks and bushes, where it is collected, and turned over to teams of weavers and pattern readers. Genuine Kashmiri shawls can be recognized by their diagonally ridged twill weave in their middle solid areas, with wide borders woven by interlocking colored weft threads on the back of the fabric (*kani* weaving). The naked eye can barely perceive the almost microscopic work of a superb Kashmiri border, whose decorative effect is stunning when worn. It took two-man teams eighteen months to make an average shawl, three years to make a superlative one. The finest could be pulled through a finger-ring.

Some sort of shawl, which is to say a large, flat, rectangular, triangular, or circular wrap, had always been a wardrobe basic in many cultures. It is possible that among the Three Graces, it was Térézia, with her typical boldness, who wore Kashmiri shawls first, or maybe she was wearing some other sort of dramatic shawl. In November of 1796, a commentator reported that Térézia had been at the theater wearing "a spangled muslin gown and a scarlet cloak." The usually accurate eyewitness the duchesse d'Abrantès recalled Térézia wearing a specifically Kashmiri shawl at a Luxembourg Palace event, which was most likely sometime in 1797 or 1798, and remarked that it was an "adornment very rare still at that time and very sought-after."

With Kashmiri shawls as with Bengali muslins, Joséphine's example ended up being the most influential. Eventually, she owned a staggering number of them. Because genuine shawls from Kashmir were, as the duchesse d'Abrantès pointed out, rare and sought-after, they were very expensive. Like the finest muslin, they were already ultimate luxury items where they came from, and fully appreciated at regal Mughal courts. In France, each shawl cost between about 8,000 and 12,000 francs. By the end of the Consulate, Joséphine owned ninety shawls, of which sixty-five were listed in an inventory as being "cachemire."

Kashmiri shawls, or their cheap imitations, became so ubiquitous in European wardrobes that it may be difficult to remember how foreign they once seemed. Most importantly, in India the shawls had been worn principally by men. They were also worn in a single prescribed way: wrapped securely around the shoulders, and tied once, with their bordered ends hanging straight down. (Waists were wrapped with patkas.) This prescribed usage explains the features originally most unfamiliar to European eyes: narrow proportions, long plain middles, and distinctly one-sided border designs. Correctly positioned by Indian standards, the plain middles were occupied by the wrap, while both borders were hung with right sides facing outward.

Joséphine was capable of imagining how these striking characteristics of Kashmiri shawls would enhance the most characteristic features of revolutionary style. A long, light straight muslin dress and a long, light straight shawl would echo each other. The folds of a draped shawl would rhyme with both knotted sashes worn under the bust and popular turban headdresses. The surprising warmth of Kashmiri wool, moreover, would compensate for the cool of cotton as well as for the abbreviation of Spencer jackets. The shawls' deep borders, with their dynamic *boteh* designs and delicate fringe, enlivened the whites and solid colors of dresses just enough. Or did Joséphine realize how well Kashmiri shawls would coordinate with revolutionary dresses simply because those muslin dresses had been adapted from the muslin Indian jama with which the shawls had in fact originally been worn?

And like revolutionary dresses, colonial shawls could pass for feminine ancient Greek or Roman drapery. If Europeans could forget that their "classical" dresses were made of Indian muslin, constructed like an Indian men's jama, sashed as if with an Indian men's patka, worn with headdresses like an Indian men's turban, they could forget one more thing. All it took for the French to forget that the shawls came from a real, colonized culture was to alter their spelling to "cachemire." In English the spelling "cashmere" sufficed.

As to the arrangement of the shawls according to an original cultural standard, Joséphine headed in the exact opposite direction, with the bravura of a woman who had already managed some astounding fashion transfers. In the many portraits she posed for, Joséphine demonstrated how expressively Kashmiri shawls could be staged, rather than fastened functionally. For an elegantly attenuated portrait by Pierre-Paul Prud'hon, for example, she took maximal advantage of exactly those qualities that made a Kashmiri shawl not like classical cloaks. She stretches out romantically on a rock seat against a natural background, her head pensively supported by bent arm and delicate hand gesture. The graceful sheath of her silvery gray dress defers to the long red drama of her Kashmiri shawl, which pours vibrant color behind her back, across her knees, and into a cluster at

Joséphine in a red Kashmiri shawl, painted by Prud'hon.

Joséphine in a green Kashmiri shawl, sketched by Prud'hon.

her hip. For another portrait by Prud'hon, a sketch, she wrapped a green shawl's plain middle around and around her torso.

Instead of the careful, consistent control of the shawl by its original wearers, Parisian fashion kept the shawl in motion: in slides, folds, trails, sweeps, and swags. Kashmiri shawls became the signature accessory of the era, in either costly authentic or cheaply imitated versions. They were interpreted as an expression of the personalities of the women who wore them, in fashion magazines, etiquette manuals, letters, and memoirs. The *Journal des dames et des modes* proposed endless wrapping options: draped evenly over both shoulders; knotted in front at the chest; looped around both arms; hung around the neck; knotted at one hip; draped around both hips; tossed over one shoulder and tied under the bust; tied high in the back; framing both shoulders; hanging off one shoulder and loosely folded at the hip. Take your pick.

Catherine Verlée, raised in colonial Indian trading posts, keeps her precious Kashmiri shawl coiled near her in a life-size portrait by Gérard.

Ambitious formal portraits record even more personal variations than fashion plates. Portrait subjects were self-consciously posing for posterity, and painters were inspired to embed intricate shawl compositions within their work. In yet another full-length portrait by Gérard, its subject, Catherine Verlée, leans toward a red-hot fireplace in a white revolutionary evening dress, ankles crossed to display her white satin shoes. She has arranged her Kashmiri shawl on a chair in such organic coils that it appears animate, like a kind of pet waiting for its mistress. The prominence of the shawl is all the more striking because its owner was notoriously born in colonial India, of French parents in a Danish trading post, and married to a British colonial official. She was called "Indian" her whole life, as a derogatory explanation for her lack of intellect. In March 1798, for instance, her most eminent lover, the diplomat Talleyrand, wrote to the leader of the Directory government, Térézia's lover Barras, to plead for her release from prison. Catherine had been arrested on suspicion of spying, but Talleyrand assured Barras, "man to man," that she was incapable of any such activity. "She is a very beautiful and very lazy Indian, the most unoccupied woman I have ever met." If ever the identity of a portrait subject gave a loud hint about the true origins of the shawl, especially in conjunction with the Caribbean mahogany wood of the furniture and the fabric of the dress, which might be silk gauze but is more probably Bengali muslin, it was in the case of this portrait. And yet . . .

Ingres meticulously documents the technical prowess of Kashmiri weavers to emphasize the authenticity of Madame Rivière's prize possession.

Though Paris fashion connoisseurs ignored the cultural origins of their favorite accessory, they looked very closely for technical signs of its authenticity, as a great portrait by Ingres records. In his image of Madame Rivière, Ingres observed how Kashmiri weaving prowess allowed a cream shawl to eddy and flow along an arm. The painter also bothered to represent the contrast between the crisp "right" side of one of the shawl's borders and the more blurred "wrong" side of the other, as well as the precise length and shape of the shawl's fringe fibers. The shawl is almost depicted with more

Joséphine combines colonial items for a portrait by Gros: Bengali muslin, Italian cameos, and Kashmiri shawls.

character than its human owner. Both the subject and the painter of the portrait were entranced by a status trophy, and both of them were boasting about their ability to style it.

No one, however, gave Kashmiri shawls more individual cachet than Joséphine. She repurposed them with consummate understatement. For a portrait by Jean-Antoine Gros, she combined three shawls with Bengali muslin and cameo pins into a colonial medley. She stands looking left toward a bust of her son, Eugène, mounted atop a column; a vase filled with flowers called *hortensias* in French refers to her daughter, Hortense. Joséphine holds a letter in her hand, whose envelope, wax seal still attached, has been dropped at her feet, so great is her haste to read its news, hinting at dispatches from Napoléon's latest battle. These details proclaim, "I am always thinking of my family." The main event of the portrait, however, is her outfit.

Joséphine fastened a muslin veil to her chignon with a classical pin. Over a muslin underdress, she attached Kashmiri shawls with cameos. She wrapped another shawl under her bust and tossed it over her shoulder, letting an end gather behind her on the ground. The outfit is completely original, harmonious, balanced—and wildly expensive. The shawls alone might have cost as much as 36,000 francs. An ordinary French craftswoman would have had to work 120 years to make that much money.

With her shawls as with her muslins and her jewelry, no single piece created Joséphine's look, but rather the way she put them all together. Joséphine employed skilled women "couturières," such as Madame Raimbaut and Madame Germont, whom Joséphine shared with her daughter, Hortense. These women probably did make and sell unusually good items. But it was Joséphine who selected them, and Joséphine who picked the elements of her outfit every morning.

And Joséphine's choices, in turn, depended on France's colonial power. Look into the revolutionary wardrobe, Joséphine's first and foremost. What was in it? The Caribbean gole, Bengali muslin, Indian jamdani, chikandari, jama, and Kashmiri shawls. Juliette, Térézia, and Joséphine were not known for wearing turbans, but many other women were, notably the political theorist Germaine de Staël, who made it her trademark. What else was there to the new style? Not much. Revolutionary fashion was called neoclassicism to preserve European pride. Maybe it should be called colony classicism instead.

With Napoléon away in Egypt, Joséphine also exercised real estate and sexual independence, like Térézia, who remained her best friend. After having rented in Paris for years, she bought an elegant château and its estate just outside of Paris in April of 1799. It may have been recommended by Térézia, who had spent time there before her first marriage, before the Revolution. Joséphine brought Napoléon to see the property, called Malmaison, before his departure and he approved. Nevertheless, she secured it primarily as a refuge for herself and her children, which it did turn out to be.

Among Joséphine's misunderstood financial transactions, her purchase of Malmaison has loomed large. For two centuries, biased critics interpreted her ability to pay for it herself as proof that she was not much more than a prostitute, married though she was to Napoléon. They assumed she traded sex for the official purchase price of 225,000 francs, perhaps with more than one man. A milder version of that explanation, which takes into account how close she was to Térézia, has been that Ouvrard provided her the money, not in exchange for sex but to curry favor with Barras, Napoléon, or Térézia.

Joséphine's recent biographer Branda, however, has proposed a more ingenious explanation for her acquisition of Malmaison. Based on his research into her finances, he argues that Joséphine probably did not really pay the fair market price of 225,000 francs, but rather obtained an enormous discount by first trading hard currency for official paper assignats. This was how Térézia had acquired her Paris villa, Barras his château de Grosbois, and Ouvrard his château Le Raincy.

Being a woman, Joséphine could not obtain hard currency the usual ways men did: through government office, like Barras; business, like Ouvrard; or military conquest, like Napoléon. But Joséphine knew another way, her biographer shows—from her mother, on Martinique. Steep profits were still being made from the sugar trade, profits multiplied by the labor of the enslaved. The government of Martinique had simply refused to recognize the revolutionary National Convention government's abolition of slavery in 1793. Slow communications and passive resistance allowed Martinique to ignore a law promulgated in Paris. The difficulty remained of getting gold surreptitiously into France, avoiding as many rules, taxes, and bribes as possible. Joséphine succeeded by having her mother send the gold through a German financier. She used her connections to facilitate each link in the transaction chain, ending with the trade into assignats. The purchase of Malmaison is indeed tarnished, not by the sexual transactions Joséphine's critics have alleged, but rather by colonial slavery.

Meanwhile, Joséphine carried on a torrid affair. She had taken Hippolyte Charles as her lover, certainly by fall 1797, possibly a year earlier. Contrary to what Barras claimed about her, the affair seems to have been about enjoying sex with Charles for its own sake. In fall 1799, Napoléon left Egypt for Paris, incensed by reports of Joséphine's affair with Charles (though he had by no means been faithful himself) and determined to get a divorce. The quarrelsome but tight Bonaparte clan had never approved of Joséphine. Napoléon's mother, brothers, and sisters resented her influence over him, her first marriage, her children, her independence, and her flair. They did not think it likely that at the age of thirty-six, she would give Napoléon an heir, and if she did, her influence would only increase. His brothers needled him endlessly over her betrayal.

Back in Paris on October 16, Napoléon arrived first at the elegantly refurnished rue de la Victoire pavilion. When Joséphine arrived, Napoléon had locked her out. She wept, he stormed. He would never take her back, he said. Luckily, Eugène de Beauharnais was there and reconciled them. After a night together, Joséphine and Napoléon woke up in bed, smiling.

Napoléon had also returned from Egypt with a political coup in mind. He toppled the Directory government on the eighteenth of Brumaire, Year VIII (November 9, 1799) and installed a new government called the Consulate. At first, it was ruled by three consuls, of whom Napoléon pretended to be one among equals. Karl Marx called his history of France "the 18th Brumaire" to mark the coup d'état as the beginning of the end of the French Revolution.

From that moment, Joséphine too sensed the beginning of an end. She knew her husband's power was waxing and her chances of staving off divorce were waning. Every year her chances of producing an heir dwindled and the Bonaparte family case against her improved. Napoléon's genuine love for her children helped her. Eugène had already served his stepfather as aide-de-camp, and distinguished himself in battle. Hortense was brought into the Bonaparte fold by being married to her step-uncle, Napoléon's younger brother Louis.

Style was still on Joséphine's side. It became her retention strategy, and for a while it worked. The pavilion on the rue de la Victoire was much too small for what was rapidly becoming Napoléon's quasi-royal court. Napoléon reoccupied the Tuileries Palace, where King Louis XVI and Marie Antoinette had last reigned before the Terror. Joséphine presided over her husband's entourage with grace and dignity, amid furnishings that mingled legacies from the monarchy with new commissions. She had no sway over Napoléon's political decisions; it was all she could do to salvage her marriage. When possible after 1800, she retreated to Malmaison, where Isabey often joined her to help design festivities, and where she reinstalled a few favorite pieces from the rue de la Victoire pavilion. Gradually, though, she let Percier's style take over her interior decoration. He was responsible both for her official residence in the Tuileries Palace and for her Malmaison retreat.

Percier designed a magnificent bedroom for her, with a big *B* for "Bonaparte" in the middle of splendid drapery behind the bed. On either side of the *B* he placed butterflies, symbols of transformation, perhaps to confirm that Rose de Beauharnais had completely morphed into Joséphine Bonaparte. A suggestively reclining female figure ornamented the bed; a couple amorously embraced on a painting above the bed; cupids pranced on the sidewalls. This was not Juliette's enticing yet withholding bedroom, or Térézia's self-sufficiently stately bedroom; it was a bedroom that catered to one man.

Percier's fashionable design for Joséphine's married bedroom.

HER best and most personal style asset remained her clothing. Napoléon continued to revel in Joséphine's taste. He noticed what she wore, as their entourage frequently remarked. He also noticed what other women wore at receptions, sometimes critically. One lady was told she had worn a dress too often and must ask her husband to buy another. Napoléon took to calling the *Journal des dames et des modes* the *Moniteur officiel de la mode*, playing on the name of his official government political journal, *Le Moniteur universel.* When he was asked for his opinion on clothing, he proclaimed: "Consult La Mésengère's magazine, it must be your *Moniteur.*"

Decades later, the duchesse d'Abrantès could still recall details of Joséphine's most striking outfits. For a ball in 1800 at Lucien Bonaparte's, Joséphine had worn a dress on which were scattered golden, sulphur, and lemon-yellow feathers, with a few red chest feathers interspersed.

> A beautiful and very strange dress . . . in white crepe, and entirely scattered with little toucan feathers; these feathers were sewn to the crepe, and at their ends were a little pearl. Madame Bonaparte wore with this dress rubies in a necklace and earrings. Her hairstyle, a masterpiece of Duplan's, was done with the same feathers, mounted into a wreath.

On another occasion Joséphine wore a different delicate natural substance, scattering a white crêpe dress with real rose petals. She favored spritzes of color, sprinkled texture, sprays of diamonds and precious gems. Observers often called her Consulate clothing "light" or "elegant"; "I was struck by the simplicity of Madame Bonaparte's toilette." Another eyewitness recalled: "The purest taste and the most subtle elegance presided over her toilette."

Napoléon, however, grew more stylistically ponderous as his policies grew more conservative. He rolled back many of the new rights granted by the Revolution. In 1802 he reinstated slavery in the French colonies. He consolidated the rule of law, which the Revolution had fought for, and enshrined it in a "*code civil*," which guaranteed many property and civil rights to men but retracted many rights that the Revolution had granted women. One of the few that remained was the right to divorce, and it was suspected divorce had been retained mostly to keep open Napoléon's option to divorce Joséphine.

Napoléon was acutely aware that his wife's favorite fabrics came from abroad. A global textile trade, with its connection to the sugar and coffee trades, was certainly in France's long-term economic interest. In the immediate present, however, Napoléon cared more about the local economic and labor pressures caused by revolutionary fashion. Fashion's swap of muslin for silk had been catastrophic for the silk industry, which employed most of Lyon, France's second-biggest city. The substitution of Indian embroideries for lace and the elimination of *passementerie* threatened French craft specialties. Napoléon wanted to jump-start the economy, and secure the loyalty of the artisanal class. He felt personally aggrieved by foreign imports.

Napoléon's authority began moving fashion away from Joséphine's original, refined elegance. He changed the tone of the country, but he would not have been able to if the public mood had not been turning against the Revolution.

After the *Journal des dames et des modes* fashion magazine's coeditor Sellèque died in the assassination attempt on Napoléon's life in December 1799, La Mésengère, the former priest who had so emphatically turned to the secular side of life, took over the magazine. The magazine's tone changed, becoming steadily more stylistically conservative. Silhouettes grew more static, fabrics more stiff, trim more ornate. La Mésengère, admittedly, was a better businessman than Sellèque had been. Under his sole leadership, the magazine's readership and influence expanded for decades. Looking back in 1834, a journalist compared La Mésengère's power to Napoléon's. He wrote that the emperor Napoléon had "conquered masculine Europe" while "feminine Europe" had succumbed to the editor. Moreover, the journalist continued, "Napoléon lost his conquests, while M. de La Mésengère retained his."

Joséphine's wardrobe when she was married in spring of 1796 had consisted mostly of cotton dresses. By the time it was inventoried in late 1804, quantities of lace had appeared, French we must assume, as well as silk organdy and silk velvet. She still owned Bengali muslin, but also lengths of white French silk. The tide was turning. Joséphine's daughter, Hortense, vividly recalled that while Napoléon was consul, he repeatedly demanded to know if she and her mother were wearing Indian muslin. Fearing his wrath, they fibbed and said it was French linen. As Hortense remembered it, he was not fooled, grabbed their dresses, and tore them apart with his bare hands. "This disaster having befallen our clothes several times, we were obliged to revert to satin or velvet."

"This disaster" was about to befall all the women's clothes the Revolution had introduced. The whole of fashion was doomed to "revert," along with most of the Revolution's other advances. Only one of the Three Graces saw the danger coming.

(416)

Chevelure à demi Découverte.

CHAPTER 13

OPPOSITION PATTERNS

(Juliette)

1799–1804

STYLE CAN BE ON THE SURFACE, and it can express an inner conviction. It can start as a spectacle of individuality, and end as a shared hope. Juliette Récamier's luminous, pure clothing principles captured the visual imagination of Europe to make her an international celebrity. A circle of celebrated men increasingly opposed to Napoléon's power seized on her image as their symbol. In the midst of their fame and their definition of politics, Juliette's celebrity and style also functioned as a form of self-affirmation, for herself, for the intellectual women around her, and for her very best friend, the greatest women's rights advocate of their generation. Revolutionary style's feminism has always been a secret hidden in plain sight.

Juliette's salon rallied the most stubborn proponents of the Revolution's principles. For these liberals, the Revolution reached its finest moments with the *Declaration of the Rights of Man and of the Citizen*, the drafting of a constitution, and the election of representatives. They considered the Terror an interruption of the Revolution, not its refutation. After briefly hoping Napoléon would consolidate the Revolution, Juliette's salon core acknowledged its error and became his vocal opponents. They remained committed to universal human rights and constitutional, elected government. Their resistance drew them ever closer together politically and emotionally.

Juliette's salon did not exclude other political persuasions. Even Eugène de Beauharnais and Napoléon's ministers attended. Napoléon exclaimed in annoyance: "Since when does my Cabinet meet at Madame Récamier's?" The true faithful, however, were the liberals. René de Chateaubriand wrote: "Madame Récamier gathered at her home, in Paris, those who were most eminent among the opposition parties, and among the thinkers who had not succumbed entirely to Napoléon." Chateaubriand and Benjamin Constant were both eager to point out in their memoirs that Napoléon's brother Lucien had been in love with Juliette. Their gleefully malicious point was that this one Napoleonic advance, at least, had been beaten back. They quoted a letter from Lucien to Juliette that she had shared with them to demonstrate her triumph over him.

> I was subjugated! I could not sufficiently admire your features, your accents, your silence, your gestures, and that expression which was made more beautiful still by your sweet indifference, for you know how to give a charm to indifference. . . . I was watching your way of walking, which is as simple and unaffected as your dress. At each of your movements, with each fold of your gown, it seemed as though flowers were opening.

Men in Juliette's salon circle like Chateaubriand and Constant penned explicitly political tracts. Constant was actively involved in the Constitution of the Year III, which established the Directory, as well as in the defense of the Directory from attempted coups d'état, which came from both the left and the right. When Napoléon overthrew the

Directory in the 18th Brumaire coup d'état, he appointed Constant to the governing body called the Tribunat, in a reluctant gesture toward political inclusion.

The French Revolution did not encourage women to play such political roles. No sooner had revolutionaries inadvertently opened the logical door to women's citizenship, with their 1789 *Declaration of the Rights of Man and of the Citizen*, than they slammed the door shut. Too late. On September 15 of 1791, Olympe de Gouges published her incendiary *Declaration of the Rights of Woman*, a clause-by-clause exposition of how the original *Declaration* should apply to women. At the same time, on the tenth, eleventh, and nineteenth of September 1791, Talleyrand delivered a long "Report on Public Instruction" to the National Assembly government to explain that because men and women were naturally different, they had different natural rights. Women, he argued, were anatomically destined for the private roles of daughter, wife, and mother. Only men could be active citizens. Women must accept the status of passive citizens. Women were naturally less intellectual and creative than men.

The great English political theorist Mary Wollstonecraft responded directly to Talleyrand in 1792 with her *Vindication of the Rights of Woman*. Women, she argued, were indeed different from men, but morally and intellectually they were equal to men. Perhaps women were naturally unsuited to active political citizenship, but they were naturally capable of intellectual self-expression. A number of French women publicly took positions similar to Wollstonecraft's, notably Constance Pipelet in her 1797 *Épître aux femmes*, and Albertine Clément-Hémery, who wrote articles in defense of women's dignity for the *Journal des dames et des modes*, and objected vociferously in print in 1801 when a law was proposed that would make it illegal to teach women to read.

By 1795, it was clear that the new revolutionary political rights of French *citoyens* were not going to be extended to *citoyennes*, a distinction masked in English by the ungendered word "citizen." In a strictly political sense, the battle for women's equality was lost when the Directory's Constitution of 1795 excluded women from full citizenship. The constitution reserved for men the rights to vote, own property unconditionally, and make basic decisions about their lives and their children. Women remained legally dependent on men.

Nor were women's equal rights recognized by art institutions for long. In rebellion against the Royal Academy, a Commune des Arts was founded in 1790, of which one in five members were women. In 1793, the Commune was replaced by the Société Populaire et Républicaine des Arts, which voted to exclude women. When the government founded an organization called the Institut in 1795 to lead French arts and letters, women were again excluded. Only men, henceforward, would be allowed to set standards for the prestigious media of painting, sculpture, architecture, and serious literature.

Nonetheless, during Juliette's ascent to fashion celebrity, women tried harder than ever to make their mark in the shrinking domain of culture left to them. They hoped they could still prove their worth in other art forms, like novels, portraits, and fashion, regardless of whether the Institut sanctioned them. A woman named Fortunée Briquet, for example, compiled a guide to the history of women's writing, proudly titled *Historical, Literary, and Bibliographical Dictionary of French Women and Women Naturalized in France*, which she published in 1804. She included an engraved portrait of herself made in 1801, wearing a revolutionary dress and hairstyle.

Despite the obstacles in their way, women began to train in unprecedented numbers for professional arts careers. It was a commonplace of the 1794–1804 Directory and Consulate régime years to exclaim in surprise at the women performing everywhere in Paris's most prestigious arts institutions, called for short the "Paris Parnassus": women giving public lectures, women conducting public scientific experiments, women selling novels, women writing plays. Napoléon, for example, wrote to one of his brothers: "Women are everywhere: at the theater, in public parks, in libraries. Only here, of all the places on earth, do they deserve to hold the rudder; consequently, men are crazy about them, they think only of women and live only through and for them. A woman only needs six months in Paris to know what is due to her and what is her empire."

Yet no matter how professional the goals, no matter how extensive the celebrity, intellectual women strivers were obliged to reconcile their new aspirations with traditional feminine roles. Even the most radical men demanded that women continue to manage the home and devote themselves to being mothers, wives, and daughters. Women who clung to some semblance of equal rights tried to prove they could meet those demands. They proposed dual identities: emotional and intellectual, stylish and smart, domestic and professional. If they could manage to reconcile what they had been taught were opposites, they hoped they might receive educations, use their minds, and influence politics. Though they could not be equal citizens before the law, they hoped they could still be respected intellectually.

Women were left with what have been called "weapons of the weak." Among those weapons was clothing. Fashion may seem like a paltry form of self-assertion, but it was a form of body politics. If it had not been perceived as an expression of women's freedom, it would not have been so virulently opposed. British caricaturists, for example, would not have attacked the French Revolution by pretending that the new style stripped women naked. Twenty-first-century people may find it difficult to understand how a style that preserved full long skirts and delicate fabrics could make any difference to women. But consider some ways in which revolutionary dresses changed women's daily lives.

If you had been laced into stays, burdened with petticoats, and festooned in silk gowns all your life, the revolutionary dress felt like miraculous relief. You were suddenly freed from constriction, load, and drag. You felt weightless and mobile. Compared to what you had been obliged to wear before, the new dress radically changed the spatial relationship between your clothes and your body. Revolutionary dresses did not merely tweak style. The combination of their fabric and construction allowed women to move. Women could feel their dynamic potential from inside their clothing. Their movement could be seen from the outside by others. Revolutionary fashion brought a very basic individual and social freedom.

The political implications of this liberation explain why American women embraced the newest in Paris fashion. American women, like French women, had been through a revolution, and enthusiastically greeted what felt appropriate to their new democracy. Word traveled fast, considering the distance. In 1798, during a visit back to Paris, the French-born Delaware transplant Gabrielle Joséphine du Pont wrote to her American friend Margaret Manigault in South Carolina: "The women were perfectly and very richly attired, generally in lovely muslins. . . . To drape oneself well is truly an art."

Some American men were delighted. In 1800, Harrison Gray Otis, then a U.S. representative, reported to his wife that he had seen a woman in one of the new dresses and "had been regaled with the sight" of her "whole legs for five minutes together." Some prominent women were ambivalent. In 1800, Abigail Adams—who famously said to her husband, John Adams, "Remember the ladies"—called the "new . . . stile of dress" "an outrage upon all decency" because it was designed "perfectly to show the whole form." She allowed, however, that it revealed the "rich Luxurience of naturs Charms."

Overall, the "new stile" swept the United States and lingered longest there, years after Paris had gone back to cages. Dolley Madison, another First Lady, wife of President James Madison, picked it up in Paris and loved it so much she never relinquished it, no matter how much fashion changed. In 1804, she showed off her revolutionary dress bodice in her famous portrait by Gilbert Stuart (now in the White House collection). She wore the same "new stile" for all her portraits up until her death in 1849. When she died, though her circumstances were much reduced, she still possessed a dress in the revolutionary style, albeit in orange velvet (now in the Greensboro, North Carolina, Historical Museum).

No woman in the United States was more aware of the new style's democratic potential for self-made celebrity than Elizabeth Patterson of Baltimore. Like Térézia and Joséphine, she was willing to court scandal. She knew their example extremely well, because the man she married on Christmas Eve of 1803 was Jérôme Bonaparte, Joséphine's brother-in-law. Elizabeth wore a wedding dress that for the United States was still thrillingly novel. Guests were titillated, and hastened to spread the word of Elizabeth's revolution. One wrote: "Several of the Gentlemen who saw her said they could put all the cloaths [*sic*] she had on in their vest pocket." After the wedding, Elizabeth and her Bonaparte husband went on a celebrity tour, west to Niagara Falls and south to Washington, DC. Wherever they went, they were invited to dinners and balls so that people could gawk at Elizabeth's outfits. (Later, Napoléon forced his brother Jérôme to dissolve his marriage to Elizabeth, in favor of one more advantageous to imperial diplomacy.)

Elizabeth Patterson's phenomenal wedding dress may have survived. The Met Costume Institute collection includes a dress she certainly did own, special enough for her 1803 wedding. One can see why people were appalled by its nothingness. It does seem like a gossamer drift in comparison with the dense heft of metal-thread brocade ancien régime gowns. Nonetheless, the dress has presence. Its white cotton embroidery on Indian muslin is composed with subtle elegance. A wide central strip of symmetrical, abstract floral motifs calmly centers the garment, then branches sideways at the hem to define the long train. A narrower strip of similar motifs under the bust barely breaks the continuous line. The perfectly proportioned volumes of the short, gathered sleeves exactly balance the height of the whole.

American women sensed the momentous social implications of the new style. To be encased in the most valuable ancien régime gowns required servants and time. Petticoats and skirts were unwieldy, stays

A dress made of Bengali muslin that belonged to Elizabeth Patterson of Baltimore, pictured in a study room of the Metropolitan Museum of Art, to which it now belongs. Like the three Graces of Paris, Patterson styled herself into a celebrity by wearing dresses like these, over slips.

laced from behind. The droves of straight pins that attached the parts of gowns were most accurately aimed by servants, while their employers stood quite still to avoid being pricked.

Meanwhile, a woman could don a revolutionary dress all by herself, in a minute, no matter how formal the occasion. In seconds, she pulled a slip over her head. In a few more seconds, she ducked into a feather-weight, one-piece dress. She looked down at the flaps lining the bodice, and tied three or four bows to keep them shut. She gathered the fabric on either side of the outer bodice on drawstrings under her bust to whatever felt comfortable that day, and another around her throat: two little bows, with the ends tucked inside. She wrapped her sash under the bodice, and knotted it according to her mood. *Voilà*. A wealthy woman could become independent. A woman of modest means could become fashionable.

Despite the wear and tear ordinary clothes usually suffer from, French museum collections include a number of cheap and cheerful cotton print dresses worn by working-class women. Their patterns and bright colors evoke flocks of working women joining the fun of fashion. Luxurious muslins and Kashmiri shawls were emulated with cheap knockoffs in sturdy cottons and ordinary wool. Fashion had welcomed a vastly expanded audience to the lower end of its price spectrum.

Even at the high end of the cost spectrum, prices had plummeted. The Peabody Essex Museum in Salem, Massachusetts, owns an exceptionally well-documented dress treasured over generations, originally made to be worn by a bride—a dress comparable to Patterson's. The dress came to the museum with a letter by the groom-to-be, who acquired its fabric. The white muslin he bought in India in 1800, he wrote, was of the best quality, appropriate for a wedding. It cost him five dollars a yard. No more than seven yards would have been required. Remembering that most of the cost of any garment was the fabric, and knowing that even an unskilled American worker was then earning about one dollar a day, this means that the most important dress of a

lifetime in the most fashionable possible material was within reach of a majority of Americans. Whereas a worker had not been able to earn in an entire lifetime the price of a European royal court costume. And the Revolution had given dresses like Patterson's or the Peabody Essex bridal dress the authority that had once been wielded by court costume. Never again would royalty govern fashion.

The technical simplicity of revolutionary style, furthermore, had direct social consequences. It was so easy to make a one-piece straight dress whose bodice was fitted with drawstrings that women no longer needed to rely on the technical knowledge of professional seamstresses or guild workshops to acquire clothing at the height of fashion. The guilds had been abolished, and printed cotton revolutionary dresses could be made by the sort of women who wore them, with the simplest cutting and sewing skills. (I say this with assurance, because I

1800 Bengali muslin wedding dress, in the collection of the Salem, Massachusetts, Peabody Essex Museum. In this photograph, the dress is displayed with the Kashmiri shawl the bride also wore, in the preserved room in which the wedding took place.

worked for several years in a theatrical costume shop. To cut and sew full-skirted, pieced-bodice gowns would challenge me for weeks, even though the master of a guild would have expelled me for the shortcuts I took. I could knock off a revolutionary dress in a morning.) The French Revolution allowed all but the poorest women to think they could wear the same styles as the richest.

When a fashion was worn by so many women, it was not going to be a reliable indicator of explicitly political opinion. Nor was it necessarily going to serve as a barometer of intellectual self-assertion. But the women who most wanted to present themselves as intellectuals did dress in the new style, especially in Paris. For these visionary women, fashion argued in favor of respect and dignity.

The women's rights advocate Constance Pipelet, notably, used portraiture to project the revolutionary significance of her clothing. Though Constance Pipelet is far from a household name today, she was one of the leading women poets of the revolutionary era, a regular member of influential salons, and a playwright whose 1794 *Sapho, tragédie melée de chants*, a lyric-verse tragedy in three acts, paid tribute to the great woman poet of ancient Greece. (Keeping track of her accomplishments is not helped by the change of her name to the princesse de Salm after a second marriage in 1803.) Constance Pipelet championed the whole cohort of women struggling to enter the arts in her rousing 1797 "Epistle to Women." She warned:

Women's rights advocate Constance Pipelet in a 1797 portrait by Désoria.

> *But already thousands condemn our courage*
> *They are shocked. They whisper, they are unnerved, they heckle*
> *They want to take our pens and our paintbrushes away.*

After divorcing in 1799, Pipelet wrote an advice piece on divorce, addressed from a mother to a daughter. She was among the political thinkers who tried to come to terms with conflicts between traditional femininity and equal rights. In 1799, reporting on "the condition of women in the Republic," she conceded that women were dependent "physical beings," yet maintained women were also "moral beings" who should be "free in essence." This tension between the physical and the moral condition of women, she lamented, burdened them with "perpetual contradictions."

In her portrait, at least, Constance Pipelet attained her goal of becoming "free in essence." Comfortable yet feminine in her revolutionary dress, with her short curls tied by one amaranth-red ribbon, Constance Pipelet looks straight at us with total confidence, dominating a vast landscape behind her, a book casually held in one hand. If a revolutionary man (in a suit) had adopted the same pose and the same gaze, we would admire his assurance.

Julie Candeille posed professionally for her portrait in 1796 with pen in hand at her writing desk, wearing a long-sleeved, blue-striped revolutionary dress. She was known for her progressive views on women's careers and on slavery. She had played the lead role in her friend Olympe de Gouges's 1789 play *The Happy Shipwreck*, which argued against slavery in France's colonies. The play and her performance were so remarkable that Candeille became a fixture of the abolitionist club the Society of the Friends of Blacks (Amis des noirs). Olympe de Gouges's opinions became such anathema to governing men that she was sent to the guillotine during the Terror, on November 3, 1793. Candeille fared better, and was hailed as a leading actress and playwright during the 1794–1804 Directory and Con-

Actor and abolitionist Julie Candeille in a 1796 portrait by Jeanne Doucet de Surini.

Art student Charlotte du Val d'Ognes in an 1801 portrait by fellow student Denise Villers.

sulate years. Her miniature portrait by Jeanne Doucet de Surigny went on public display in 1796, and Constance Pipelet's oil portrait in 1798, where they exhibited for all the world to see the possibility of an expanded sense of self.

Among the great portraits of revolutionary women's new identities, the one that uses visual devices the most compellingly is of an art student, by an art student. The sitter for the portrait was Charlotte du Val d'Ognes, who at the time, 1801, was training in a new studio in the Louvre dedicated to women. Ever since the portrait was acquired by the New York Metropolitan Museum of Art in 1917, it has been a visitor favorite. For decades, art historians thought the painting was so good it must be a masterpiece by David. Evidence to the contrary surfaced, and the painting was attributed to Denise Villers, one of those young Consulate women breaking into the painting profession. The portrait then became a feminist icon, as a lesson in how history had forgotten women's achievements.

The gaze of the sitter is direct and brave, her hold on her drawing pad forthright, her energetic body backlit by a magic illumination, at once solar and lunar. Add to that the fashion statement of a fitted long-sleeve version of the new dress worn with a white neckerchief, accessorized by a sash and shawl in shades of pink. According to the memoir of women's rights advocate Albertine Clément-Hémery, who trained in the same studio, students were equally adept at painting and fashion; in between lessons they invented new ways to wear ribbons and paraded their styles in the adjacent Tuileries Gardens, where their innovations immediately caught on.

In the portrait, through a cracked window, we see across the Seine

River to a tiny version of Charlotte, dressed in the same clothes, in a couple with a man, and behind them, to her home. Thanks to this use of perspective, our gaze oscillates between work in the foreground and love in the background. The artist found an optical way to help us see how the ambitious intellectual women of her generation were trying to balance career and family, revolution and tradition.

Women dressed to think appeared in ever greater numbers as the Directory ended and the Consulate began. Collectively, they suggested that women could visibly occupy the public intellectual world. The most explicit, adamant, and vocal of them all was Germaine de Staël. Not coincidentally, she was the woman who had the strongest impact on Juliette Récamier. And vice versa. Juliette's style guided Germaine de Staël's advocacy in a powerfully new direction.

Juliette did not meet Germaine until 1798, the last full year of the Directory. Even then, although the two were instantly struck by each other, their great friendship did not begin in earnest until the Consulate years of 1799–1804. It was the second of the extraordinary bonds between women that marked the fashion revolution, the first being, of course, Térézia and Joséphine's.

Juliette and Germaine met when Monsieur Récamier purchased the Paris town house that was going to showcase Juliette. It is odd that Juliette and Germaine had not encountered each other in person earlier, considering how many acquaintances they shared, but sources agree on this, including Juliette. She remembered instantly taking note of both Germaine's

Equal rights advocate Germaine de Staël in a circa 1800 portrait.

Juliette in a portrait by Massot.

clothing and her spirit, communicated through her eyes.

Her garb was strange; she wore a casual morning dress and a little decorated hat, ornamented with flowers; I took her for a stranger. I was struck by the beauty of her eyes and gaze. . . . It was then only an apparition in my life, but the impression was vivid. Afterward, I thought only about Madame de Staël, so deeply had I felt the effect of this character so ardent and so strong.

Germaine de Staël, however, had been famous for a long time. Given the circles Juliette moved in, she must have known Germaine by reputation. Born in 1766, Germaine's father, Jacques Necker, was a controller general of King Louis XVI between 1777 and 1781, tantamount to a finance minister or secretary of the Treasury. He was not noble, but rather a Swiss Protestant commoner, and a banker, like Térézia Tallien's father and Juliette's husband. Necker, unlike most fathers at the time, was convinced his daughter had genius, and launched her while she was only a child. Although Germaine felt no man could ever be as marvelous as her father, in 1786 she married a titled Swede, the Baron de Staël, in order to become legally an adult.

Already by 1792, the press mocked Germaine's public support of women's rights. In salon conversations, in pamphlets, tracts, novels, and histories, she argued that women and men were equal human beings. Fortunée Briquet, the historian of women writers, placed Germaine in the first rank, saying "her knowledge is surprising for its variety and extent" and extolling her prose for its "great superiority." She was the first person, Briquet asserted, to have applied the philosophy of "perfectibility" to literature. Perfectibility admitted women's weaknesses, but promised that if women were educated as intellectual equals, they would gradually be perfected. The key assumption of perfectibility was a belief in women's creative potential, which Germaine endeavored to prove with every performance of her intellect. Her expository verve drew rapt audiences, including people who disagreed with her.

Among the men both attracted to and daunted by her intelligence was Talleyrand, who had a sexual affair with her. When he married the "beautiful" and "lazy" Catherine Verlée, Talleyrand pronounced à propos of Germaine de Staël: "One had to have loved a woman of genius to savor the pleasure of marrying someone stupid."

Opinions about Germaine de Staël were divided. On the negative side, notably, was Barras, leader of the Directory government and Térézia's lover.

> I declare that I never really knew to which sex Madame de Staël belonged. The virility of her form, face and carriage, her manner of wearing her clothes, the strength of her intellectual conceptions, her exuberant vigor and energy—all, in short, would have led me to believe that she belonged rather to our sex than to the other.

On the positive side, when Benjamin Constant met Germaine de Staël, he was instantly smitten. "I met, by an accident that had a long influence on my life, the most famous person of our century, due to her writings and her conversation. I had never seen anything like it in the whole world. I fell passionately in love."

Once Juliette and Germaine got to know each other, they became best friends. Germaine wrote:

> It's been eight days, beautiful Juliette, that you haven't answered one word to my last letter. Why are you at once so seductive and so flighty, someone so generous and who can do so well without those she saves? In the end why, in love as in friendship, is no one

necessary to you? . . . Dear Juliette, if I return to Paris, isn't it true that you will get used to needing me?

The people who knew Juliette and Germaine best recognized how intensely attached they were to each other. Some of the letters Juliette and Germaine exchanged were read by their mutual friends, who said the letters "had a charm almost like love." The women eventually exchanged portraits, which they hung prominently in their homes so they could see each other even when they were separated. On her deathbed, Germaine wrote to Juliette: "I embrace you with all that is left of me."

To explain this exceptional bond, the women's closest allies invoked Juliette's unusual relationship to her father. "This friendship was fortified by a deep emotion they both felt: filial love." "Filial love" was an understatement. Germaine was so enamored of her father that she may have been the only person who could completely understand how a very young Juliette had been persuaded to marry hers.

Contemporaries were fascinated by how Juliette and Germaine complemented each other. Together, it was said, they formed one perfect whole. Benjamin Constant expounded:

> The speed with which one expressed a thousand new thoughts, and the rapidity with which the other seized and judged them, this masculine, strong mind which unveiled everything, and that delicate, fine mind which understood everything . . . it all formed a reunion [*réunion*] which it is impossible to represent without having had the Happiness to have witnessed it oneself.

More summarily, a young man plopped down on a sofa between Germaine and Juliette, and announced he had landed between Mind and Beauty.

Despite these contemporary observations, biographers and historians have been loath to take Juliette and Germaine's relationship seriously. It did not help timorous scholars that both women destroyed almost all the many letters they exchanged. We can ponder this erasure of evidence as itself a sort of evidence. We can feel certain the two women were aware how extraordinary their friendship was, how nonconforming. What did they need to hide? One simple answer would be explicit statements that Juliette's husband was her biological father. Or perhaps their passionate love for each other had a sexual dimension, despite their many romantic flirtations or relationships with men. Another possibility might be overt encouragement of each other's public ambitions. I do wonder, in particular, whether Germaine applauded Juliette's celebrity as a form of self-affirmation, or praised the politics of her style. Any one of these themes, let alone a combination of them, would have shocked their society and jeopardized their reputations.

A major testament to their mutual inspiration that does survive, gloriously, is the single most enduringly famous and popular of all Germaine de Staël's writings. Her novel *Corinne* has been in print ever since it was published in 1807; it remains one of the landmark works of both Romantic literature and nascent feminism. Excerpts were published in the *Journal des dames et des modes*, with special attention to Corinne's clothing. It went through more than forty printings in French by 1872, and was translated three times into English before the 1930s. It was read by Jane Austen, Mary Godwin Shelley, the Brontë sisters, George Eliot, and George Sand. The book tells the human story,

A scene from Germaine de Staël's most famous novel, *Corinne*, by Gérard.

through its eponymous heroine, of an entire revolutionary generation's hope for equal rights, and the tragic defeat of those dreams. Corinne is a genius. Not, like most artistic heroines of the period, a talented but tentative amateur who works in some marginal medium, but a flat-out brilliant tormented epic genius of poetry who declaims in public live for crowds of ardent fans—wearing fabulous outfits.

Germaine had been writing novels to articulate the possibility of a feminine literary genius before she met Juliette. After she became best friends with Juliette, she imagined a feminine genius who united literature and fashion. Germaine de Staël did not write the novel that galvanized women writers for a century until she had basked in Juliette's friendship, style, and self-made celebrity. We have written evidence that Germaine identified with Corinne. She sometimes referred to herself as Corinne in her letters, and friends sometimes called her Corinne. Of all her heroines, the one she identified with was the one who united her creative qualities with Juliette's.

Juliette reciprocated the feeling. From 1820 until she died, she hung a huge painting of a scene from *Corinne* in her living room, one in which Corinne's costume is the focal point of the whole composition. The installation was a perpetual endorsement of her best friend's vision. Painting or no painting, how could we ever have thought that Juliette Récamier's willpower, her ability to endure enforced virginity within a sham marriage for decades, her adamant adherence to a rigorously absolute style, was not sustained and empowered by a best friend who told the world there was such a thing as feminine genius?

Not to mention the pressure of Napoléon's rise to power. With each passing year of the Consulate, Napoléon's dislike of intellectual women and all other forms of opposition grew more threatening. His incremental control of legal and police power made the menace of arrest, confiscation of property, financial ruin, or exile in retaliation for what Juliette and Germaine did and what they stood for all too real. Yet

Juliette persisted. Napoléon never managed to drive a wedge between this pair of friends.

Even more famous and influential than Germaine's novel *Corinne* is the work of art of which Juliette is indubitably the driving force and star, her portrait by David. Just to begin with, the painting has caused the type of sofa she reclines on to be called a "Récamier sofa" to this day. The portrait is one of the iconic attractions of the Louvre Museum, seen by millions of visitors a year. It has been count-lessly reproduced, imitated, reprised, and parodied, hailed as the quin-tessence of the revolutionary era and of neoclassical style. Ever since it was made, its ambiguities have retained attention. Unlike more facile

Juliette's salon in 1848.

Juliette's iconic 1800 portrait by David, who was unable to finish it.

or charming portraits, this one perplexes. Juliette's wary gaze, her partial turn away from us, her distance from us, and the emptiness of the scene are at once elegant and elusive.

For a large-scale, formal, oil-on-canvas portrait, Juliette dared to wear nothing but an absolutely simple white dress. Her arms and throat are bare, as well as her feet. One solid ribbon binds her natural curls. Pristine cotton skims her body. The light, thin, but opaque dress registers every curve of her turning torso and limbs as she looks over her shoulder at us. Her style concentrates on the essential. It eliminates color, pattern, adornment, ornament, volume, and detail. The painting's setting echoes her abnegations, with its single, linear piece of furniture, its extinguished Roman brazier, and its empty space.

The portrait may be the most famous unfinished painting in the history of Western art, and scholars have asked why David abandoned it. Harvard art historian Ewa Lajer-Burcharth has researched David's authorship of this portrait as completely and astutely as anyone probably ever will. She factors in the cohort of women intellectuals in Juliette's and Germaine's generation, women of the Fortunée Briquet, Julie Candeille, Constance Pipelet, Albertine Clément-Hémery, Nisa Villers sort. She considers what women wore and what rights they demanded. She gauges the sexuality of their behavior. Taking all of that into account from the perspective of David, closely analyzing his composition and his own statements, she concludes that David felt too much psychological challenge to be able to finish the portrait. This was not the revolution he had anticipated. As he stood at his easel, he was confronted with a woman who had fashioned herself and her fame. It was so disturbing that he could not go on. He rudely claimed to have lost interest in the project, and ceased.

We need only swivel Lajer-Burcharth's insights around to Juliette's point of view. She was staring down the most eminent artist of her era, a man backed by Napoléon's military and political power, alone in a big dark room. All she had on her side was a dress. And a best friend who eloquently demanded rights for women. And a salon full of friends who defended the principles of democracy. And a generation of women who wagered that in the long run, history would not forget their revolution.

Coëffure à la Cérès. Sautoir en Serpent.

PART III

AFTER
THE
REVOLUTION

—

(494)

Costume négligé d'un jeune homme.

CHAPTER 14

ORDER IN THE
WARDROBE

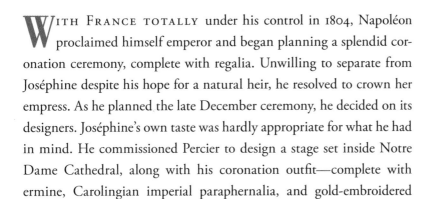

WITH FRANCE TOTALLY under his control in 1804, Napoléon proclaimed himself emperor and began planning a splendid coronation ceremony, complete with regalia. Unwilling to separate from Joséphine despite his hope for a natural heir, he resolved to crown her empress. As he planned the late December ceremony, he decided on its designers. Joséphine's own taste was hardly appropriate for what he had in mind. He commissioned Percier to design a stage set inside Notre Dame Cathedral, along with his coronation outfit—complete with ermine, Carolingian imperial paraphernalia, and gold-embroidered silks. For all the other clothing, including Joséphine's, Napoléon turned to Isabey. Given Isabey's effortless Directory and Consulate elegance, Joséphine might have hoped for something just a little bit chic. But Isabey too had been vanquished.

The whole coronation was such a propaganda enterprise that all of Isabey's costume designs were recorded in a book. Vigilant eagles and stolid gold borders surround the outfits and set the tone. Isabey designed both formal and superformal regalia for Joséphine. The thick white satin of Joséphine's formal "petit costume" skirt was weighted with emphatically French gold-metal-thread embroidery and a dense red velvet train. Around the neckline bristled a French lace collar, and a bulbous tiara fenced in her head.

Joséphine's "petit costume" merely hinted at her superformal "grand costume." The grand costume lace ruff reared formidably high, gold-metal thread invaded almost every square centimeter, and twisted gold fringe brushed the ground. Lest we think the execution of Isabey's costumes did not meet specifications, an embroidered velvet train designed for a lesser female ceremony attendant survives, and it does correspond to its design. Each of the ladies-in-waiting attending the ceremony was given 10,000 francs for her expenses, of which the principal was her costume, along with a gift of diamonds in Joséphine's name. (Remember that only eight years earlier, Joséphine's own entire wardrobe had been valued at 729 francs.) Louis Hippolyte Leroy, who previously had sold finished clothing, was brought in to supervise the fabrication of the

Isabey's 1804 design for one of Joséphine's conciliatory coronation outfits.

Isabey's 1804 design for Joséphine's most splendid and heavy coronation outfit.

coronation costumes, and Joséphine's seamstress Madame Raimbaut was required to follow his instructions. It marked the start of Leroy's career at the imperial court, elevating him into what doyenne French costume historian Madeleine Delpierre called the "star couturier and grand coordinator of imperial elegance."

The train for Joséphine's *grand costume* caused a family crisis. Reinforced straps were created to attach it to her shoulders, but she still could not drag the thing behind her down the aisle of a cathedral. The train was just too colossal, with its twenty-two meters (over twenty-four yards) of amaranth velvet, weightily embroidered with gold bees and leaves, and lined with ermine. Napoléon demanded his sisters carry the train. Serve Joséphine so personally? they shot back. Never. He commanded. They complied.

On one day, December 2, 1804, in one grandiose ceremony trumpeted to the world, the fashion revolution went into reverse. Ostensibly, Joséphine was crowned empress of France. From a fashion point of view, however, the ceremony staged her abdication from revolutionary design leadership and proclaimed her submission to imperial style authority. Talleyrand, of course, adapted to yet another political régime and dutifully attended the ceremony. Loyal only to his aesthetic convictions, he privately skewered the whole Bonaparte family's clothing pretensions. Their "luxury sort of pedantry" (*espèce de luxe érudit*), Talleyrand sniffed, lacked both the gravity of France's old monarchy and the élan of new democracy.

> This family of Bonapartes, which had come out of a distant island, barely French, where it lived in a petty state, had for chief a man of genius, whose elevation was due to a military glory acquired at the head of republican armies, themselves from an ebullient democracy; should it not have rejected old luxury, and adopted, even for the frivolous side of life, an entirely new route? Would it not have been more imposing with a noble simplicity, which would have inspired

confidence in its strength and endurance? Instead, the Bonapartes deluded themselves into thinking that callow imitation of the kings whose throne they took would be a way to succeed them.

Joséphine crowned empress of France by Napoléon.

Indifferent to Talleyrand's verdict, Napoléon commissioned David to idealize the grandeur of the coronation with an epic painting. He wanted some awkward family issues fixed. David painted Napoléon's mother into the audience to correct her refusal to attend the ceremony (too pretentious, she had said). To placate the sisters who had not wanted to carry Joséphine's train, David substituted ladies-in-waiting. The key political issue was the choice of moment to represent. Napoléon considered the moment he crowned himself, but decided it might be too provocative. Instead, he chose the more romantic moment he crowned

Joséphine. His authority would not be compromised, because though she would be at the center of the painting, she would be kneeling to him, head bowed, wearing what he had ordered her to wear.

THE painting turned out to be a resplendent scene, with dozens of accurate full-length portraits—including Talleyrand's, who stands on the right wearing a calf-length red cloak, his nose, predictably, turned up.

David's painting of the imperial coronation now hangs in a place of honor in the Louvre, not far, ironically, from his *Portrait of Madame Récamier*. Without being conscious of it, visitors see the zenith and the nadir of the Fashion Revolution together.

Radical style retreated. At last alerted to Napoléon's formidable imperial authority, Térézia realized her illegitimate relationship with Ouvrard had to end. In Germaine de Staël's salon, Térézia met and enchanted the Belgian François Joseph Philippe de Riquet, comte de Caraman. She was thirty-one and he was thirty-three. His father was horrified that he wanted to bestow himself and the family title on a woman with her past. Térézia came with six children by three fathers. Four of her children were so openly illegitimate they carried their mother's maiden name, Cabarrus. The young comte could not be dissuaded. Térézia sought an annulment of her first marriage from the Catholic Church. It was granted, thanks to a letter from her mother. Madame Cabarrus testified that Térézia had been married against her will while only a child. Térézia's second marriage was ignored because it had been ratified by only a civil ceremony, not a religious one.

On August 3, 1805, Térézia became a comtesse when she married Caraman. Soon after the wedding, the

groom's maternal uncle died without a son, and the new couple unexpectedly added to their Caraman titles the titles of prince and princesse de Chimay. They went to Italy for their honeymoon. Térézia was presented at the court of Florence, wearing a stiff silk velvet gown embroidered in Lyon. Though the dress was striking enough, of its sort, to be reported in the press, and imitated, the fashion revolution was over for her too. In Rome she was graciously received by the pope. Her prince charming hoped the pope's religious sanction would sway his father. The elder Caraman remained obdurate. Térézia's social sins were too scandalous to be forgiven.

Napoléon held the same opinion. Was he jealous that she had given birth to four babies in four years, while he longed for an heir? Had he never forgiven her for snubbing him when he joined her salon back in 1796? In any case, he forbade Joséphine from ever seeing Térézia again. He wrote Joséphine a letter, calling Térézia's husband a "wretch" and alleging two extra children.

> My friend . . . I forbid you to see Madame Tallien no matter what the pretext; I will accept no excuse. If you value my esteem and you want to please me, do not ever break this present order. If she comes to your apartments, to spend the night, forbid your porter to let her in. A wretch married her with eight bastards! I despise her even more than I used to. She may have been a lovely girl, but she has become a horrible, infamous woman.

Joséphine tried one more time. "What do I not owe her? She is better than good. She only devotes herself to others. She has taken every opportunity to help everyone, at her expense." Napoléon remained inflexible, and Joséphine succumbed. Térézia sadly accepted his verdict, though she would not renounce her feelings for Joséphine: "My friendship can resist every test and will only end when I die."

Napoléon softened slightly after Joséphine's death, after he had been defeated by the monarchies of Europe, when the issue was moot. In his memoirs, he recalled from exile on the island of Saint Helena a secret annual rendezvous at masked balls in the early years of the empire with "a very lovely woman, very good and very beautiful." She asked him every time if he would not relent and admit her to his court. He claimed to have responded that although she was "charming," "you have had two or three husbands and children by everyone. . . . Put yourself in my position as Emperor and consider: what would you do in my place ? . . . Especially because I am expected to bring back a certain decorum!"

The Fashion Revolution was over, and with it one of the great style collaborations of all time.

Small children consulting a fashion magazine along with a fashion doll, plate 206 of the *Journal des dames et des modes.*

(181)

Mise Ordinaire

CHAPTER 15

EPILOGUES

JOSÉPHINE, *Empress of France*

After Joséphine was crowned empress, her attire became the stuff of imperial propaganda. Countless exhibitions and books have celebrated Empire decorative arts. Napoléon used the arts on an international stage so flagrantly that what Joséphine wore after 1804 was bound to become part of the Napoleonic legend.

Yet Joséphine's revolutionary design vitality was gone. Talleyrand got Empire style just about right: too much, too heavy, not democratic. The great creative years had ended. Joséphine refreshed her look by incorporating neomedieval elements into her outfits, especially soft hats with feathers, and she became adept at swansdown and fur borders. These were minor touches in comparison with the bold tactics of 1794–1804.

Joséphine did get an extraordinarily large wardrobe in exchange for her obedience. Once she was empress, she received an annual personal expense allowance of 600,000 francs, plus another 120,000 francs for personal charity—much more than Marie Antoinette's budget. Still, she, like Marie Antoinette, often could not pay her clothing bills. Napoléon blamed her purveyors. One day a milliner named Mademoiselle Despéaux showed up to propose a bonnet, and Napoléon was so incensed at her invoice that he had her arrested and put in jail. Joséphine soon intervened and the milliner was freed. Suspecting routine inflation of bills, Napoléon told those in charge of Joséphine's household to never pay in full.

Within the new boundaries Napoléon set, Joséphine chose her own outfits. A lady-in-waiting remembered: "The Empress had continued, as in the past, to decide all these details of her toilette by herself, and perhaps no other lady of the Empire could have helped her with this choice, because no one else had the taste of Her Majesty." Six to eight women assisted at two dressing sessions, one for the day at nine in the morning, and one for the evening at six. Her entourage marveled at her insatiable love of fashion. One lady said she bought for the pleasure of buying, rather than to possess. Another said, "It is almost incredible that this taste for attire, so completely satisfied, was never blasé."

NAPOLÉON sometimes appeared in her dressing room to override her choices, Joséphine's personal maid, Mademoiselle d'Avrillion, recalled.

> It was extraordinary for us see a man whose head was so full of important matters enter into such minute detail and indicate which clothes and jewelry the Empress should wear on this and that occasion. One day he happened to stain a gown with ink because he did not care for it, and in order for the Empress to wear something else. Whenever he touched her jewel caskets he left everything in disarray.

❀ ❀ ❀

IN 1809 Napoléon finally decided to repudiate Joséphine in order to marry an Austrian archduchess who could give him an heir. Joséphine was devastated, but not so devastated that she didn't show up looking fabulous for her termination. Just a few days before the official divorce, Napoléon's valet recalled, the emperor could not take his eyes off her perfectly fitted white dress edged in swansdown, utterly devoid of ornament, or her hairdo, punctuated by silver sprays with blue flowers. Playing the Juliette Récamier minimalist style card, Joséphine appeared at the reading of the divorce decree on December 15, 1809, dressed all in white.

Her wardrobe had reached an impressive peak. Besides 60 Kashmiri shawls, at that point she owned 666 dresses, 431 chemises, 269 pairs of stockings, and 25 pairs of shoes.

Joséphine retained Malmaison, the title of empress, and a munificent allowance. Twice a year, she inspected her wardrobe and decided what she would not wear in the future, including clothes she had never worn. The rejects were given to her staff. In 1812, an entire chamber at Malmaison dedicated to Joséphine's clothing was lined with closets and drawers.

Napoléon abdicated on April 6, 1814. A few weeks later, Joséphine caught a cold while on a walk at Malmaison. The morning of the twenty-ninth of May, she asked to be very nicely dressed. When she died that day, with her children at her side, she was decked out in ribbons and pink satin.

TÉRÉZIA, *Princesse de Caraman-Chimay*

Térézia had been banned from Napoléon's French court, but the Chimays were a Belgian family anyway. The new prince brought her to the ancestral château. It had been originally built in the eleventh century, and repeatedly redesigned. All the tenants and neighbors around the Château Chimay palace adored Térézia. She had found a harbor in the nick of time. Napoléon bankrupted Ouvrard by exercising his absolute authority over military contracts and the French banking system.

Térézia had four more children by the prince de Chimay. One lived only six months. This brought her total number of pregnancies to eleven by five men, with nine surviving children by four fathers. One was the child of a radical, violent revolutionary and three were the children of a prince. She loved all the children equally. One day she went to the Louvre with Théodore de Fontenay on one arm, holding Rose Thermidor Tallien by the other hand, who in turn held hands with the little future prince, Joseph de Caraman Chimay. People stared and whispered about their remarkably various paternities, more and more loudly. She hustled the children away from the crowd. A friend who was with her had never seen her so upset. It was the intrusion on her family outing that bothered her, not the revelation of a secret to the children. She had never hidden anything from them. They knew her history so well that after her death in 1835, three of the children by Ouvrard changed their last names from Cabarrus to Tallien. Rose Thermidor had already changed her given name to the less provocative Laure Joséphine, emulating her mother's best friend's name change from Rose to Joséphine. Térézia's youngest, noble, child transmitted her stories to her first biographer, Arsène Houssaye, without a trace of shame.

When Laure Joséphine married in 1815, Térézia invited the bride's father, Tallien, to the quiet wedding. He had warned her when their daughter reached marriageable age that she should be careful to dress Laure Joséphine more conservatively than she dressed herself: "Oblige her to be more reasonable than you are. . . . You paid your tribute to fashion, and all your inconveniences come from that." Though he chided her, he still loved her. She continued to try to help him. He wrote her: "Your visit, my friend, brought me joy; you are truly

Our Lady of Charity [Notre-Dame de Bon Secours]." When Tallien died in 1820, and the news was brought to Térézia, she felt unable to continue to entertain guests, demurring with utmost courtesy: "Ladies, the death of Monsieur Tallien has been announced to me; you will excuse me if I retire to my apartments."

Térézia was in Paris in 1815 when Napoléon attempted a return to power, and still in Paris when he left for the Battle of Waterloo. She uttered no complaint, but only mused on the tumultuous history she had lived through. After the battle, its victor, the Duke of Wellington, called on her at home. In 1821, when she heard Napoléon had died in exile on the island of Saint Helena, she wrote: "What a death! What a destiny! How it causes one to reflect on the grandeurs of this world!"

Only Térézia's exclusion from royal court troubled the last act of her saga. Her husband the prince was awarded the official role of "chambellan du roi" after

the dissolution of the Napoleonic empire attached the principality of Chimay to the Kingdom of Holland. The reigning monarch declared Térézia's past irredeemable. He just couldn't handle the combination of illicit sex and participation in a revolution that had guillotined a fellow king. The ladies at the court of Holland had poisoned the king's mind. They were "jealous of the beautiful Tallien's past. . . . These nebulous ladies feared a star," or so her Caraman Chimay daughter claimed.

Térézia professed to be saddened by this royal pronouncement, mostly on behalf of her husband, whom she feared she embarrassed. She missed her Caraman Chimay children when they accompanied their father to court. She wrote to the prince: "I enjoy no pleasure, I only love solitude and painting and only want to see you and your children, but to see you happy, for I would bury myself in a cottage, on an inaccessible mountain if I had to see you sad and unhappy because of me, you who are the dearest objects of my heart and for whose contentment I would not hesitate to sacrifice my life." Perhaps it was not so terrible to stay at home in her own château. After all, Térézia got to be a princess without enduring stuffy court etiquette, or wearing a provincial court version of the corsets, hoops, and huge bell skirts that had inexorably returned to European fashion. The latest Paris fashion continued to fascinate her, and she followed it from Chimay. Isabey came to visit her in her château and paint with her.

A rare surviving self-portrait could have been made during one of these Isabey visits. In her image, she crowned herself with a duplicate of the flower wreath she had worn for her great formal portrait by Gérard, and ringed herself with the four youngest of her children.

Térézia, princesse de Chimay, wrote to her son the future prince de Chimay: "Enjoy the sweet, benevolent happiness one feels when one has done good to one's fellows. It's the only happiness unmixed with sorrow that heaven grants us. Time, which withers everything, which weakens everything, cannot impair the memory of the good deeds one has done." In 1826, she wrote to a friend: "What a novel my life has been!" She died in January 1835 of a liver disease, at the age of sixty-one, surrounded by her children. She had asked to be taken out into the open air, one last time.

An 1816 self-portrait by Térézia, princesse de Chimay, with her last four children.

JULIETTE RÉCAMIER, *as Always*

Napoléon had ousted Constant from government office in 1802, and exiled both him and Germaine in 1803. Next he turned to Juliette. He drove her husband Récamier into bankruptcy in 1806 the same way he had bankrupted Térézia's lover Ouvrard, by manipulating the national banking system and military contracts. Juliette would never again have the means to entertain on the scale that had launched her celebrity.

Exile and hindsight combined to give Juliette Récamier, Germaine de Staël, Benjamin Constant, and René de Chateaubriand the perspective with which to appreciate one another better than ever. Constant published his most famous novel, *Adolphe*, a model of Romantic literature, in 1806. Shocked by Germaine's death in 1817, he turned to Juliette to have someone with whom he could endlessly reminisce. It is unclear whether he fell in love with Juliette, or fell in love with her love for Germaine. Together, they chastely kept their friend's memory vivid.

Juliette almost married Prince August of Prussia in 1807, then thought better of it. She would have had to divorce her husband/father (who did not die until 1830) and Napoléon had made divorce very difficult in 1803, in his *code civil*. Perhaps by 1807 Juliette had decided that to go down in history as the incarnation of purity she would have to remain virginal for the rest of her life. But as a souvenir, she gave Prince August the iconic portrait of her by Gérard. In 1827, the great Romantic philosopher Wilhelm Schlegel saw the portrait and wrote to the artist: "I recently had the pleasure of seeing again in Berlin, at prince August's, your portrait of Madame Récamier, which one cannot contemplate without being delighted."

Juliette hung on to the furniture from her great Consulate salon, to portraits of Germaine and Chateaubriand, and to the massive scene of Corinne demonstrating a woman's genius. When Juliette was allowed to return to Paris, she reinstalled these cherished tokens in a small apartment in the Abbaye-au-Bois on the rue de Sèvres. She continued to recline on the same chaise longue (reupholstered in dark orange). She continued to dress in the same style, all in white. Political and literary personalities continued to come and pay homage to her and to the ideal of the revolution, though in dwindling numbers. She became a white ghost of France's revolutionary past.

Louis XVI's two younger brothers were restored to the French

Juliette in her room at
l'Abbaye-au-Bois in 1826

throne, one after the other. A revolution overthrew the Restoration
monarchy in 1830, and installed a constitutional monarchy. Louis-
Philippe reigned until 1848, when yet another revolution instituted
a second Republic. Juliette weathered these upheavals, and died in
1849. The devoted niece who edited her memoirs stayed with her to
the end. Juliette's reputation remained as she had created it: steadfast
and pure.

The year of her death, and the next, 1850, saw the posthumous publication of Chateaubriand's *Mémoires d'outre-tombe*, which became a
fixture of the French literary canon. One of its most prominent sections
is all about Juliette Récamier.

Chapeau de Castor. Fichu Garni d'une Fraise.

(155)

Bokay.

CHAPTER 16

CONCLUSION

REAL REVOLUTIONS WILL ALWAYS BE RESISTED.
The mid-nineteenth century tossed Térézia's and Germaine's reputations in the trash. Juliette was protected by Chateaubriand's Romantic prose; Joséphine was protected by the aura of Napoléon. Her grandson, by her daughter, Hortense, had become the next emperor of France in 1851, under the name Napoléon III. In 1864 Edmond and Jules Goncourt published their *History of French Society during the Directory*. It instantly became the orthodox interpretation of the Directory. The book proved perennially popular, and kept on being published in new editions throughout the rest of the century.

There is no way around the Goncourts' history of the Directory. It has to be confronted. The Goncourt brothers lived together and published together, until Jules died of syphilis. They resented modernity. They resisted anything that threatened their superiority. Unfortunately, that sort of angry fear can be peculiarly persuasive. The Goncourts did their homework, and cited original sources, which lent their vitriol credibility. Their idea of a Directory dominated by depraved women in transparent dresses insinuated itself into every history of the French Revolution.

Read against the grain, the Goncourts' argument that the two most important figures in the history of the Directory were Germaine de Staël and Térézia Tallien has its merits. Putting aside the Goncourts' palpable horror at the politics of the one and the style of the other, at least they recognized the impact of both women. Germaine, they announced, was the single greatest champion of the republican principle of the Revolution. Only she was fully capable, they declared, of separating the purest idea of democracy—the universal rights of man—from the practice of the Terror. This may seem correct to today's advocates of democracy, but the Goncourts thought that because democracy was based on a principle, it was bad. Térézia, they scolded, was the "pretty ambassadress sent to reconcile women with the Revolution, and men with Fashion." For the Goncourts, any "reconciliation" with democracy or modern fashion sowed social chaos.

Térézia, the Goncourt brothers argued, aghast, set the tone for all of Directory society. They recoiled at what they acknowledged was her unprecedented celebrity. "Madame Tallien, besieged by mute homages, parts the breathless crowd and saunters slowly through this hedge of impatient curiosity." Her powers, they maintained, were not natural because her authority over every detail of style was so absolute and immediate. They called her a "fairy," or "Circe." By fairy they meant an evil fairy, and by Circe they meant a wicked witch.

The Goncourts concluded that if women were the political and style leaders of the Directory, then the Directory must have been sexually deviant. They thought calling Germaine de Staël "a great mind . . . a man of genius" would cancel her, because what could be worse for a woman than to be called either a great mind or a man? As for Térézia, they alleged her loose morals and dresses corrupted the whole nation. "The most dissolute monarchies show no comparable example of the annihilation of man, or the triumph and thunder of woman."

The Goncourt brothers did not exactly lie. As historians, they prided themselves on their fidelity to original documents. They did observe the flat laced shoes of the new style. They did note the handbag "revolution against pockets." They admitted that evidence recorded dresses worn without slips or a knit base-layer only during one week in the revolutionary Year V, and only by two women. Though they dwelt with glee on one doctor's claim that more women had died from wearing thin dresses in the Parisian winter than had died in the previous forty years, they wrote that it would have been worse if women had soaked their dresses with water to make them cling, not that they did soak their dresses. Nonetheless, through clever turns of phrase and breathless lists of invective, they left their readers with the impression that women during the Directory had been naked: "In the audacity even of nakedness there was further audacity."

The *Journal des dames et des modes* definitely proves this was a hysterical lie. Out of 499 plates published from 1797 through 1804, one, exactly one, showed an outfit with a see-through dress. That one is the exception that proves the rule, because the outfit was designed to be worn only indoors in the solitary privacy of home.

DESPITE all resistance, the French fashion revolution has been vindicated. The men's part, which burst into action in 1789, remained victorious and unquestioned. Very, very slowly, women's fashion has come around to all the revolutionary ideas Térézia, Joséphine, and Juliette dared to introduce in the 1790s.

For a short time at the start of the twentieth century, revolutionary style was revived; the designer Paul Poiret, whose entire oeuvre picked up Directory inventions, named one of his creations "the Joséphine dress," and a second *Journal des dames et des modes* was published in homage to the first one. The Roaring Twenties also brought back the Revolution's straight line, to such an extreme that all but the skinniest women had to wear long tight girdles. Some sort of girdle lasted until the 1960s, and has returned in the hourglass form of today's Spanx and other "body shapers." Our contemporary underwear restrictions, however, are entirely optional, and we have the alternative of a knit base-layer, mercifully restored to us in the early twenty-first century.

Now we face the next fashion revolution, the first one of real historical importance since 1789. The crucial lesson of the French fashion revolution is that what is important about our clothing is not the details, like how wide our skirts are, or whether our jeans are stone-washed or not. What matters is how clothing expresses the power dynamics among human bodies and how we manage the natural resources that go into our clothing materials. What matters are fundamental issues like which gender is given social permission to wear skirts, how our jeans use water and dump chemicals, and which people are forced into sweatshop labor to churn out shoddy skirts and jeans. The next frontiers are sexuality, sustainability, and fair trade, which, unlike hemlines or silhouettes, truly defy the entrenched axioms of fashion. Nothing fundamental has changed since the Graces. Their revolution leveled social class, freed women, and stopped expressing social authority with naturally precious materials.

In the 1980s, women caught up with the revolutionary men of 1789 and got the practical pantsuit. LGBTQ+ movements have eased the boundaries between feminine and masculine. Advance signs indicate a reversal of the Great Renunciation, with a few men embracing color, pattern, and texture again. Skirts for men have been glimpsed on some daring stars and on designer runways. Covid-19 pandemic shelter-wear dealt a mortal blow to formal clothing, where gender rules are strictest, and pushed luxury leisure to new craft heights, eroding distinctions between public and private.

Today, fundamental assumptions about style must be abandoned to save our planet. The clothing industry is now by many measures the second-worst threat to our natural environment. Fashion has to stop meaning escalating purchases of cheap new clothes made with toxic chemicals. People of every gender, I am convinced, will always want to strut and seduce in clothes from refreshed wardrobes. We will find ways to make that primal impulse compatible with our world's future. We will invest "new" and "sexy" with sustainable meanings.

I wanted to tell a story about revolutionary style to show how radically we have been able to change clothes. We can do it again. When we do, we will be led by Graces who, like Térézia, free us; like Joséphine, find us something different to wear; and, like Juliette, have an idea.

Chapeau de Paille, garni de Rubans Cannelés.
Spencer à la Russarde.

How This Book Happened

BY WAY OF ACKNOWLEDGMENTS

THIS BOOK STARTED A LONG WAY BACK.

My father, Patrice Higonnet, has passionately devoted much of his career to the French Revolution, and believed his daughters should go along for that ride. One evening I overheard my tiny sister Etelle ask our father for a bedtime story: "Daddy, tell me again what caused the French Revolution." Forty-five minutes later the story hadn't ended, and my sister lay happily in the dark, her eyes shining.

In reaction to so much erudition, I learned a craft in college. Years of theater costume work in Harvard's Loeb Drama Center taught me about textiles, cut, construction, and the history of clothing. I was left with the occupational liability of seeing all garments in terms of their yardage, fiber content, and seam placement.

Yet when I committed to an academic art history career, I dedicated my research and writing to the "fine arts," chiefly painting, because I was supposed to. Among the paintings I became entranced by while still a graduate student was a mysterious 1801 portrait at the New York Metropolitan Museum of Art of a woman drawing in front of a cracked window. At the time, neither the subject nor the author of the portrait was securely identified, and though I wanted to know more, I had no idea how.

Years later, I began teaching at Barnard College of Columbia University, near the Met and that 1801 portrait. I began to research its subject, and plunged into the fashion world of the French Revolution. Like all scholars of the period, I relied on the illustrations of the dominant Paris fashion magazine, the *Journal des dames et des modes*. To study the *Journal*'s scattered and very rare fashion plates, I roved from library to library, in both France and the United States.

Then chance brought me right back home. Checking the footnotes of my essay on the 1801 portrait, a Columbia graduate student, Kathryn Krenmitzer, spotted a garbled entry in the catalogue of the Morgan Library and Museum. It implied, cryptically, that the Morgan might own a complete set of *Journal des dames et des modes* plates, including the rarest first seven years, 1797–1804. Improbable, I sighed, because the specialist who had dedicated an entire book to the *Journal des dames et des modes*, Annemarie Kleinert, had listed all the collections that owned parts of the *Journal*, and the Morgan wasn't one of them. But the Morgan was only a subway ride away. So off I went with Kathryn.

Six volumes were brought to us in the quiet Morgan reading room. We opened the first. Plate 1, 1797. Plate 2. Plate 3 . . . We kept turning the pages. The Morgan, unbeknownst to itself or anyone else, owned a complete set of the rarest fashion plates in the world. Their quirky catalogue entry had hidden them ever since they had been bought by the legendary, elegant, first great librarian of the Morgan, Belle da Costa Greene. The Morgan curator of books, John Bidwell, listened sympathetically when I proposed something the Morgan doesn't usually do. I asked if the Morgan would digitize the plates and allow graduate students in a Columbia University seminar to build a website about them. He agreed.

You can access the website at https://stylerevolution.github.io. It includes all 499 1797–1804 plates and several useful features for navigating the plates, among them translations into English of the plates' French captions; a mapping feature to find where in Paris the plates were made or marketed, as well as Paris locations mentioned in the captions; comparisons with competing British fashion plates; color and fabric glossaries; and a macroscope of all 499 plates.

Still, that was only the picture part of the *Journal des dames et des modes*. Even rarer than the images of the magazine were its words. Dealers had routinely discarded the text to sell just the plates, to the Morgan's Belle da Costa Greene, for example. I lamented to students in a seminar that I had only one lead left to a complete text: a Danish museum I couldn't locate. A Barnard exchange student, Ana Cornelia Pade, exclaimed: "I know that museum! I used to work there. You're using the wrong museum name, which was changed to the Design Museum Denmark."

Thanks to Ana Cornelia's intercession, I learned that the Design Museum did have the entire magazine, both images and text, for the years 1797 to 1804, possibly the only truly complete surviving copy of the text in the world. Thanks to a Tow grant from Barnard, the museum digitized the text for me. Finally, I had a complete version of the most important years of the *Journal des dames et des modes*. The text and pictures clicked together into a startling vision of fashion during the French Revolution. It was the crucial missing evidence for a radical movement history had forgotten, whose loss had misled historians for more than two centuries.

I wondered if I could corroborate the revelations of the *Journal des dames et des modes* with actual surviving clothing. Wondering will not get you into a museum costume collection, even if you are a bona fide professor of art history. Fair enough, because the academic field of art history has not included the art of clothing. I had to beg.

My first break came from the Boston Museum of Fine Arts in 2017. That was where I first realized that my French subject was not completely French. "We're sorry to tell you that our 'French' dresses you asked to see are all made with Indian fabric." I was not sorry. As I realized that revolutionary Paris chic had depended on Indian textiles from head to toe, turban to Kashmiri shawl, I saw the scope of my project expand across continents and cultures.

To move into that broader domain, I turned to my former PhD student Siddhartha Shah, then curator of Indian art at the Peabody Essex Museum. He convinced his colleagues Karina Corrigan (Asian Export curator), Petra Slinkard (Fashion and Textiles), Paula Richter (curator for exhibitions and research), and Lan Morgan (assistant curator for exhibitions and research) to organize an intimate and lengthy costume-study session. The PEM collection includes many more revolutionary muslin dresses than one would imagine because the area's maritime global trade ports were then at their peak. Siddhartha also steered me to the invaluable Indian textile expertise of art historian Sylvia Houghteling as well as Victoria and Albert Museum curator Avalon Fotheringham.

Rie Nii may have let me in to her collection at the Kyoto Costume Institute only because she was surprised I would go all the way to Japan. It was worth the trip. More than any other collection, Kyoto's mirrors the actual patterns of revolutionary style, including fabulous shoes made for striding.

Armed with new purpose, I petitioned for entry into costume collections with more assurance. Michele Majer at the Cora Ginsburg collection, one of the great dealers in historic clothing and textiles, allowed not only me but a whole seminar of students to measure and touch dresses, including one that had been picked apart. I began to understand how revolutionary dresses had fit women, and how they had been worn.

At this point, my history project reconnected me to my clothing-craft experience. I learned the history of revolutionary fashion in my fingers as well as in my brain. Two entirely distinct aspects of my life had made contact. But could their meeting become a book?

No program could better foster an intellectual experiment than the Radcliffe Institute (now named the Harvard Radcliffe Institute). When I was lucky enough to land there in 2019–20, Meredith Quinn, Sharon Bromberg-Lim, and Rebecca Haley organized the sociability that broke through disciplinary boundaries. Lectures, but also conversations during meals, in neighboring offices, and especially at the coffee machine opened my mind.

At the Radcliffe Institute, political scientist Tali Mendelberg introduced me to Virginia Sapiro, who taught me about the politics and portraits of Mary Wollstonecraft, which led me to the work of Wollstonecraft scholar Eileen Hunt Botting. Music historian Margot Fassler pushed me to borrow several books a day from the superb Harvard library system, led me to music historian Julia Doe, and from there to the style arena of revolutionary theater. Historian Manisha Sinha patiently talked me through book logistics and even more patiently kept taking me to Zumba, at which she is great and I am terrible. Anthropologist Lindsay Montgomery gave me the words with which to say how Bengali muslin, Kashmiri shawls, patka sashes, men's turbans, and men's jama were used by French fashion.

After a talk I gave at the Radcliffe Institute, religion historian Todne Thomas and public health expert Camara Phyllis Jones suggested I investigate the history of clothing on the Caribbean islands colonized by the French. By coincidence, I was about to visit Guadeloupe to participate in events at Mémorial ACTe. There, I asked the questions Todne and Camara had posed. The whole Mémorial ACTe staff leapt in to answer, especially then-director Laurella Yssap-Rinçon. Laurella took me on an expedition into Pointe-à-Pitre to hunt for Indian madras handkerchiefs, which brought to life the colonial link between Indian cotton and Caribbean slavery. At the very last minute in this project, I was able to see a vivid record of Antilles fashion in paintings by Agostino Brunias thanks to the welcome of Robert B. Simon and Dominic Ferrante at Robert Simon Fine Art.

The Radcliffe Institute matches its fellows with Harvard undergraduates in a Research Partners program. Kelsey Chen and Tanisha Mugwimi saw style from a fresh perspective, and calculated for me just how rarely revolutionary dresses were ever see-through.

At this point, my malleable project was shaped by Alane Mason, Norton editor extraordinaire. She proposed starring roles for Joséphine Bonaparte, Térézia Tallien, and Juliette Récamier. After recovering from the assault on my (starless) academic habits, I realized she was completely right. A history of the fashion revolution would have been hollow without the three leaders at its heart. Her comments, Willem Marx's, and Mo Crist's have steered me infallibly through successive drafts. Sarah Johnson caught my inconsistencies.

It did also take the wise experience of Radcliffe Institute fellow and science historian Allan Brandt for me to figure out what the difference between writing a history of revolutionary clothing and writing about three women's revolutionary celebrity would entail.

How to break it to my colleagues that I was reorganizing my history around fashion personalities? The first big step was delivering a paper at the Stanford University Center for the Study of the Novel. There, my stylish colleagues Emily Apter, Margaret Cohen, and Rhonda Garelick assured me they, at least, would not denounce me. Nor did Yoon Sun Lee or Sue Lanser blanch when I suggested a talk about the new direction my project had taken for their Mahindra Center seminar on eighteenth-century studies. Reactions to the talk convinced me that eighteenth-century studies scholars have capacious sensibilities, notably Ewa Lajer-Burcharth, Meredith Martin, Andrew McClellan, and Susan Wager. Ewa's research on David's portrait of Juliette Récamier has been foundational for me, as has Meredith's on Paris Indomania. Literary scholar Maurice Samuels kindly condoned my interpretation of Germaine de Staël.

After years of negotiations with the Met Costume Institute, eased by Jessica Glasscock but interrupted by Covid-19, I was finally ushered into its inner-sanctum study rooms by Marci Morimoto in fall of 2021. Her expertise reminded me that only costume curators know the insides of clothing as well as the outsides.

Even longer negotiations were required to make my way into the two greatest French collections of revolutionary costume. Convincing a French curator that an American truly appreciates anything French has never been easy. It is indeed impossible to match their knowledge of their domain. Denis Bruna at the national Musée des Arts Décoratifs wryly combines a panoramic sense of style with an awareness that the devil is in the details. During the summer of 2022, I finally got to meet the elusive Pascale Gorguet-Ballesteros, curator at the Paris Galliéra costume museum. I can only hope she now believes I really do care about muslin. I especially want to thank Hélène Renaudin, who knew that deep in the MAD storerooms, the shoes of my three heroines had been preserved together.

Without pictures, the text of this book would have been forlorn, and getting the pictures would not have happened without Margot Bernstein. She has heroically pursued the countless clues that lead to hidden collections and owners of reproduction rights. At lightning speed, Zoe de Bretagne caught my typos and stray phrases.

Karissa van Tassel and Valerie Asher visualized for me what the author of a book about fashion should look like.

Radcliffe Institute alums Francine Berman, Elizabeth Chiarello, and Alexandra Lahav stuck with the writing of this book from beginning to end. Fran warned me every time I shuffled into academic nonsense. Liz said, *Vous Pouvez*. Alexi put the parts in their correct places. They are this book's Graces.

Chevelure en porc-épic. Schall à Mouches. Rubans en Cothurnes.

Dess. d'ap. Nat. sur le Boulevart des Capucines.

Notes

INTRODUCTION

xvi **"You will be next":** This was the story she told as soon as she was released. It was first written down in June of 1796 right after a lunch with her and Joséphine. Charles de Constant, letter dated June 4, 1796, in "Lettres de Charles de Constant," in *Nouvelle revue rétrospective* (Paris: Aux bureau de la nouvelle revue retrospective, 1895), premier semestre (July–December 1894): 83.

1. SUMPTUARY DICTATES (JOSEPHINE)

4 **On a typical Antilles:** Dale Tomich, *Slavery in the Circuit of Sugar: Martinique and the World Economy, 1830–1848,* 2nd ed. (Albany: State University of New York Press, Fernand Braudel Center Studies in Historical Social Science, 2016), 310–43.

5 **In 1806:** Françoise Wagener, *L'impératrice Joséphine, 1763–1814* (Paris: Flammarion, 1999), 89–90.

6 **Those in this category were allowed:** Séverine Bulteau and Sylvie Tersen, eds., *Flâneries Vestimentaires* (Pointe-à-Pitre, Guadeloupe: Musée Sant-Jean Perse, 2004), 2–3.

6 **free and skilled:** Elizabeth Léo, *La société martiniquaise aux XVIIe et XVIIIe siècles 1664–1789* (Paris: Karthala, and Fort-de-France: Société de l'Histoire de Martinique, 2003); Frédéric Régent, *Esclavage, métissage, liberté: La Révolution française en Guadeloupe, 1789–1802* (Paris: Grasset, 2004).

6 **The 1754 edict divided:** Ordonnance du 7 septembre, 1754. Bulteau and Tersen, *Flâneries Vestimentaires,* 2–3.

7 **The 1754 sumptuary edict:** Séverine Laborie, "Joseph Savart (1735–1801), 'maître-peintre' à Basse-Terre,"

Bulletin de la Société d'Histoire de la Guadeloupe 163 (September–December 2012): 1–16.

8 **Sundays and holidays:** Most White writers agreed that people of color took every opportunity to dress up, especially on Sundays and holidays, and resented it. Moreau de Saint-Méry, for instance, wrote about enslaved women on Saint-Domingue in 1797, using the racist language of his time: "One can hardly believe to what point the expenditures of a negress can go; her glory, and one of her greatest pleasures, is to have lots of *linge* [underwear]. . . . Negresses have been known to have as many as a hundred *deshabillés* . . . worth 200 écus." The amount Moreau de Saint-Méry cited was absurd, but it expressed a perception that women of color spent a lot of money on the straight, white, cotton dresses he called "*deshabillés.*" According to him, they also owned multiple headscarves, red or predominantly red. "The luxury of Mulatto women was pushed to the highest degree." Médéric Louis Elie Moreau de Saint-Méry, *Description topographique, physique, civile, politique et historique de la partie française de l'isle Saint-Domingue,* ed. Odette Roy Fombrun (1797; repr., Port-au-Prince, Haiti: Le Natal, 1983), 11, 13, 17.

8 **It was instead:** The gole was a dress intended to be worn in public, unlike another loose white cotton dress intended to be worn at home, fastened higher at the neck, called a "*deshabillé*" or "*peignoir.*" The gole and *deshabillé* were enough alike that they may have been confused with each other, for example when Moreau de Saint-Méry claimed that enslaved women owned as many as a hundred *deshabillés.*

9 **Moreover, Antilles style:** Nicole Vanony-Frisch, "Les

Esclaves de la Guadeloupe à la fin de l'ancien régime d'après les sources notariales (1770–1789)," *Bulletin de la Société d'Histoire de la Guadeloupe* 63–64 (1985): 86.

10 **Luckily for us:** Kay Dian Kriz, *Slavery, Sugar, and the Culture of Refinement: Picturing the British West Indies, 1700–1840* (New Haven: Yale University Press, 2008), 36–69. See also Robert S. DuPlessis, *The Material Atlantic: Clothing, Commerce, and Colonization in the Atlantic World, 1650–1800* (Cambridge: Cambridge University Press, 2016), 151–59.

10 **Agostino Brunias:** Anne Lafont has discussed the economic and textile-trade context of Brunias's "tax-onomic" racial impulses in: *L'Art et la race: L'Africain (tout) contre l'oeil des Lumieres* (Paris: Presses du Réel, 2019), 258–74. Madeleine Dobie discusses these issues, in the context of textile trade, in: *Trading Places: Colonization and Slavery in Eighteenth-Century French Culture* (Ithaca, NY: Cornell University Press, 2010). See also the important monograph on Brunias: Mia L. Bagneris, *Colouring the Caribbean: Race and the Art of Agostino Brunias* (Manchester, UK: University of Manchester Press, 2018); Beth Tobin Fowkes, "Taxonomy and Agency in Brunias's West India Paintings," in *Picturing Imperial Power: Colonial Subjects in Eighteenth-Century British Painting* (Durham, NC: Duke University Press, 1999), 138–73; Danielle C. Skeehan, "Caribbean Women, Creole Fashioning, and the Fabric of Black Atlantic Writing," *Eighteenth Century* 56, no. 1 (Spring 2015): 105–23, 146.

11 **"We must have":** *Roses for an Empress: Josephine Bonaparte and Pierre-Joseph Redouté*, trans. Anna Bennett (London: Sidgwick & Jackson, 1983), 13.

11 **He wrote his father:** Pierre Branda, *Joséphine: Le paradoxe du cygne* (Paris: Perrin, 2016), 32.

12 **In 1786:** Jacques de Marsay, *De l'âge des privilèges au temps des vanités: Essai sur l'origine et la valeur des prétensions nobiliaires* (Paris: Champion, 1932), 83–84.

12 **the 400,000 livres:** Caroline Weber, *Queen of Fashion: What Marie Antoinette Wore to the Revolution* (New York: Henry Holt, 2006), 16.

12 **the 270 livres:** Clare Haru Crowston, *Fabricating Women: The Seamstresses of Old Regime France, 1675–1791* (Durham, NC: Duke University Press, 2001), 92–93.

13 **the collective authority:** Steven L. Kaplan, *La fin des corporations* (Paris: Fayard, 2001), xiii.

13 **In eighteenth-century Paris:** Kaplan, *Fin des corporations*, xiii–xiv.

17 **one formal court gown:** Crowston, *Fabricating Women*, 162.

18 **It seemed as if sumptuary laws:** Martha C. Howell, "The Dangers of Dress," in *Commerce before Capitalism in Europe, 1300–1600* (Cambridge: Cambridge University Press, 2010), 211.

19 **rapid-fire series of edicts:** Denis Bruna and Chloé Demey, eds., *Histoire des modes et du vêtement* (Paris: Les éditions Textuels, 2018), 147.

19 **The laboring poor:** Crowston, *Fabricating Women*, 92–93; J. Sgard, "L'Échelle des revenus," *Dix-Huitième Siècle* 14 (1982): 425–33.

19 **Marie Antoinette:** Kimberly Chrisman-Campbell, *Fashion Victims: Dress at the Court of Louis XVI and Marie-Antoinette* (New Haven: Yale University Press, 2015), 27.

20 **thirty-six new outfits:** Bruna and Demey, *Histoire des modes*, 206.

2. STYLE ENTERPRISE (TEREZIA)

25 **In summer 1785:** Christian Gilles, *Madame Tallien: La reine du Directoire 1773–1835* (Biarritz, France: Atlantica, 1999), 21–23.

26 **All over Paris:** Michael Sonenscher, *Work and Wages: Natural Law, Politics, and the Eighteenth-Century French Trades* (Cambridge: Cambridge University Press, 1989); Cissie Fairchilds, "The Production and Marketing of Populuxe Goods in Eighteenth-Century Paris," in *Consumption and the World of Goods*, ed. John Brewer and Roy Porter (London: Routledge, 1993).

27 **the physiocrats:** In 1776, a physiocrat tried to abolish the guilds. The controller general of France, basically the chief of finances, Anne-Robert-Jacques Turgot, issued six edicts to liberalize trade and commerce, one of which declared an end to the guilds. Not everyone was convinced, however, notably Antoine-Louis Séguier, attorney general of the powerful Parlement law courts of Paris. Turgot was dismissed, and the king reinstated the guilds. That same year, the founder of modern economics, Adam Smith, promised that markets would balance supply and demand if they were left to their own devices and would generate "The Wealth of Nations," as he titled his great book.

27 **a boutique run by *couturières*:** Crowston, *Fabricating Women*, 1–5.

27 ***marchandes des modes*:** "Mode, marchande, et marchandes de," in *Encyclopédie, ou dictionnaire raisonné des sciences, des arts et des métiers, etc.*, ed. Denis Diderot and Jean le Rond d'Alembert (Paris: Chez Samuel Faulche & Compagnie, Libraires & Imprimeurs: 1765), 10:598–99.

28 **"It was the establishment of colonies":** Legoux de Flaix, *Essai historique, géographique et politique sur l'Indoustan avec le tableaus de son commerce* (Paris, 1807), 2:134–35, cited in Richard Roberts, "West Africa and the Pondicherry Textile Industry," *Indian Economic and Social History Review* 31, no. 2 (1994): 117.

29 **a staple of the Indian economy:** Giorgio Riello, *Cotton: The Fabric That Made the Modern World* (Cambridge: Cambridge University Press, 2013), 1.

29 **Most of their business:** Felicia Gottman, *Global Trade, Smuggling, and the Making of Economic Liberalism: Asian Textiles in France 1680–1760* (London: Palgrave Macmillan, 2016), 22, 37.

29 **the French East Indies Company:** Riello, *Cotton*, 92.

29 **A bewildering plethora:** Riello, *Cotton*, 30; Gottman, *Global Trade*, 19, 28–29. Glossaries are diabolically difficult to establish, because the hundreds of fabric names used for cottons, wools, linens, silks, and mixes among them are further complicated by linguistic changes over time, compounded by language differences when dealing with trade among far-flung parts of the world. Is it more useful, for instance, to refer to a fabric by its Indian name of origin, or its French name of destination? Add to this nomenclature mess the absence of any standardized widths of woven fabric, or of length measurements, even within a relatively unified country like France, until the French Revolution. The British used a length measurement called the "ell," while the French preferred the *"aune."* An *aune* in Marseilles, however, might not be the same as in Paris. This is why historians resort to talking about "pieces" of fabric, and why comparative price calculations can only be approximate and qualitative. When I feel sorry for myself about this problem, I imagine what it must have been like to be a fabric merchant.

30 **The same seamstress:** Crowston, *Fabricating Women*, 160–61.

31 **Imported cotton:** Riello, *Cotton*, 176.

31 **the ban against cotton:** Gottman, *Global Trade*, 19.

31 **the biggest loophole of all:** Gottman, *Global Trade*, 42–49.

32 **another sort of effect:** Daniel Roche, *La Culture des Apparences* (Paris: Fayard, 1989). Roche patiently studied inventories of people's possessions taken after death. Because clothes remained so valuable, every clothing item was listed. Roche was able to count what people wore, how many clothes they had, and what the clothes were made of. He also found that whereas around 1700, 7% of wage earners' clothes were made of cotton, the same percentage as those of nobles, by the start of the Revolution, 38% of wage earners wore cotton, and so did 25% of nobles.

33 **a dress that cost:** Crowston, *Fabricating Women*, 160–61.

35 **"All eyes will be fixed on you":** Weber, *Queen of Fashion*, 59.

35 **"hurtling toward an abyss":** Weber, *Queen of Fashion*, 117.

35 **"ornaments of royalty":** Cited in Chrisman-Campbell, *Fashion Victims*, 180.

35 **Rose Bertin:** Michelle Sapori, *Rose Bertin: Ministre des modes de Marie Antoinette* (Paris: Librairie Académique Perrin, 2010).

35 **"odd personage":** Clare Haru Crowston, *Credit, Fashion, Sex: Economies of Regard in Old Regime France* (Durham, NC: Duke University Press, 2013), 202; and Nicole Pellegrin, *Les vêtements de la liberté: Abécédaire des pratiques vestimentaires françaises de 1780 à 1800* (Paris: Alinéa, 1989), 26.

36 **so many of her clothes:** Cited in Chrisman-Campbell, *Fashion Victims*, 27.

3. Strained Seams (Juliette)

42 **"For all time":** Cited in Edouart Herriot, *Madame Récamier*, trans. Alys Hallard (London: W. Heinemann, 1906), 9.

42 **Juliette's exceptional beauty:** Amélie Cyvoct Lenormant, ed., *Memoirs and Correspondence of Madame Récamier*, trans. from the French and further edited by Isaphene M. Luyster, 2nd ed. (Boston: Roberts Brothers, Lenormant, 1868), 8.

42 **"long hours at the toilette":** Lenormant, *Memoirs and Correspondence*, 4.

45 **"One could propose":** *Cabinet des modes, ou les Modes nouvelles, décrites d'une manière claire & précise, & représentées par des planches en taille-douce, enluminées* (Paris: Chez Buisson, 1786), cahier 3, 15 déc. 1785, 19–20; cahier 5, 15 janv. 1786, 39.

45 **"Was not our century":** *Cabinet des modes*, cahier 13, 15 mai 1786, 97.

45 **"the originality of Asiatic costumes":** Meredith Martin, "Tipu Sultan's Ambassadors at Saint-Cloud: Indomania and Anglophobia in Pre-Revolutionary Paris," *West 86th: A Journal of Decorative Arts, Design History, and Material Culture* 21, no. 1 (2014): 57.

47 **cotton elevated to an imperial level:** Sylvia Houghteling, "The Emperor's Humbler Clothes: Textures of Courtly Dress in Seventeenth-Century South Asia," *Ars Orientalis* 57 (November 2017).

47 **Bengali muslin's superiority:** Houghteling, "Emperor's Humbler Clothes."

47 ***Phuti karpas:*** Zaria Gorvett, "The Ancient Fabric That No One Knows How to Make," BBC, March 16, 2021, https://www.bbc.com/future/article/20210316 -the-legendary-fabric-that-no-one-knows-how-to -make.

48 **Tipu Sultan gifted Queen Marie Antoinette:** Chrisman-Campbell, *Fashion Victims*, 253–54.

49 **A French traveler:** Cited in Ritu Kumar, *Costumes and Textiles of Royal India* (London: Christie's Books, 1999), 152.

49 **the most lavish Indian embroidery:** Avalon Fotheringham, *The Indian Textile Sourcebook* (London: Thames & Hudson, 2019).

50 ***chikandari:*** Fotheringham, *Indian Textile Sourcebook.*

51 **so acutely aware of fashion:** Silvia A. Centeno, Dorothy Mahon, and David Pullins, "Refashioning the Lavoisiers," Metropolitan Museum of Art, September 1, 2021, https://www.metmuseum.org/perspectives/ articles/2021/9/david-lavoisier-conservation.

53 **"Under this transparent dress":** *Cabinet des modes*, cahier 11, 15 avril 1786, 82.

53 **"seeing death was inevitable":** Bernardin de Saint-Pierre, *Paul et Virginie*, 1788 ed., Jean Ehrard collection folio classique (Paris: Gallimard, 2020), 224–25.

53 **never cease wearing gowns:** Duhamel, *Cabinet des modes*, cahier 21, An II, 10 juin 1787, 161.

4. Off with Their Silks

59 **"stunningly beautiful":** Gilles, *Madame Tallien*, 107.

59 **"ready to choose domestic happiness":** Cited and translated in *Roses for an Empress*, 21.

60 **"correct herself":** André Castelot, *Joséphine* (Paris: Perrin, 1964), 42.

60 **"Make your arrangements":** Castelot, *Joséphine*, 48.

61 **"my consolation":** Cited in Branda, *Joséphine*, 45.

61 **"a casual fine linen ball dress":** Castelot, *Joséphine*, 63.

61 **"This woman":** Castelot, *Joséphine*, 63.

63 **"My mother":** Gilles, *Madame Tallien*, 32.

64 **"both beautiful and pretty":** Gilles, *Madame Tallien*, 41.

65 **"the Great Renunciation":** J. C. Flügel, *The Psychology of Clothes* (London: Institute of Psycho-Analysis and Hogarth Press, 1930).

66 **October 7, 1666:** David Kuchta, *The Three-Piece Suit and Modern Masculinity* (Berkeley: University of California Press, 2002), 1.

66 **"clothing come from the English":** Edmond Jean François Barbier, *Journal historique et anecdotique du règne de Louis XV*, 4 vols. (Paris: Renouard, 1847), 1:228.

66 **"an outfit very little flattering":** *Mercure de France. Dédié au Roy. Février 1726* (Paris: Chez Cavilier, 1726), 403–4.

66 **the new style from across the Channel:** *Cabinet des modes*, cahier 16, 1 juil. 1786, 121–23.

66 **"Everything is *à l'anglaise*":** Gouverneur Morris, *The Diaries and Letters of Gouverneur Morris*, ed. Anne Cary Morris, 2 vols. (London: Kegan Paul, Trench and Co., 1889) 1:31.

67 **Before the Estates General:** For the story of the clothing of the Estates General see: Georges Lefebvre and Anne Terroine, *Recueil de documents relatifs aux séances des Etats Généraux, mai-juin 1789* (Paris: Editions du Centre National de la Recherche Scientifique, 1953), 1:64–82.

68 **"a different costume":** Mirabeau, *Lettres à ses commettants*, cited in Lefebvre and Terroine, *Recueil de documents*, 78.

70 **turned to their ally David:** The Committee of Public Safety, of which David was a member, charged him with the design of a neoclassical revolutionary government uniform by decree on 25 Floréal Year II (May 14, 1794). On 28 Fructidor Year III (September 14, 1795), a representative in the next government, the Directory, reiterated the plea for a magnificent uniform.

70 **"closer to our customs":** Cited in Jean-Marie Bruson and Christophe Leribault, "Les idées, les arts, les lettres et les institutions," in *Au temps des merveilleuses: La société parisienne sous le Directoire et le Consulat* (Paris: Musée Carnavalet, 2005), 214.

71 **complaints against guilds:** Cited in Kaplan, *Fin des corporations*, 557.

72 **"No person of one sex":** *Moniteur Universel*, 1re décade, Brumaire, An 2 (October 22–31, 1793).

73 **"One of the great crimes":** Paul Louis de Giafferri, *Histoire du costume féminin: De l'an 1037 à l'an 1870* (Paris: Editions Nilsson, n.d., ca. 1925), Album 7e, "Révolution," article 71, n.p. [1].

73 **"relative to the Jews":** Lynn Hunt, ed., *The French Revolution and Human Rights: A Brief Documentary History* (Boston: Bedford St. Martin's, 1996), 99.

73 **"without distinction of color":** Hunt, *French Revolution*, 99.

76 **tricolor cockades:** Pellegrin, *Vêtements de la liberté*, 48.

5. Cut to Nothing

81 **Hoche:** Paul Barras, *Memoirs of Barras*, ed. George Duruy, trans. C. E. Roche (New York: Harper & Brothers, 1895), 2:60.

81 **"It's so hard":** Wagener, *L'Impératrice Joséphine*, 103.

82 **Heedless of this dire warning:** Gilles, *Madame Tallien*, 93.

82 **the memory of a witness:** Gilles, *Madame Tallien*, 107.

83 **When Tallien:** Françoise Kermina, *Madame Tallien* (Paris: Perrin, 2006), 42, 67.

84 **"Take it all":** Jean-Claude Fauveau, *La Tallien: La Terreur à Bordeaux (mai 1793–avril 1794)* (Bordeaux: Féret, 2016), 16–17.

84 **one noblewoman remembered:** Marquise de La Tour du Pin, *Journal d'une femme de cinquante ans 1778–1815* (Paris: Librairie Chapelot, 1916), 1:335–39. By the time she wrote her memoirs, the comtesse de Gouvernet had married into a new name.

84 **complaints against Tallien's leniency:** Gilles, *Madame Tallien*, 96.

85 **One atrocity in particular:** Antoine de Baecque, "La Mort de la Princesse de Lamballe, ou le sexe massacré," in *La Révolution terrorisée* (Paris: CNRS Editions, 2017).

85 **"The police chief":** Cited in Kermina, *Madame Tallien*, 114.

87 **her biological father:** In the middle of the nineteenth century, the secret, to the extent that it was a secret, was published in print behind the thinnest of veils. In her later years, Juliette lived with an informally adopted niece of her husband's. This niece, Amélie Cyvoct Lenormant, was sincerely devoted to her aunt, and took it upon herself after Juliette died to assemble, edit, and publish the records of Juliette's illustrious career in 1868. Lenormant had direct testimonials from many of those who had known her aunt in her glory years, supplemented, she affirmed, by her aunt's own recollections. The prudish norms of the Victorian era reigned by 1868, and the French Revolution was then a controversial era. Nevertheless, the difficult issue of Juliette's marriage to Récamier was addressed. There had already been too much talk for it not to be. "The tie between them was never anything but a nominal tie. Mme. Récamier received from her husband only his name. . . . This fact may create astonishment, but I am not bound to explain it." Juliette's niece, however, did explain it in the following sentences: "M. Récamier's relations to his wife were of a strictly paternal character. He treated the young and innocent girl who bore his name like a daughter." Lenormant, *Memoirs and Correspondence*, 7.

87 **he plainly wrote:** Herriot, *Madame Récamier*, 12–13.

6. Desperate Measures (Terezia & Josephine)

92 **solitary confinement:** Cited in Marie-Hélène Bourquin-Simonin, *Monsieur et Madame Tallien* (Paris: Perrin, 1987), 211.

92 **"executioners drunk with blood":** Gilles, *Madame Tallien*, 166–67.

92 **Robespierre tried to bribe her:** Gilles, *Madame Tallien*, 165–66.

92 **Robespierre had added insult:** "Lettres de Charles de Constant," 82–85.

92 **When Tallien freed her:** Letter from Térézia to her children, Château de Chimay archives, cited in Gilles, *Madame Tallien*, 201. Lest this seem like a self-aggrandizing memory, it should be noted that the children to whom Térézia was writing were not Tallien's.

93 **"*Vive Notre-Dame de Thermidor!*":** Gilles, *Madame Tallien*, 195–96; Jean-Claude Jumièges, *Madame Tallien: Ou une femme dans la tourmente révolutionnaire* (Lausanne: Edition Rencontre, 1967), 189.

93 **shut the Paris Jacobin Club:** Jumièges, *Madame Tallien*, 188–89.

93 **William Pitt:** Possibly November 1794, cited in Gilles, *Madame Tallien*, 203.

93 **"Long Live Forever the Republic":** Louis Gastine, *Reine du directoire, la belle Tallien* (Paris: Albin Michel, 1909), 127.

93 **"Madame Tallien":** Charles Lacretelle, *Dix années d'épreuves* (Paris: A. Allouard, 1842), 196.

94 **to a friend back in Bordeaux:** Cited in Gilles, *Madame Tallien*, 197–98.

94 **"la citoyenne Cabarrus":** Cited in Bourquin-Simonin, *Monsieur et Madame Tallien*, 263.

95 **"It was embraces":** Lacretelle, *Dix années d'épreuves*, 198–203.

95 **unrepentant royalists:** After the French Revolution ended, the labels *Incroyables* and *Merveilleuses* were used indiscriminately for anyone who wore any version of the new style.

96 **"You will no doubt":** Cited in *Roses for an Empress*, 45.

96 **The two men became close enough:** Gilles, *Madame Tallien*, 216.

97 **"Madame Tallien":** Cited in Kermina, *Madame Tallien*, 197.

100 **There is also a chance:** A portrait of Candeille by Adélaïde Labille Guiard dated 1791 hints at a gole.

102 **The single most useful:** *A Sketch of Modern France. In a Series of Letters to a Lady of Fashion, Written in the Years 1796 and 1797, During a Tour through France*, ed. C. L. Moody (1708; facsimile repr., London: Pickering & Chatto, 2009).

102 **"females":** *Sketch of Modern France*, 259.

102 **"'It matters not, however'":** *Sketch of Modern France*, 266–69.

104 **paintings chart fashion revolution:** Paintings can be difficult to date precisely. It helps when they were exhibited in the regular public Paris Salons, for which records were kept. It also helps if detailed documents of an artist's whereabouts have been studied. This portrait of Emilie Sériziat, for instance, was displayed in the Salon of 1795, which opened in September, so it had to have been finished by then, and biographical study of David suggests it was painted in May of that year.

105 **Maria Nugent:** Maria Nugent was born in New Jersey before the American Revolution began, to a loyalist family that fled to Britain. She then moved to Jamaica when her husband became the island's governor. The dress that puzzled her was given to her in 1802, by Pauline Bonaparte, by that time Joséphine's sister-in-law. Maria Nugent, *Lady Nugent's Journal of Her Residence in Jamaica from 1801 to 1805*, ed. Philip Wright (Barbados: The University of the West Indies Press, 2002), 106, 112, 126, 132–33.

7. AT EASE (TEREZIA)

111 **"a Directory dinner":** Charles-Maurice de Talleyrand, *Mots, propos, aphorismes: Paris, 1754–1838* (Paris: Editions Horay, 2016), 74.

111 **a social set:** Cited in Gilles, *Madame Tallien*, 210.

111 **"a savage in flesh-colored tights":** Herriot, *Madame Récamier*, 24.

112 **a notarized contract:** Contract cited in Bourquin-Simonin, *Monsieur et Madame Tallien*, 265–66.

112 **"Let him tell us":** Gilles, *Madame Tallien*, 212–24.

112 **on the floor of the National Convention:** Gilles, *Madame Tallien*, 212–24.

113 **the Cottage:** Kermina, *Madame Tallien*, 211.

113 **"more expensively undressed":** Talleyrand, cited in Kermina, *Madame Tallien*, 157.

114 **"more severity than levity":** Madame de Chastenay, cited in Kermina, *Madame Tallien*, 211.

114 **"a semi-Greek costume":** Duchesse d'Abrantès, *Histoire des salons de Paris: Tableaux et portraits du grand monde, sous Louis XVI, le Directoire, de Consulat et l'Empire, la Réstauration et le règne de Louis-Philippe*, 4 vols. (Paris: Garnier Frères, 1893), 137–39.

114 **"her bust half-naked":** Louis-Victor, duc de Broglie, *Souvenirs 1785–1870*, ed. Albert de Broglie (Paris, 1886), 1:23.

115 **de Staël frequently attended:** Arsène Houssaye, *Notre-Dame de Thermidor* (Paris: Plon, 1867), 447.

115 **"the least favored by fortune":** Gabriel Julien Ouvrard, *Mémoires de G.-J. Ouvrard: Sur sa vie et ses diverses opérations financières*, 3 vols. (Paris: Moutardier, 1827), 1:19.

117 **she became disillusioned:** Houssaye, *Notre-Dame de Thermidor*, 438.

117 **sincerely shocked:** Lacretelle, *Dix années d'épreuves*, 201.

117 **"Too much blood":** Gilles, *Madame Tallien*, 225.

117 **"crossing a tempest":** Cited in Houssaye, *Notre-Dame de Thermidor*, 13.

117 **"in her home":** Ouvrard, *Mémoires*, 1:19.

118 **"an immense fortune":** Talleyrand, *Mots, propos, aphorismes*, 106.

118 **During parties:** Cited in Jacques Castelnau, *Madame Tallien: Revolutionnaire, favorite, princesse* (Paris: Hachette, 1938), 183.

118 **"Gentle, good, sympathetic":** Étienne Denis, duc de Pasquier, *Histoire de mon temps: Mémoires du Chancelier Pasquier*, 10 vols. (Paris, E. Plon, Nourrit, 1893–95), 1:126.

118 **"Amid all these gentlewomen":** Barras, *Memoirs of Barras*, 2:61–64.

8. ALTERED FORTUNE (JOSEPHINE & NAPOLÉON)

121 **"It has been a long time":** Cited in *Roses for an Empress*, 45.

122 **"Well, my friend":** Gilles, *Madame Tallien*, 234.

123 **"belle citoyenne":** Castelnau, *Madame Tallien*, 197.

123 **"none of her attractions":** Barras, *Memoirs of Barras*, 2:63.

124 **"a friend of the beautiful Madame Tallien":** Cited in *Roses for an Empress*, 52.

124 **"her figure":** Cited from the comte Montgaillard in *Roses for an Empress*, 8.

124 **"not a person of remarkable intellect":** Cited from the comtesse de Rémusat in *Roses for an Empress*, 53.

125 **"I would be so happy":** Cited in Branda, *Joséphine*, 93.

125 **"prettiest possible"**: Cited in Branda, *Joséphine*, 92–93.

125 **"libertinism"**: Barras, *Memoirs of Barras*, 2:62.

125 **"It was even said"**: Barras, *Memoirs of Barras*, 2:64.

126 **false rumor**: Branda, *Joséphine*, 70–78.

127 **"I awake"**: Napoléon Bonaparte, cited in *Roses for an Empress*, 51.

127 **"The following day"**: Eugène de Beauharnais, cited in *Roses for an Empress*, 47.

127 **Hortense fondly exaggerated**: Rose de Beauharnais, cited in *Roses for an Empress*, 50.

129 **"The public"**: Général Baron Thiébault, cited in *Roses for an Empress*, 54.

129 **"Barras has taken charge"**: Lucien Bonaparte, cited in *Roses for an Empress*, 54.

9. MINIMALIST PRINCIPLES (JULIETTE)

131 **When she and Juliette Récamier met**: Accounts differ. Some memoirs recall Juliette being present at Directory parties hosted by Barras in 1794–95, at which Térézia and Joséphine presided. Others say the first meeting was just between Térézia and Juliette, and in 1796. One contemporary recalled seeing Juliette go with Térézia and Joséphine into Barras's apartment in the first year of the Directory. François-Yves Besnard, *Souvenirs d'un nonagénaire: Mémoires de François-Yves Besnard, publiés sur le manuscrit autographe par Célestin Port*, 2 vols. (Paris: H. Champion, 1880) 2:146–47. Another wrote about the end of the Terror: "Paris once more reigned supreme in matters of fashion and taste. Two women, both of them famous for their beauty, Mme. Tallien, and a little later Mme. Récamier, took the lead." *Mémoire de M. le comte Thibaudeau* (Paris: 1834), chap. 11, cited in Herriot, *Madame Récamier*, 28.

131 **"When she appeared in a salon"**: Houssaye, *Notre-Dame de Thermidor*, 28.

132 **Judgment was quickly delivered**: Charles de Constant, November 2, 1796, reproduced in *Revue rétrospective* (Paris: Aux bureau de la nouvelle revue retrospective I, 2 1894): 185.

133 **"Her beauty"**: Chateaubriand, *Mémoires d'outre-tombe*, ed. Maurice Levaillant and Georges Moulinier (1839; Paris: Gallimard, 1951), 156.

133 **"In the midst"**: Chateaubriand, *Mémoires d'outre-tombe*, 169.

134 **"From your earliest youth"**: Cited in Chateaubriand, *Mémoires d'outre-tombe*, 209.

134 **would not deign**: Cited in Chateaubriand, *Mémoires d'outre-tombe*, 159.

135 **"Madame Récamier"**: Mathieu Molé, *Souvenirs de jeunesse: 1793–1803*, ed. Jean-Claude Berchet (Paris: Mercure de France, 1991), 210.

137 **entrusted the interior redecoration**: Lenormant, *Souvenirs et correspondances* (1860), 1:25.

140 **"An instinct for beauty"**: Cited in Chateaubriand, *Mémoires d'outre-tombe*, 161.

140 **"the depths of every soul"**: Benjamin Constant, cited in Herriot, *Madame Récamier*, 4, 338n4.

140 **A visitor noted**: Johann Friedrich Reichardt, *Un hiver à Paris sous le Consulat et l'Empire 1802–1803* (Paris: Tallandier, 2003), 133.

141 **"the ethereal bed"**: Reichardt, *Un hiver à Paris*, 133.

141 **"Madame Récamier's bed"**: Mary Berry, *Voyages de Miss Berry à Paris (1782–1836)* (Paris: A. Roblot, 1905), 107.

141 **"My friendship for you"**: Cited in Herriot, *Madame Récamier*, 44–45n1 (fourth letter of Mme. R. to Paul David, M. Ch. de Loménie's papers).

141 **"One finds in her"**: Pierre Simon Ballanche, *Vie de Madame Récamier*, ed. Kurt Kloocke (Frankfurt: Peter Lang, 1999).

142 **"Nearing my end"**: Chateaubriand, *Mémoires d'outre-tombe*, 1983 ed., II, 3e partie, livre 29, chap. 23, 222.

10. A DIRECTORY OF ACCESSORIES

146 *Journal des dames et des modes*: Annemarie Kleinert, *Le "Journal des dames et des modes" ou la conquête de l'Europe féminine 1797–1839* (Stuttgart: Thornbecke, 2001).

146 **"The degree of civilization"**: *Journal des dames et des modes*, 1797, no. 1, p. 1.

146 **Its initial price**: Kleinert, *Conquête de l'Europe féminine*, 33. The price subsequently rose due to stamp taxes, which the editors decried.

147 **the editors announced**: *Journal des dames et des modes*, 1797, no. 1, p. 5.

147 **"the genius of *la mode*"**: *Journal des dames et des modes*, December 17, 1797, tome 1, no. 63, p. 9.

147 **"decent dresses"**: *Journal des dames et des modes*, 1797, no. 7, p. 5.

148 **Purses . . . had been around**: For essays on the history (by Claire Wilcox) and psychology (by Adam Phillips) of handbags, as well as pictures, see: Judith Clark, *Handbags: The Making of a Museum* (New Haven: Yale University Press; London: Simone Handbag Museum, 2012).

149 **"pockets revolution"**: *Journal des dames et des modes*, 1798, tome 1, no. 19, p. 1; *Journal des dames et des modes*, December 9, 1798, tome 1, no. 24, p. 10, "Explication de la gravure no. 24."

149 **even rebus puzzles**: Baudelaire was intrigued by the modernity of the handbags displayed in the *Journal des dames et des modes*, especially those with rebus puzzles, such as the one in plate 71. T. H. Parke, "Baudelaire et La Mésangère," *Revue d'Histoire littéraire de la France* 86e Année, no. 2 (March–April, 1986): 248–57.

149 **"two steps in Paris"**: *Journal des dames et des modes*, 1798, tome 1, no. 19, p. 1; *Journal des dames et des modes*, December 2, 1798, tome 11, no. 23, p. 13, "Explication de la gravure."

152 **"The most elegant coiffure"**: *Journal des dames et des modes*, 1797, no. 2, p. 2.

152 **"to be à la mode"**: *Journal des dames et des modes*, 1797, no. 4, p. 4.

152 **Some women**: Cited in Gastine, *Reine du Directoire*, 263, 266–67.

156 **the hat she was famous for**: Jules Bertaut, *Madame Tallien* (Paris: Fayard, 1946), 88. No matter how much the French professed to admire ancient Greece, they almost always used the Roman names for divinities, hence "Minerva."

156 **"the Graces"**: Houssaye, *Notre-Dame de Thermidor*, 23.

156 **set the Three Graces subject herself**: Hugh Honour, "Canova's Three Graces," in *The Three Graces: Antonio Canova*, exhibition catalogue (National Gallery of Scotland, 1995), 19–20.

156 **"Beauty without grace"**: Talleyrand, *Mots, propos, aphorismes*, 68.

11. Freedom from Clothes (Térézia)

159 **Though he had been jilted**: Houssaye, *Notre-Dame de Thermidor*, 462.

160 **"The tender memories"**: Jean-Lambert Tallien to Térézia Tallien, Rosette, 17 Thermidor, An VI (August 4, 1797) in *Correspondance intime de l'armée d'Egypte, interceptée par la croisière anglaise*, ed. Lorédan Larchey (Paris, R. Pincebourde, 1866), 67–68.

160 **the divorce proceedings lingered**: Houssaye, *Notre-Dame de Thermidor*, 462.

160 **Some biographers**: Bourquin-Simonin, *Monsieur et Madame Tallien*, 314–15.

160 **in effect publicly announced their illegitimate intimate relationship**: Louis-Marie de la Larevellière-Lépeaux, *Mémoires de Larevellière-Lépeaux, publiés par son fils sur le manuscrit autographe de l'auteur et suivis des pièces, justificatives et de correspondance inédites*, ed. Robert David d'Angers, 3 vols. (Paris: E. Plon, Nourrit, 1895), 1:338.

161 **a villa with a large garden**: Gilles, *Madame Tallien*, 291.

161 **She herself told her children**: Houssaye, *Notre-Dame de Thermidor*.

161 **the place was now hers**: *Au Temps des merveilleuses*, 84.

162 **The Paris rue de Babylone villa and park**: *Au Temps des merveilleuses*, 85.

162 **"Her mind"**: Cited in Gilles, *Madame Tallien*, 262.

162 **"Mme Tallien was extremely elegant"**: Cited in Gilles, *Madame Tallien*, 265.

162 **a country**: A royal tax collector and financier named Bordier had built the first château of Le Raincy in the seventeenth century. Between 1769 and 1793, the estate was owned by the royal (but regicide) Orléans family, which put in a fashionably rambling *jardin anglais*. The execution by guillotine of the duc d'Orléans in November of 1793 automatically turned Le Raincy into a "propriété nationale." The Comité du Salut Publique turned it the following year into an "établissement rural" public park, with a collection of confiscated animals, and a café in the *jardin anglais*. This public service project came to naught, and ownership of Le Raincy obscurely passed to someone named Danguin de Livery, who may have been a front man for Ouvrard. The main building was torn down, and replaced by a neoclassical building, with a central peristyle and six Ionic columns. In 1799, the estate was officially rented to Ouvrard, who bought it outright in 1806.

163 **the couple threw lavish parties**: Jean-Pierre Sarrazin, *Gabriel Julien Ouvrard: Grandeur et misère d'un financier de genie sous l'Empire* (Paris: L'Harmattan, 2014), 85–88.

163 **a stunning bathroom**: Sarrazin, *Ouvrard*, 86.

164 **the great love of his life**: Sarrazin, *Ouvrard*, 88.

164 **"RESPECT NATIONAL PROPERTIES"**: *Rapsodies du jour*, An 5, cited in Gastine, *Reine du Directoire*, 264.

165 **Barras bought the château de Grosbois**: Gastine, *Reine du Directoire*, 318.

166 **He remembered it being politically progressive**: Antoine Vincent Arnault, *Souvenirs d'un sexagenaire*, 4 vols. (Paris: Duféy, 1833), 2:313.

167 **"You prescribed":** Cited in Gilles, *Madame Tallien*, 272.

167 **a nasty, anonymous roman à clef:** Cited in Jean-Marie Bruson and Anne Forray-Carlier, "Quelques merveilleuses," in *Au temps des merveilleuses*, 81.

168 **"a new fashion":** Gorvett, "Ancient Fabric," https://www.bbc.com/future/article/20210316-the-legendary-fabric-that-no-one-knows-how-to-make.

169 **Rose Thermidor recounted:** Gilles, *Madame Tallien*, 215.

170 **her children:** Child #1: by Comte Devin de Fontenay: Antoine-François Théodore-Denis Ignace de Fontenay, born May 2, 1789, died February 9, 1815. Child #2, by Jean-Lambert Tallien: Thermidor-Rose-Thérésia Tallien, born May 17, 1795. Child #3, by Jean-Lambert Tallien or Paul Barras: stillbirth, December 20, 1798. Child #4, by Gabriel Julien Ouvrard: Clémence-Isaure Cabarrus, born February 1, 1800. Child #5, by Gabriel Julien Ouvrard: Jules-Joseph Edouard Cabarrus, born April 19, 1801. Child #6, by Gabriel Julien Ouvrard: Clarisse-Gabrielle-Thérésa Cabarrus, born May 21, 1802. Child #7, by Gabriel Julien Ouvrard: Stéphanie-Caroline Thérésa Cabarrus, born September 2, 1803. Child #8, by Prince François-Joseph-Philippe de Riquet-Caraman: prince Joseph de Chimay, born August 20, 1808. Child #9, by Prince François-Joseph-Philippe de Riquet-Caraman: Alphonse de Chimay, born June 16, 1810. Child #10, by Prince François-Joseph-Philippe de Riquet-Caraman: Marie-Louise de Chimay, born August 6, 1813 (dies after six months). Child #11, by Prince François-Joseph-Philippe de Riquet-Caraman: Louise de Chimay, born February 19, 1815.

12. DRESSED FOR SUCCESS (JOSEPHINE)

176 **"My maxim":** Cited in Branda, *Joséphine*, 116.

176 **"There are funds now":** Cited in Branda, *Joséphine*, 145.

176 **she commissioned:** Branda, *Joséphine*, 145.

177 **Total value of the wardrobe:** *Joséphine*, exhibition catalogue, Musée du Luxembourg, 2014 (Paris: Réunion des Musées Nationaux, 2014), 37.

177 **Another inventory:** *Joséphine*, exhibition catalogue, 37.

178 **One of Térézia's biographers:** Castelnau, *Madame Tallien*, 146.

178 **"kingdom of tulle and muslin":** Castelnau, *Madame Tallien*, 185.

179 **"beautiful Indian muslin":** Cited in Gastine, *Reine du Directoire*, 254.

179 **"a white muslin dress":** Louis Constant Wairy, *Mémoires intimes de Napoléon 1er par Constant, son valet de chambre* (Paris: Mercure de France, 1967), 65.

179 **"She was charming":** Abrantès, *Histoire des salons de Paris*, 32.

179 **"dress in Indian muslin":** Abrantès, *Histoire des salons de Paris*, 356.

180 **The effect:** *Jean-Baptise Isabey, portraitiste de l'Europe (1767–1855)*, exhibition catalogue (Paris: Réunion des Musées Nationaux, 2005), 136.

181 **As she reigned:** Cited in Diana Scarisbrick, "Love and Glory: Joséphine's Jewelry," in *Joséphine and the Arts of the Empire*, ed. Eleanor Delorme (Los Angeles: J. Paul Getty Museum, 2005), 180.

182 **"The Empress is no more exempt":** Cited in Scarisbrick, "Love and Glory," 177.

183 **copies of medals:** *Joséphine*, exhibition catalogue, 75.

184 **Eventually she acquired:** Scarisbrick, "Love and Glory," 183–84.

184 **the national jewelry collection:** The collection was archaically called the *Trésor de la Couronne*. Scarisbrick, "Love and Glory," 176.

184 **"a fashionable lady wears":** Cited in Diana Scarisbrick, "The Incomparable Josephine," Sotheby's, December 1, 2021, https://www.sothebys.com/en/articles/the-incomparable-josephine.

185 **"Madame Bonaparte showed us":** *Roses for an Empress*, 65.

187 **Genuine Kashmiri shawls:** Monique Lévi-Strauss, *The Cashmere Shawl* (New York: Harry N. Abrams, 1986), 14–15.

187 **Térézia . . . wore Kashmiri shawls first:** An eyewitness, Charles Constant, reported she wore one on June 3, 1796. See Bourquin-Simonin, *Monsieur et Madame Tallien*, 304.

187 **"a scarlet cloak":** Henry Swinburne, *The Courts of Europe at the Close of the Last Century* (London: H. Colburn, 1841), 2:139–40, 181.

187 **"adornment very rare":** Cited in Gastine, *Reine du Directoire*, 54, 268.

188 **each shawl cost:** Lévi-Strauss, *Cashmere Shawl*, 19.

188 **Joséphine owned ninety shawls:** *Joséphine*, exhibition catalogue, 40.

191 **"man to man":** Talleyrand, *Mots, propos, aphorismes*, 71.

191 **a loud hint:** The same idea that Indians could accomplish nothing persisted where shawls, too, were concerned. The Scottish town of Paisley made a nineteenth-century fortune by imitating and rebranding Kashmiri shawls as "paisley shawls." In 2013 the Met described the design of the shawl in the portrait of Catherine Verlée as "paisley." Kathryn Calley Galitz, "François Gérard: Portraiture, Scandal, and the Art of Power in Napoleonic France," *Metropolitan Museum of Art Bulletin* (Summer 2013): 25. This despite the illustration of the essay with a picture of a shawl whose caption correctly identifies its origins as "Kashmir, India."

193 **Joséphine employed skilled women:** Marie-Jeanne-Pierette Avrillion, *Mémoires de mademoiselle Avrillion: Sur la vie privée de Joséphine, sa famille et sa cour*, ed. Maurice Dernelle (Paris: Mercure de France, 1986), 278.

193 **recommended by Térézia:** Branda, *Joséphine*, 180–83.

194 **a more ingenious explanation:** Branda, *Joséphine*, 56–60.

196 **Percier's style:** In 1804, Napoléon banished his rival General Jean-Victor-Marie Moreau to the United States. Joséphine acquired some of Moreau's furniture, including Madame Moreau's bed, because it was in her favorite style. Napoleonic decorative arts scholar Eleanor Delorme has identified an 1802 drawing of the bed installation by Percier (*Joséphine and the Arts*, 110–11). It does tell us something about Joséphine and Napoléon that they were happy to occupy a bed that had once belonged to a man and a woman they had utterly defeated. Napoléon, however, was not satisfied. Soon after their coronation as emperor and empress, he demanded she get a more imperial bed, with more bulk, more gold, and much more ornament.

197 **"Consult La Mésengère's magazine":** Kleinert, *Conquête de l'Europe féminine*, 85.

197 **"A beautiful and very strange dress":** Abrantès, *Histoire des salons*, 494.

197 **a white crêpe dress:** Abrantès, *Histoire des salons*, 495.

197 **"the simplicity of Madame Bonaparte's toilette":** Abrantès, *Histoire des salons*, 357.

197 **"The purest taste":** Cited in *Joséphine*, exhibition catalogue, 16.

198 **a journalist compared:** Kleinert, *Conquête de l'Europe féminine*, 1.

198 **it was inventoried:** Céline Meunier, "Histoires de garde-robe," in *Joséphine*, exhibition catalogue, 40.

199 **"This disaster":** Hortense de Beauharnais, *The Memoirs of Queen Hortense*, ed. Prince Napoléon, trans. Arthur K. Griggs and F. Mabel Robinson, 2 vols. (London: Thornton Butterworth, 1928), 1:56.

13. Opposition Patterns (Juliette)

202 **"Since when":** Cited in Chateaubriand, *Mémoires d'outre-tombe*, 174.

202 **"I was subjugated!":** Cited in Herriot, *Madame Récamier*, 47n3 (*Souv. et Corr.*, 1:27–35).

204 **"Women are everywhere":** Cited in Gilles, *Madame Tallien*, 233–34.

206 **"perfectly and very richly attired":** Mrs. Victor du Pont to Mrs. Gabriel Manigault, Paris, December 10, 1798, in Betty-Bright P. Low, "Of Muslins and *Merveilleuses*: Excerpts from the Letters of Josephine Du Pont and Margaret Manigault," *Winterthur Portfolio* 9 (1974): 45–46.

206 **"whole legs":** Harrison Gray Otis to his wife, January 18, 1800, in Samuel Eliot Morrison, ed., *The Life and Letters of Harrison Gray Otis, Federalist, 1765–1848*, 2 vols. (Boston: Houghton Mifflin, 1913), 1:137.

206 **"an outrage upon all decency":** Abigail Adams to Mary Cranch, March 15–18, 1800, in *New Letters of Abigail Adams, 1788–1801*, ed. Stewart Mitchell (Boston: Houghton Mifflin, 1947), 241–42.

207 **"Several of the Gentlemen":** Cited in Charlene M. Boyer Lewis, *Elizabeth Patterson Bonaparte: An American Aristocrat in the Early Republic* (Philadelphia: University of Pennsylvania Press, 2012), 33.

207 **phenomenal wedding dress:** Met curators believe the dress dates to shortly after Elizabeth Patterson's wedding, to 1804–5. I am not so sure, based on a comparison with the very similar wedding dress belonging to the Peabody Essex Museum and securely dated to 1800. Some style leaders move fast.

210 **"already thousands condemn":** From Constance Pipelet, *Ouvrage divers en prose, suivi de mes soixantes ans par Mme la Princesse de Salm* (Paris: Firmin Didot, 1835), 2:149–50.

211 **"physical beings":** Constance Pipelet, *Rapport sur un ouvrage du Ctn Theilemin, intitulé "De la Condition des Femmes dans Une république"* (Paris: 1799), cited in Carla Alison Hesse, *The Other Enlightenment: How French Women Became Modern* (Princeton: Princeton University Press, 2001), 134.

214 **"Her garb was strange":** Maurice Levaillant, ed., *Une amitié amoureuse: Madame de Staël et Madame Récamier; Lettres et documents inédits* (Paris: Editions Hachette, 1956), 19.

214 **Briquet asserted:** Reprinted in Fortunée Briquet, *Dictionnaire historique des Françaises connues par leurs écrits*, ed. Nicole Pellegrin (Strasbourg: Presses universitaires de Strasbourg, 2016), 293–94.

215 **"a woman of genius":** Talleyrand, *Mots, propos, aphorismes*, 71.

215 **"I never really knew":** Barras, *Memoirs of Barras*, 116. The occasion was Germaine de Staël's introduction to Barras of Benjamin Constant.

215 **"I met":** Benjamin Constant, *Cécile*, cited in Léonard Burnand, Stéphanie Genand, and Catriona Seth, eds., *Germaine de Staël et Benjamin Constant: L'esprit de la liberté* (Paris: Perrin, 2017), 75.

215 **"It's been eight days":** Levaillant, *Une amitié amoureuse*, 69.

216 **"almost like love":** Cited in Chateaubriand, *Mémoires d'outre-tombe*, 168.

216 **"I embrace you":** Cited in Thomas, "Mme Récamier, Mme de Staël," in Delphine Gleizes and Sarga Moussa, *Juliette Récamier dans les arts et la littérature: La fabrique des representations* (Paris: Hermann, 2011), 55n17.

216 **"This friendship":** Chateaubriand, *Mémoires d'outre-tombe*, 2:985–86.

216 **"The speed":** Cited in Chateaubriand, *Mémoires d'outre-tombe*, 1:168.

216 **Mind and Beauty:** Cited in Maurice Levaillant, *The Passionate Exiles* (New York: Farrar, Straus & Cudahy, 1957), 11.

217 **most enduringly famous and popular:** Avriel H. Godberger, "Germaine de Staël's *Corinne*: Challenges to the Translator in the 1980s," *French Review* 63, no. 5 (April 1990): 800–9.

218 **called her Corinne:** Burnand, Genand, and Seth, *Germaine de Staël et Benjamin Constant*, 150.

220 **David's authorship of this portrait:** Ewa Lajer-Burcharth, *Necklines* (New Haven: Yale University Press, 1999).

14. ORDER IN THE WARDROBE

226 **Each of the ladies-in-waiting:** Claire Elisabeth Jeanne Gravier de Vergennes, *Mémoires de Madame de Rémusat, 1802–1808*, ed. Paul de Rémusat, 3 vols., 14th ed. (Paris: Calmann-Lévy, 1880), 54–56.

227 **"star couturier":** Madeleine Delpierre, *Le Costume Consulat-Empire*, La grammaire des styles (Paris: Flammarion, 1990).

227 **The train:** Alphonse Maze-Sencier, *Les fournisseurs de Napoléon Ier et des deux impératrices: D'après des documents inédits tirés des archives nationales, des archives du Ministère des affaires étrangèrs et des archives des Manufactures de Sèvres et des Gobelins* (Paris: Laurens, 1893), 4.

227 **"This family of Bonapartes":** Talleyrand, *Mots, propos, aphorismes*, 48.

230 **"My friend":** Bertaut, *Madame Tallien*, 112–13.

230 **"What do I not owe her?":** Cited in Gilles, *Madame Tallien*, 296–97.

230 **"My friendship":** Cited in Gastine, *Reine du Directoire*, 338.

231 **"a very lovely woman":** Gastine, *Reine du Directoire*, 353.

15. EPILOGUES

234 **"The Empress":** *Mémoires de Mademoiselle Avrillion*, 29.

234 **"almost incredible":** Vergennes, *Mémoires de Madame de Rémusat*, 2:347.

234 **"It was extraordinary":** *Roses for an Empress*, 86.

235 **minimalist style card:** *Joséphine*, exhibition catalogue, 44.

235 **an impressive peak:** *Joséphine*, exhibition catalogue, 45.

235 **decked out in ribbons:** *Joséphine*, exhibition catalogue, 18.

236 **One day:** Gilles, *Madame Tallien*, 317.

236 **after her death:** Kermina, *Madame Tallien*, 309.

236 **"Oblige her to be more reasonable":** Jean-Lambert Tallien, cited in Kermina, *Madame Tallien*, 296.

236 **"Your visit":** Cited in Gilles, *Madame Tallien*, 323.

237 **"the death of Monsieur Tallien":** Cited in Gilles, *Madame Tallien*, 331.

237 **"What a death!":** Cited in Gilles, *Madame Tallien*, 333.

237 **"jealous of the beautiful Tallien":** Houssaye, *Notre-Dame de Thermidor*, 478.

237 **"I enjoy no pleasure":** Cited in Gilles, *Madame Tallien*, 330.

238 **fashion continued to fascinate:** Houssaye, *Notre-Dame de Thermidor*, 487.

238 **"the sweet, benevolent happinesss":** Cited in Gilles, *Madame Tallien*, 336.

238 **"What a novel":** Gilles, *Madame Tallien*, 339.

239 **"I recently had the pleasure":** Wilhelm Schlegel to François Gérard, Bonn, September 27, 1827, in Henri Alexandre Gérard, *Lettres adressées au baron François Gérard, peintre d'histoire, par les artistes et les personnages célèbres de son temps*, 2nd ed., 2 vols. (Paris: A. Quantin, 1886), 2:234.

16. CONCLUSION

244 **the Goncourts' argument:** Edmond and Jules de Goncourt, *Histoire de la société française sous le Directoire* (Paris: Didier, 1864; Paris: G. Charpentier and E. Fasquelle, Éditeurs, 1892), chap. 10, 290–302.

244 **They recoiled:** Goncourt, *Histoire*, 293.

244 **"a great mind":** Goncourt, *Histoire*, 290.

244 **"The most dissolute monarchies":** Goncourt, *Histoire*, 294.

244 **did not exactly lie:** Goncourt, *Histoire*, 413.

245 **wearing thin dresses:** Goncourt, *Histoire*, 411–12.

245 **"the audacity even of nakedness":** Goncourt, *Histoire*, 413.

245 **Out of 499 plates:** The plates of the *Journal*, reinforced by the magazine's text, and corroborated by portraits, put sheer dresses in museum collections into fashion context. The magazine routinely described a knit base-layer, a slip, or both. The beauty and value of these underlayers was often displayed by having them fill in a neckline over the throat, or extend down the arms past sleeveless or short-sleeved dresses. The magazine's combined captions and text descriptions also specify the type of social occasion for which a particular outfit was intended. It turns out that the sheerest dresses were supposed to be worn on formal occasions, especially for balls. When women wore such dresses for portraits, they were showing off exceptional attire.

Image Credits

All but one of the period fashion illustrations in this book, with great thanks to the curators of the Morgan Library and Museum, New York, are selected from *Journal des dames et des modes*, 1797–1804, PML 5687-5707. Purchased by Pierpont Morgan, by 1906. (The collection can be browsed in full here: http://stylerevolution.github.io/plates). For fine art and other illustration credits, please see below.

28 "Marchande des Modes," in Rey, M. Michel., Brunet, B., Stoupe, J. George Antoine., Panckoucke, C., Richomme., Benard, R. (1777). *Suite du recueil de planches, sur les sciences, les arts libéraux et mechaniques, avec leur explication: deux cents quarante-quatre planches*. A Paris: chez Panckoucke Libraire. Photo courtesy of the author.

33 Elisabeth Louise Vigée Le Brun, *Marie Antoinette in a Chemise Dress*, 1783. Oil on canvas, 89.8 × 72 cm (35 3/8 × 28 3/8 in.) Museum Schloss Fasanerie, Eichenzell, Germany. © Hessische Hausstiftung, Kronberg i. T., Germany.

43 Philibert Louis Debucourt, *The Palais Royal Gallery's Walk*, 1787. Color aquatint on paper, 38.2 × 57 cm (plate); 39 × 58 cm. The Art Institute of Chicago, Gift of Mr. and Mrs. Potter Palmer, Jr. 1924.1344.

46 Charles-François-Gabriel Le Vachez, *View of the Interior of the Nouveau Cirque of the Palais Royal and the Ambassadors of Nabab Tipou*, 1788. Etching, roulette, bister, 27.5 × 36 cm (10¾ × 14 in.). Département des Éstampes et Photographie, Bibliothèque Nationale de France, Paris. FRBNF40251881.

47 Elisabeth Louise Vigée Le Brun, *Portrait of Muhammad Darvesh Khan, Ambassador to Tipu Sultan*, 1788. Oil on canvas, 245 × 161 cm, (96½ × 632/5 in.). Islamic Arts Museum, Malaysia. ©Islamic Arts Museum Malaysia.

50 Kashmiri artist unknown, *Kashmir Shawl belonging to Sarah Peirce-Nichols*, about 1801, Cashmere and wool, 65 3/4 × 64 1/2 in. (167.01 × 163.83 cm) L × W, Gift of the estate of Miss Charlotte Sanders Nichols, 1938. 123590.2 Courtesy of the Peabody Essex Museum. Photographed at Peirce-Nichols House by Walter Silver/PEM.

52 Jacques Louis David, *Antoine Laurent Lavoisier and Marie Anne Lavoisier (Marie Anne Pierrette Paulze)*, 1788. Oil on canvas, 259.7 × 194.6 cm (102 ¼ × 76 5/8 in.). The Metropolitan Museum of Art, Purchase, Mr. and Mrs. Charles Wrightsman Gift, in honor of Everett Fahy. 1977.10.

58 Left: Michel Garnier, *Rose de Beauharnais*, c. 1790–93. Oil on mahogany panel, 12.75 × 10.5 inches. Snite Museum of Art, University of Notre Dame. Gift of Michael and Susie McLoughlin, 2015.079). Right: Anonymous, Madame Tallien, original ca. 1789–93. Engraving and stipple, Image: 16.3 × 11 cm; Plate: 22 × 15.8 cm; Sheet: 37.8 × 28.5 cm. Photo courtesy of the author.

69 Auguste Couder, Opening of the General Assembly, 5th of May, 1789, 1839. Musée national des châteaux de Versailles. MV 2275. Erich Lessing / Art Resource, NY.

71 Jean-Louis Laneuville, *Bertrand Barère de Vieuzac*, 1793–94. Oil on canvas, 51.1 × 38.1 in. (130 × 97 cm). Kunsthalle, Bremen. Kunsthalle Bremen—Lars Lohrisch / ARTOTHEK.

75 *Françaises devenues libres : . . . et nous aussi, nous savons combattre et vaincre . . .* (Paris: chez Villeneuve, 1790). Engraving, W. 9 cm × H. 11 cm. Bibliothèque nationale de France, Département des Éstampes, Paris. FOL-QB-1 (1789–07–14). Photo Alamy.

80 Jacques-Louis David, *Portrait de Marie-Antoinette reine de France, conduit au supplice*, 1793. Pen and brown ink, 14.8 × 10.1 cm. Collection Edmond de Rothschild, Louvre Museum, Paris. Photo: Thierry Le Mage. Collection Rothschild. © RMN-Grand Palais / Art Resource, NY.

103 Top: Jacques-Louis David, *Madame Pierre Sériziat, née Émilie Pécoul, soeur de Mme. David, née Marguerite-Charlotte Pécoul, et un de ses fils, Émile, né en 1793*, fourth quarter of the eighteenth century (1795); Salon of 1795. Oil on wood, 131 × 96 cm. Musée du Louvre, Paris. RF 1282. Photo: Frank Raux. © RMN-Grand Palais / Art Resource, NY. Bottom: Jean-Antoine Laurent (1763–1832), *Les Demoiselles de Tourzel, assises près d'un ruisseau*, undated. Miniature on ivory, 25 × 19 cm. Musée du Louvre, Paris. RF 30764-recto. © RMN-Grand Palais / Art Resource, NY.

104 Top: Louis-Leopold Boilly, *Artist in her Studio*, 1796; Salon of 1796. Oil on canvas, 49.5 × 60.5 cm. Staatliches Museum, Schwerin. Inv. Nr. G 240. Photo: Elke Walford. bpk Bildagentur / Art Resource, NY. Bottom: Andrea Appiani the Elder, *Josephine Bonaparte Crowning the Myrtle Tree*, 1796. Oil on canvas, 98 × 73.5 cm (38 5/8 × 29 in.). Private Collection. Image courtesy of Robilant+Voena.

110 Jean-Bernard Duvivier, *Portrait of Madame Tallien*, 1806. Oil on canvas, 125.7 × 93.3 cm (49 ½ × 36 ¾ in.). Brooklyn Museum, New York. Healey Purchase Fund B. 1989.28.

116 Detail of a fan, ca. 1795–1799. H. 16 cm. Paris Musées / Palais Galliéra, Musée de la Mode de la Ville de Paris. 1981.95.76.

122 Jean-Baptiste Isabey, *Portrait of Josephine at Malmaison*, 1798. Watercolor with white heightening, 16.5 × 12.4 cm. Châteaux de Malmaison et Bois-Préau, Rueil-Malmaison. M.M.2017.5.1 Photo: Franck Raux. © RMN-Grand Palais / Art Resource, NY.

125 James Gillray, *Ci-devant Occupations; or, Madame*

Talian and the Empress Josephine Dancing Naked before Barrass in the Winter of 1797.—A Fact!, published February 20, 1805 by Hannah Humphrey, London. Hand-colored etching, sheet: 31.6 × 45.7 cm (12 7/16 × 18 in.); Harris Brisbane Dick Fund, 1917. The Metropolitan Museum of Art, New York. 17.3.888–61.

126 James Gillray, *La belle Espagnole,-ou-la doublure de Madame Tallien*, published on February 25, 1796 by Hannah Humphrey, London. Hand colored etching, 30.9 × 21.7 cm. 1851,0901.777. The British Museum, London.

132 Marguerite Gérard, *La Confidence, ou Portraits de Thérésa Tallien et Juliette Récamier*, undated (1). Oil on canvas, 55 × 44.5 cm. Mairie de Bordeaux, Musée des Beaux-Arts, photo, F.Deval. Bx E 493.

135 François Gérard, Portrait de Juliette Récamier, née Bernard, 1777–1849, 1802–1805. Oil on canvas, 257 × 183 cm. Musée Carnavalet, Paris. P1581.

136 Antoine Cardon after Richard Cosway, *Madame Récamier (née Jeanne Françoise Julie Adelaide Bernard), (1777–1849)*, ca. 1802. Etching and color stipple, 19.8 × 27.7 cm. Musée Carnavalet, Paris. G.41976.

137 Eulalie Morin, *Juliette Récamier (1777–1849)*, 1799. Oil on canvas, 116 × 90 cm. Musée national des châteaux de Versailles. MV 5344. Photo: Franck Raux. © RMN-Grand Palais / Art Resource, NY.

138 François Gérard, *Jean-Baptiste Isabey and his Daughter*, 1795. Oil on canvas, 195 × 130 cm. Musée du Louvre, Paris. INV 4764. Photo: Angele Dequier. RMN-Grand Palais/Art Resource, NY.

139 Louis Léopold Boilly, *Isabey's Studio (Réunion d'artistes dans l'atelier d'Isabey)*, 1798. Oil on canvas, 72 × 111 cm. Musée du Louvre, Paris. RF 1290 bis / INV 1290 BIS. Photo: Adrien Didierjean. © RMN-Grand Palais / Art Resource, NY.

140 Robert Smirke, *Elevation of one wall of Madame Récamier's bedroom, Hôtel Récamier*, Paris, 1800. Watercolor on paper, 28 × 35.8 cm. Royal Institute of British Architects Library, London. Inv. SD 84/2 (2).

150 Top: Guillaume Lethière, *Girl with Portfolio*, c. 1799. Oil on canvas, 63.5 × 56.4 cm. Worcester Art Museum, Worcester, Massachusetts. 1954.21. Credit: Worcester Art Museum, Massachusetts, USA© Worcester Art Museum /Bridgeman Images. Bottom: Jean-Baptiste Isabey, Portrait of a Woman, c. 1795. Watercolor and bodycolor on ivory, ormolu frame, 68 mm diameter/ 6.8 × 6.8 cm (2.7 × 2.7 cm). Private Collection Austria/ Sotheby's.

151 *Baron François-Pascal-Simon Gérard, Portrait* of the *Comtesse de Morel-Vindé and Her Daughter (The Music Lesson)*, 1799 (An 7). Oil on canvas, 200.7 × 142.9 cm (79 × 56 1.4 in.). Fine Arts Museums of San Francisco. Museum purchase, Mildred Anna Williams Bequest Fund and the William H. Noble Bequest Fund. 1979.8.

153 Top: Stipple engraving by W Bend after a portrait by I .G. Marguerier, *Madame Tallien*, 1803. British Museum, London. 1885,1212.67. Bottom: After Jean-Baptiste Isabey, *Portrait of Theresa de Cabarrus (1773–1835) also known as Madame Tallien*, 1895. Colored lithograph printed by Boussod, Valadon and Company. Bibliothèque Nationale, Paris, France/ Bridgeman Images.

154 *Costumes parisiens 53, Journal des dames et des modes*, An 6 [special insert]; Design Museum Denmark.

155 Philibert-Louis Debucourt, *L'Orange, ou, Le moderne jugement de Paris*, 1800. Aquatint and etching, printed à la poupée with hand-coloring, image: 10 1/16 × 15 1/4 in. (25.6 × 38.8 cm). The Clark Art Institute, Williamstown, MA. 1955.2327. Acquired by Sterling and Francine Clark before 1955.

167 *Parisian Ladies in their Winter Dress for 1800*, published by S.W. Fores, London, November 24, 1799. Hand-colored engraving, 39 × 26 cm. Library of Congress Prints and Photographs Division, Washington, D.C. 2007677627.

171 Top: Louis-Léopold Boilly, *Portrait of Madame Tallien, full-length, seated in a garden*. Oil on panel, 20 1/2 × 16 1/2 in. (52 × 42 cm.) © 2023 Christie's Images Limited. Bottom: After Boilly, *Portrait of Thérézia Tallien with her daughter Rose-Thermidor in the park*, Bibliothèque Nationale de France.

172 Top: Louis Léopold Boilly, *The Artist's Wife in his Studio*, c. 1795–99. Oil on canvas, 40.6 × 32.9 cm (16 × 12 15/16 in.). Clark Art Institute, Williamstown, Massachusetts. 1955.646. Acquired by Sterling and Francine Clark, 1925. Bottom: John Keenan (fl. 1791–1815) after John Opie (1761–1807), Oil portrait of Mary Wollstonecraft, 1804. Oil on [?], 39 × 36 × 5 in. (framed). The Carl H. Pforzheimer Collection of Shelley and his Circle at the New York Public Library. NYPL catalog ID (B-number): b19980492.

173 François Gérard, *Portrait of Theresia Cabarrus (1773–1835), wife of Tallien, then Princess of Caraman-Chimay*, c. 1805. Oil on canvas, 212 × 127 cm (83.4 × 50 in.). Musée Carnavalet, Paris. P2738.

177 Pierre-François-Léonard Fontaine and Charles Percier, *View of Napoleon's Library at Malmaison*, 1800. Musée national des châteaux de Malmaison et Bois-Préau, Reuil-Mailmaison, France. 84–001274. Photo:

Daniel Arnaudet / Jean Schormans, 1984. © RMN-Grand Palais / Art Resource, NY.

179 Jean-Baptiste Isabey, *The Empress Joséphine*, c. 1810–1814. Miniature; watercolor on paper, 13.5 × 9.4 cm. The Wallace Collection, London. M216. UK/Bridgeman Images.

180 François-Pascal-Simon Gérard, *Portrait of Joséphine, the Wife of Napoleon*, 1801. Oil on canvas, 178 × 174 cm (70 × 68.5 in.). The State Hermitage Museum, St. Petersburg. ГЭ-5674. IanDagnall Computing / Alamy.

181 The Gonzaga Cameo, Portraits of Ptolemy II and Arsinoe II, 3rd century BCE. Sardonyx, silver, copper, 15.7 × 11.8 cm. The State Hermitage Museum, St. Petersburg. ГР-12678 Dmitriy Moroz / Alamy.

183 Top: Jean-Baptiste Isabey, *Empress Joséphine*, miniature in a hemmed octagonal frame with a blue enamel border. Without frame: 70 mm × 31 mm; with frame: 81.42 mm. Private Collection. Image courtesy of Osenat Auction House; Photo: Michel Bury. Bottom: Andrea Appiani, *Joséphine Bonaparte épouse du Premier consul*, c. 1800–1802. Private Collection.

184 Top: Antoine-Jean Gros, *Portrait of Empress Joséphine*, 1809. Rueil-Malmaison, châteaux de Malmaison et Bois-Préau, France. MM.40.47.6874. Photo: Daniel Arnaudet / Gérard Blot. © RMN-Grand Palais / Art Resource, NY. Bottom: Martin-Guillaume Biennais, Empress Joséphine's jewelry box and writing case, 1802–1804. Mahogany, steel, silver and wood veneer. Rueil-Malmaison, châteaux de Malmaison et Bois-Préau, France. M.M.93.5.1. Photo: Daniel Arnaudet © RMN-Grand Palais / Art Resource, NY.

185 Left: Breguet N°611 Small (médaillon) tact watch (open). Blue-enameled gold case, diamond-set pointer, touch studs of large round diamonds, silver dial, ruby cylinder escapement. Diam. 39mm. Sold February 18, 1800 to Mrs. Bonaparte, later Empress Joséphine, for the sum of 3000 francs. Collection Montres Breguet SA. Right: Breguet N°611 Small (médaillon) tact watch (closed). Blue-enameled gold case, diamond-set pointer, touch studs of large round diamonds, silver dial, ruby cylinder escapement. Diam. 39mm. Sold February 18, 1800 to Mrs. Bonaparte, later Empress Joséphine, for the sum of 3000 francs. Collection Montres Breguet SA.

186 Detail of *Jahangir Receives Prince Khurram at Ajmer on His Return from the Mewar Campaign: Page from the Windsor Padshahnama*, c. 1635. Opaque watercolor and gold on paper. Image dimensions: 11 15/16 × 7 15/16 in. (30.4 × 20.1 cm). Royal Collection Trust Royal Collection Trust / © His Majesty King Charles III, 2023/ Bridgeman Images.

189 Top: Pierre-Paul Prud'hon, *L'impératrice Joséphine*, 1805. Oil on canvas, 244 × 179 cm. Louvre Museum, Paris. RF 270. Photo: Mathieu Rabeau © RMN-Grand Palais / Art Resource, NY. Bottom: Pierre Paul Prud'hon, *Portrait of Empress Joséphine*, c. 1800. Oil on canvas, 74 × 60 cm. Rueil-Malmaison, châteaux de Malmaison et Bois-Préau, France. M.M.80.1.1 Photo: Daniel Arnaudet / Jean Schormans. © RMN-Grand Palais / Art Resource, NY.

190 Baron François Gérard, *Madame Charles Maurice de Talleyrand Périgord (1761–1835)*, c. 1804. Oil on canvas, 88 7/8 × 64 7/8 in. (225.7 × 164.8 cm). The Metropolitan Museum of Art, NY, The Wrightsman Fund, 2002. 2002.31.

191 Jean-Baptiste-Dominique Ingres, *Madame Rivière*, 1805. Oil on canvas, 117 × 82 cm. Musée du Louvre, Paris. MI 1446. Photo: Franck Raux. © RMN-Grand Palais / Art Resource, NY.

192 Antoine Gros, *Joséphine*, 1808–09. Musée Masséna, Nice, France. Inv. 2842. Erich Lessing / Art Resource, NY.

196 Charles Percier, *Design for a Bedroom for Joséphine*, c. 1802. Ink, wash, and watercolor on paper. Private Collection.

207 A dress worn by Elizabeth Patterson, ca. 1804–05. Costume Institute, The Metropolitan Musuem of Art, NY. 1983.6.1. The Metropolitan Museum of Art, Purchase, Gifts in memory of Elizabeth N. Lawrence, 1983 (1983.6.1).

209 Indian muslin wedding dress, 1800, Peabody Essex Museum, Salem MA. Wedding dress of Sarah Peirce-Nichols photographed at Peirce-Nichols House. Courtesy of the Peabody Essex Museum. Photo by Walter Silver.

210 Jean-Baptiste-François Désoria, *Portrait of Constance Pipelet*, 1797; Salon of 1798. Oil on canvas, 130 × 99.1 cm (51 1/4 × 39 in.). Art Institute of Chicago. Simeon B. Williams Fund. 1939.533.

211 Jeanne Doucet de Surigny, *Femme écrivant, assise devant une table* (Possibly a Portrait of Julie Candeille (1770-c. 1806), undated [19th century]; Salon of 1796. 7 × 7 cm. Musée du Louvre, Paris. RF 30686. Photo: Martine Beck-Coppola. © Musée du Louvre, Dist. RMN-Grand Palais / Art Resource, NY.

212 Marie Denise Villers, *Marie Joséphine Charlotte du Val d'Ognes*, 1801. Oil on canvas, 63 1/2 × 50 5/8 in. (161.3 × 128.6 cm). The Metropolitan Museum of Art,

Index

Page numbers in *italics* indicate a figure on the corresponding page.